The

Latina

President

A Novel

By Joe Rothstein

LCCN 2016911716
ISBN-13 978 0997699913
ISBN-10 0997699913

The Latina President is a publication of
Gold Standard Publications
1025 Connecticut Avenue
NW, Washington, D.C. 20036
(202) 857-9742
TheLatinapresident.com
jrothstein@rothstein.net
Cover by Akira
Photography by Mia
Copy Editor, Michelle McSweeney

To Our Immigrant Past, and Future

All four of my grandparents fled from the lands of their birth and the authoritarian tyranny that almost certainly would have claimed their lives had they remained. They fled to the United States of America, a nation that promised to be their refuge. Because they immigrated, my family and I have had the great fortune to live the promise that brought my grandparents to these shores. In one form or another, my family's story is shared by almost everyone I now know or have ever met.

To our immigrant past, and, hopefully, its future, this book is dedicated.

Joe Rothstein

Prologue

At 8:09 p.m. two District of Columbia police cars piloting the presidential motorcade turned onto Virginia Avenue in Southwest Washington where it intersects Second Street, next to the Washingtonia Grand Hotel. The cars were quickly followed by six lead police escort motorcycles, two black limousines and two identical black SUVs. Behind them came three vans, one especially equipped for use by the counter insurgency and hazardous materials mitigation teams. Another van delivered communication equipment and operators. A third van carried members of the day's media pool. Finally, as always in a presidential motorcade, an ambulance, four more trailing police motorcycles and two police cars.

Elevated railroad tracks hovered on concrete piers over the south side of the narrow street. The hotel, spanning a city block, was the only structure on the north side. The escort vehicles filled the street space in between. Police barricades blocked all other traffic. On this small stretch of pavement, the night now belonged to the flashing red and blue lights of the world's tightest personal security force.

Eight Secret Service agents jumped out of the SUVs. Six hurried into the hotel through the Virginia Avenue employee entrance. Two others took positions at the door. Two agents emerged from the second limousine and opened a heavily armored rear door. Into a narrow slice of incandescent light cutting a triangular path through the near total darkness, the soft-outwash from hotel signs and windows, stepped U.S. President Isabel Aragon Tennyson. Alone, except for the tight embrace of her Secret Service escort, she moved quickly through the mild early November night, leaving her wool coat behind. Dozens of spectators drawn by the lights and sirens, but held back by barricades a half-block's distant, could glimpse little but her moving shadow.

Inside the hotel, more than 1,000 partisans of the new National Security Immigration Act had been ushered from a cocktail reception to tables assigned by numbers matching their $200 meal tickets.

The National Security Immigration Act had become law thirty months earlier. It was a stunningly quick conclusion to a decades-long debate. The architect of the triumph was President Tennyson, the first U.S. president of Hispanic heritage. The tide that swept her into the White House lifted into Congress the votes needed to overcome immigration reform's frenetic resistance. Now, two and one-half years after passage, the final serious legal challenge had been overcome. Tonight's celebration needed no qualifiers. No remaining asterisks. After so many years of promise, disappointment, bitter conflict. Settled. Done. The leaders of that battle were assembled tonight to toast victory. Organizational heads, community workers, members of Congress. And, in a few minutes, their heroine, their leader, the president.

Tonight's gala would be a poignant capstone to the epic U.S. immigration reform battle. Just weeks before, the U.S. House of Representatives had voted to impeach President Tennyson. Within days, the U.S. Senate would decide whether to remove her from office.

A two-story elevator ride lifted the president and her security team to the ballroom floor. Hotel manager Glen Freiberg greeted her as the elevator doors opened into the hotel's enormous kitchen, alive with staff in the final stages of preparing the largest sit down dinner the new hotel had ever served. The president asked to take one last look at herself before becoming the center of attraction. Freiberg escorted her to a bathroom to the left of the elevator doors. Check your hair, your lipstick, assess your appearance and how you will look close up on television. Take a few deep breaths to calm yourself. It was a ritual she followed through her political career.

Four minutes later, a brisk walk through the kitchen with frequent handshakes—cooks, waiters and other staff, many of whom themselves secured by the new immigration law. Now she was behind a curtain veiling her from the banquet floor, greeted by long-time friend and ally Leon Rivas, chairman of the

Immigration Reform Coordinating Committee. They embraced warmly and exchanged whispered words.

"Ready?" he asked. She nodded.

"Great night," he added.

She breathed deeply and closed her eyes.

Rivas cued the evening's master of ceremonies, Florida Senator Carson Coulter. Coulter had been filling time on stage, introducing notables, raising the emotional temperature of the crowd for the president's arrival. With the signal from Rivas, Coulter lifted his arms dramatically as if to levitate everyone in the room.

"Ladies and gentlemen," his rich baritone boomed, "the president of the United States."

A brassy "Hail to The Chief" bounced off the ballroom's hard surfaces, amplifying both the sound and the excitement. President Tennyson strode quickly onto the stage, an energetic, hands-waving entrance, the image of victory.

The ovation was deafening, sustained, overriding the orchestra. Many in the room had lived their adult lives with the uncertainty of place and belonging. For so many, the war now was over. Victory achieved. This was V-J Day and for tonight, this ballroom was Times Square.

Television cameras were live, as they were at most of the president's events these days, recording what could be the last moments of her historic presidency. The images shown now were caviar to cable television directors, a rich visual feast of expressive faces, tears, embraces. The president, triumphant, love enveloping her, love she requited with each air blown kiss.

Then the cameras went dark. Black. Suddenly and ominously. All of them at once. Those watching on television could no longer could see anything.

Those in the ballroom saw hell.

***

The television trucks parked on the east side of the Washingtonia Grand hotel, where satellite reception was best, were hurled against the building by the explosion's force. Most were set afire. Channel 6, a local Washington, D.C., news channel, had arrived late to the event and, prime locations already occupied, found space on the less desirable west corner, near the hotel's main lobby entrance, where the building had shielded it from fire and the blunt force of the shock waves.

Gloria Graham, a Channel 6 news intern, was bounced from one wall of the truck to the other and landed on the floor at the feet of video engineer Bruce Brimberg.

"What happened," she screamed.

Brimberg checked all of his screens. "Gone," he yelled back. "Nothing at all coming from the hotel."

With expert hands trained through decades piloting remote television broadcasts, Brimberg continued to work his controls. To his surprise his satellite signal was still strong enough to feed a live broadcast. "Harley!" he yelled.

Harley Littlefield, the backup tech, had been half-dozing in the front seat. Whether the blast was real or just a punctuation point in his nap was unclear to him until he heard the yells from Graham and Brimberg.

"I'm on it!" Littlefield grabbed the spare camera and fired it up.

"Gloria," Brimberg yelled again, "get ready to go on air live."

Gloria pulled herself up from the truck's floor and steadied her legs by leaning against an equipment console.

"Me? I don't know what to do."

"Figure it out. Get the hell out there."

Littlefield thrust a microphone into one of her hands and roughly pulled her out of the truck with the other. He positioned her so that the camera could see both Gloria and the hotel's smoke and flames in the same frame.

"You're crazy," she yelled. "I don't know what happened. I don't know what to do."

Harley's red light went on.

"You're live," yelled Brimberg. "Start talking."

The small television audience watching local Channel 6 coverage of the banquet now saw a strange and jumbled picture. A young woman wearing jeans, a gray sweatshirt and a red Washington

Capitals windbreaker fumbling with her microphone, uncertain how close to hold it to her face, her head disconcertingly jerking from eye contact with viewers to the scene behind her, smoke, fire, people running from the hotel.

"Talk," yelled Brimberg.

In a high-pitched, excited voice that immediately signaled to viewers that they were watching an unfolding horror story, Gloria talked.

"Oh, my God! I'm standing in front of the Washingtonia Grand hotel where, honestly, I have no idea what just happened," she yelled. "It sounded like an explosion of some kind. Then there was this huge fire ball. Now we see all this black smoke like a chimney gone crazy."

Littlefield widened the frame to show as much of the hotel as the lens would allow from this distance.

"It happened in the last five minutes. We're here to cover a speech by the president…"

And then she realized…

"Oh my God! The president's inside that hotel! Oh, my God! And more than a thousand people at a dinner! Senators and congressmen!

Gloria did not know, could not know, that hers was the first reported word of the explosion. The only live broadcast from the only remote television unit that survived. Television viewers whose screens had gone black on other channels switched around until they came upon Gloria. Suddenly Channel 6, a channel whose bread and butter programming focused on Washington area meetings, local news and weather, had an audience rapidly building into the millions.

***

At the headquarters of the Secret Service, less than a mile from the hotel, across the National Mall, Sid Farnham, the night's control officer, didn't need television or a phone call to know that something terrible had happened. His office shook until he thought the windows would shatter. Within seconds communications chief Charley Friar yelled out, "Comm's gone. Lost connection with POTUS."

LOST CONNECTION WITH POTUS!

No contact with the president of the United States. Dreaded words. After twenty-two years in the service, Farnham instantly understood the enormity of the moment. Instinct ruled hesitation. He spun in his chair to face his deputy manning a bank of screens behind him.

"Daniels, get a team to the hotel. Go!"

"We're alpha one," Farnham called out through the building's intercom system. "Alpha One. This is NOT a drill!"

"Hillman, get Samoza at the vice president's house. Total lockdown. Send eight to help him there.

"Milly, locations of House and Senate leaders and spouses. Tell Saperstein to round them up and take them to Location 10A."

"Simmons, DC PD. Capitol police. Open direct lines.

"Charley, anything from the FBI?"

"They're under way. DC fire, police, Hazmat all rolling."

"Pentagon?"

"Looks like they're scrambling Andrews."

Someone punched numbers on the office television remote until it landed on Channel 6. On a sixty-five-inch screen, like a mirage appearing from desert heat waves, the hotel emerged framed by a curtain of smoke. A hanging portrait of disaster, punctuated by flashes of flame, some reaching as high as the hotel's eighth floor.

Farnham looked up from his desk to see live, in full color, the worst nightmare the Secret Service could ever experience, the entire reason for its existence, failed. "Good God," said Farnham. "The president's dead." To himself he thought, and probably every one of the agents he sent there to keep her alive.

***

Lincoln Howard, the Washingtonia Grand's chief of security, quickly regained his feet and raced up two flights of stairs from the security office to the ballroom level. The dark cloud blowing through the ballroom doors flashed scenes etched in his memory from two tours in Iraq. Howard ducked into a bathroom, surprising three women standing immobile at the sinks. "Get out!" he shouted to them. "Get out of the hotel!" They ran. He grabbed fistfuls of cloth hand towels, soaked them in water and raced into the ballroom through a door closest to the stage, wet towels covering his face.

Howard was no stranger to dead and wounded. But his years in the Marine Corps never produced a scene like the one at the other end of his flashlight beam. It was as if a deranged choreographer had positioned a vast expanse of bodies on the floor, bodies partially hidden by white table cloths. Shrouds. Shrouds adorned with memorial wreaths of flowers, scattered from dinner tables by the force of the explosion.

Despite the arc of horror framed by the blackness beyond flashlight range, the stench of something, what, chemicals of some kind, he took a few tentative steps on a floor now slippery, sticky with salad oil and vinegar, water from overturned vases, wine, the color of blood, mixing with the still bleeding bodies all around him. Howard edged into the ballroom swinging his light's beam, searching for movement, any sign that someone was alive, anyone who might claim priority for removal from this grotesque tableau.

Back and forth he swung his light, one delicate step after another, feeling the terrible softness of draining life under his shoes. Then he saw her. With disbelieving eyes, he saw her. On her back, as still as the parquet floor beneath her, a woman in a green suit, right sleeve hanging from her shoulder, skirt pock-marked with what appeared to be charred holes from tongues of flame, blood painting her forehead and cheeks. The president of the United States was in the tight beam of his flashlight, for the moment, a star, spot-lit, the center of his attention, his alone, her eyelids tightly shut. Nothing about her suggested life.

***

The vice president's residence is at No. 1 Observatory Circle, on the spacious grounds of the Washington Naval Observatory, an urban estate once owned by the Rockefeller family, five miles from the Washingtonia Grand Hotel. Its neighborhood is known locally as Embassy Row, a cluster of embassies and ambassadorial residences.

Tonight the vice president, Roderick Theodore Rusher, was dining alone, his wife Anna away in Richmond, visiting with their son and his family. As dessert was being served, Oscar Samoza, the vice president's on-duty senior Secret Service agent, strode urgently into the dining room.

"Mr. Vice President, please come with me," said Samoza, a commanding voice and presence, hands motioning haste, a manner not open to discussion.

"What's up," said the vice president.

"The president may be dead. Assassinated. We may be under some kind of attack. Please, come with me."

Rusher rose quickly and followed Samoza down a flight of steps to a basement recreation room, below ground, accessible only through the door they just used.

"What's happening?" asked Rusher.

"Explosion at the Washingtonia Grand. No communication yet, not even with our people. We'll know soon. If she died, we have to find a place to swear you in. I'll be back as soon as I hear. Please don't leave." Samoza ran back up the stairs, leaving Rusher alone with this incredible news.

The president dead? My God! Assassinated! Images raced through Rusher's mind like waves crashing ashore one after another hurled by a gale. Tonight! This isn't how he wanted it.

The U.S. Senate was just days away from a decision on whether to remove President Isabel Aragon Tennyson from office. There had been months of hearings. Lurid hearings. Tales of gun running, money laundering, complicity with Mexican drug cartels, murder. Roderick Rusher was prepared to inherit that office, eager for it, a goal he had worked toward for decades. But not like this. Not assassination!

Disoriented, Rusher felt an overwhelming need to do something, anything. Impulsively he grabbed his private cell phone, thumbed through his contacts, found a number he had never expected to use, and pressed the round call button. A voice answered. A thick, accented voice.

The Aragon Years

1

"Isabel. "Isabel? No, I don't think so."

"But that's my name!"

"Not cool. It's not…. I don't know…. it's not how people should know you."

"What difference does it make?"

"Well, I don't know. I'm just thinking about the first few days of school. You're new there. Everybody else knows each other. People are funny. You don't want them making fun of you. It's important."

It had been a year since Isabel Aragon Tennyson moved with her family to Los Angeles from Mexico City. A year of private tutors and home schooling. A year learning to speak, read and write English. A year aligning her knowledge of math and science and history with her age group at Blackburn International, the private girls' school where she was now enrolled.

She met Carmen Sandoval only days after her family arrived in Los Angeles. Carmen's father worked at Southern California Trust and Savings, the bank Isabel's father, Malcolm Tennyson, was sent to Los Angeles to manage. Isabel was Carmen's project to "Americanize," to mentor for peer acceptance. In a few days Isabel would be leaving the secure nest of personal tutors to enter Blackburn and a world of preteens, a world that could be cruel for newcomers. Carmen was doing her best to manage the transition.

"You see, they call me Carmie, not Carmen. It's friendly. It's easy. Hey, Carmie, not hey, Carmen. That's what we need for you. We can't say, hey, Issy. That's weird. Don't get me wrong. Isabel's a nice name. I like it. I'm just thinking it's too formal or something. It should be friendlier for right now. Later on it won't matter."

The friends were sitting on Isabel's front porch, lazing the last days of summer freedom, sipping lemonade, idly scanning the molded green hills and traffic patterns of the San Fernando Valley, appearing from this height like animated plant rows. The Tennyson home was on a high perch near Mullholland Drive. Often, smog made the vista a ghostly gray apparition. On many mornings coastal fog poured down the hills like steamed casement. Today, a brisk and comforting breeze had cleared all obstructions. The world below was in sharp focus, changeable, watchable.

"My brother calls me Bell."

Carmie could not help laughing at that.

"What's wrong with Bell?"

"Cow bell? School bell? Tinker Bell?" I can hear 'em all laughing. Not in front of you for sure, but when you're not there. Don't be mad. This is stupid, I know. But it's the way it is. You've got to get started right. We start meeting people and I say this is my friend blank. We need to fill in the blank."

"So what are the other girls' names?"

Carmie thought for a minute.

"Suzy for Suzanne. Lindy for Linda. Becky for Rebecca. You see, how it works. Problem is we can't use your first name."

They sat quietly for a few more moments.

"Oh," said Carmie, finally struck with an idea she liked, "We'll use your last name."

"Tennyson? That doesn't sound fun and friendly."

"No, no. We'll make it Tenny. Hi, Suzy. Meet my friend Tenny. Tenny. Yes, that's it. I like it. We'll call you Tenny. Do you like it?"

"I don't know. It's different. I've never known a Tenny. It sounds a little stupid. To me Tenny sounds like an old shoe. But if you think it helps…"

"That's why it's good. It's familiar. Like you've been around a while. Like an old friend."

2

Decades later the world would know her as Tenny. She accepted the name as an easier entry into the world of new school friends. Later she would live with it for its political value. The name was a lever, a tool, a verbal masquerade. But it was never a name that appealed to her. She was an Aragon, a direct descendent of the Duke of Aragon, whose wife, Queen Isabella of Spain, was venture capitalist to Christopher Columbus. Aragons sailed to the New World with the conquistadors and built a legacy of economic and political power in Mexico. Her grandfather, Miguel Aragon, had vastly expanded the family's fortune through deft assembly of a business conglomerate known as Groupo Aragon.

Groupo Aragon was Miguel Aragon's life mission. His travel bags were always packed. Even when in Mexico City Miguel was a rare sighting in his family home. His wife, Alicia, accepted his absence as one of the bargains of their marriage. She had long since come to terms with a comfortable life that seldom included her husband. Their daughter, Maria Rosa, was not as charitable. No one asked Maria if she would accept childhood and adolescence without a father. If they had, she would have declined permission. Each passing year deepened her core resentment like rings on a tree trunk.

Maria paid back her father's years of separation by separating herself from him as soon as she completed high school. She enrolled in NYU as an art student and moved into a tiny apartment in New York's Greenwich Village. Maria's arrival coincided with one of the Village's most memorable eras, a time when it served as a birthing cradle for Beat Generation writers and abstract expressionist artists. Robert Motherwell, Jackson Pollock, and Mark Rothko were neighbors. Jack Kerouac was a frequent presence. The bar scene was alive with free spirits from the New York School of Poets.

In Maria's rebellion from family tradition and opulence, the Village was an ideal escape. Within a year she moved in with a fellow rebel, Malcolm Tennyson, a one-time Yale business major from Boston turned poet. When Maria learned she was pregnant, she and Malcolm married. News of the marriage came to Miguel in a brief and formal letter. No family member had been invited to the wedding. In fact, there had been no wedding, just a brief civil ceremony.

Malcolm was the antithesis of the husband Miguel had always envisioned for his daughter. An American, of little means, and without the courtesy to even ask Miguel for permission to marry his daughter, a request that Miguel most certainly would have rejected.

Soon there was the birth announcement. Federico, six pounds, three ounces, also had joined the family. Then, silence with infrequent contacts. Until five years later news of a second Tennyson child, a daughter, Isabel.

Isabel, for Isabella, queen of the Aragon dynasty. Years and distance had softened Maria's resentments. Maria meant the name as a peace offering to her father. Miguel, whose life had been a collage of deals, understood the gesture and was prepared to make his own offer. If Maria and Malcolm would move to Mexico City, he would arrange a fine home for them in the family compound and an executive position for Malcolm in the family business. After years of struggling financially in New York, and with another child to care for, and with loneliness for her family and friends a constant companion, Maria accepted.

Mexico City's Lomas de Chapultepec neighborhood was the first home Isabel knew. Wide gardened streets, arbors of flowers, homes that to a little girl's imagination evoked the magic and mystery and grandeur of castles. Papa Miguel had built four large classic California Mission style homes on adjoining wooded and terraced lots. They backed onto nearly an acre of enclosed courtyard, a private park, really, shaded by violet jacaranda trees and alive with blankets of bougainvillea.

There were many places for young Isabel to play, to hide, to be alone with her dreams. Mexico City once was known as the City of Palaces. In Isabel's young world, her home was a palace and she was a princess. How could she not be, when Papa's home, where she spent so much time, greeted her with an entry wall of Aragon history? Portraits and photos of Aragons past, Beautiful women with glittering tiaras. Tall and handsome men in uniforms, swords at their sides, infallibility on their oiled lips. And always the stories, the greatness of the crest, the expectations.

Papa told Isabel and Federico tales of his father and grandfather and ancestors going back to colonial times. He could trace them. He knew who they had been and what they had become. That he was the principal heir and guardian to this legacy Papa had no doubt. He reveled in the challenge of guardianship even as he bore its weight. Papa never tired of recalling the past. The children never tired of listening. Adventure stories, not written by others, but by their own family. Not fictional characters, but Papa and all others memorialized on the walls of their home. Papa made sure they understood, one day this would be theirs.

Despite the fact that the Tennyson family was now living just steps away from Miguel, there was little thaw in the icy barrier between Maria and her father. Miguel tried at first. Not hard and not well. He tried, but long-held resentments were too deeply embedded to be excised. While he could not unwind the past he could avoid repeating past mistakes. He could write a new chapter much more easily than trying to edit an old one.

That he did, with his grandchildren. He was able to give them the world—most importantly, his time and love. Federico and Isabel returned that love to Papa, as they called him. His pet name for Isabel was his little treasure, *pequeño tesoro*. It wasn't only the gifts, the toys, the clothes, and the adventures money could buy. He became the person closest to their lives. Maria was a kind and loving mother, but she was authority while Papa was pure joy. Their father, Malcolm, shared his wife's love for their children, but he was cut from grayer cloth than Miguel and the comparison was not to his advantage. Isabel knew there was tension. Her mother seldom visited next door when Papa was home. When they encountered one another, Isabel heard the harsh words. At those times she would just run away to her trees and flowers and dolls and dreams. If there was trouble in the adult world, in Isabel's there was only happiness.

Tension eventually overcame paradise. Friction between Maria and her father festered into open wounds and finally into the intolerable. A new bargain was struck. Malcolm would be reassigned to manage a minor Los Angeles bank, the only U.S. investment in Groupo Aragon's portfolio of assets. The Tennysons would move to Los Angeles, but Federico would remain, continuing his education with Miguel's guidance, apprenticing to one day replace

Miguel as the next generation's keeper of the Aragon flame. Maria was trading her son, temporarily she hoped, for her freedom.

A year later Isabel was entering school, speaking a new language, responding to a new name, Tenny. Was the name change necessary? She could never be sure. What she did know was that "Tenny" was easily accepted. Her transition was seamless. Her command of English quickly evolved into the idioms of young life. She loved her classes, her teachers, the world of information and thought that was opening for her. Her bonds with Carmie tightened with each passing year. As they came of age together they shared each other's clothes and deepest secrets. Together they experimented on the edge of adolescent danger, with boys and alcohol and drugs. Maria had passed along her rebellious genes to her daughter.

Classmates called them the *salvajes*, the wild ones. When partying with those who didn't know them well Tenny and Carmie would often call themselves *las hermanas*, sisters. Not that they looked alike. But they were about the same height and body builds. Each had chestnut hair that they wore shoulder length. More than appearance, it was the similarity of their personalities that gave credence to the sisters' ruse. They were perpetually buoyant, moving with confidence and usually with infectious good humor, feeding off each other's energy.

Tenny had dark, deep-set green eyes common to generations of Aragons, strikingly similar to those who in earlier centuries had stood for portraits, or who allowed a single instant in time to shape their identity through photographs. Her eyes were unusually large for her oval face, eyes you noticed immediately, eyes that didn't just see you, but locked into you, reading you, storing information about you. Her lips also pressed the boundaries of normal, shaped like the Man-Ray painting, "The Lovers." As she transitioned from the world of boys to men her lips often became lures to the unwary. She understood their attraction and used them to tease, taunt or reel in, as she pleased. Her five foot eight body veered from the overstuffed flesh of the Aragon line. Having grown up among relatives whose tortilla consumption she considered excess, and whose bodies showed it, Tenny was determined to stay trim. For most of her life she succeeded. While not born beautiful, Tenny, by the way she dressed, wore her hair, moved her body and exuded confidence, evolved into the attractive young woman she believed a princess should be.

High school ended for her on a high note, and then it was on to the University of Southern California. Her parents preferred Stanford, where she had also been accepted. But Carmie was enrolling in USC, and Tenny would go with her.

Both were excelling in their undergraduate classes. At the other end of the candle they were in high demand on the fraternity party circuit. It was just after the start of their sophomore year, a time when the new car feel of college life was giving way to the comfort of established friends and routine. Carmie and Tenny had developed a party protocol. One or the other would drive, drink moderately and see that to it they both got home with lives and honor intact. In theory it was a sensible plan. In practice it had worked well. Until the Phi Iota party and Andres Navarro.

Andres was a six foot three god of a male, as sharp as a sling blade in his tailored blue suit, an expanse of curly black hair framing his blue eyes and *GQ* cover smile. Tenny actually felt her knees buckle at first sight.

"I saw you across the room," said Andres in a rich baritone. "You're beautiful."

Carmie was not there for protection. Tenny was very much alone as Andres held out his hand. Every alarm bell inside her went off as she reached for his.

"Thanks, so are you. I'm Tenny."

"I know. My sister Bettina's told me about you. She thought we should get acquainted. "

"Dance?" said Tenny.

"Let's go over to the bar and talk for a while," he answered.

In a crowded room there's little white space. They drank standing close, heads even closer to be heard. They danced. They drank again.

"I'm going to leave with Andres," Tenny told Carmie when they took a break together in the bathroom.

"Really? Think that's a good idea? How much have you had to drink?"

"Not much. I can handle it."

"I don't know. You look pretty shaky to me. He's got you going."

"Well, he's gorgeous, but don't worry. I'll be okay."

Actually, she didn't want to be okay. Inside she was on fire.

They parked on a dark street off of Coldwater Canyon road. Boy-girl sex? Yes, she had been there. This was different, this was real. This was like nothing she had ever experienced. Half-clothed, insatiable passion that steamed the windows and vaporized reason.

Near dawn she quietly edged through the door of her home, body and mind in turmoil as she made the transition from girl to woman, her head somewhere other than its usual sensible place on her body. Heaven, maybe.

Sleepless, sleep not even considered on this first morning of her new life, she showered, dressed in shorts and tank top and dropped onto a patio lounge chair to watch the rising sun turn hilltops gold. At 7:00 a.m. she phoned Carmie.

"I'm in love, Carmie. In love."

Carmie mumbled a reply, unintelligible, from residual sleep.

"I mean it. This is real."

Carmie's eyes and lips were now open, her head still stuffed into her pillow, reluctant to move.

"I knew I shouldn't have left you alone. Backseat, front seat or what?"

"It was fantastic. But so's he, Carmie. Smart, funny, the talk was as good as the sex."

"What time should I pick you up? You can tell me all about it before classes."

"I'm not going to class today. Andres and I are going for a drive along the coast. I would have followed him home if I could."

Carmie was awake now, sitting up.

"Hey, don't get carried too far with this. He's a guy and you fell for him. Work him into your life. Don't change your life for him."

"Can't help it, Carmie. He's all I can think about."

Within a month Tenny and Andres were engaged, a month when Tenny did little but be with Andres or dream about being with him. It was a month when she became devoted not only to Andres but to sex.

Maria and Malcolm Tennyson readily accepted young Navarro as a suitable match for their daughter. Andres was a pre-med student, planning to join his father's lucrative private orthopedic practice. For grandfather Miguel it was more than acceptance. Relief that Isabel had chosen to continue the ancestral bloodline with one of their own. The Navarro family, like the Aragons, traced roots back to the early colonial days. Andres' grandparents had emigrated to Los Angeles from Puebla, Mexico, lured by the opportunity to own land in the San Fernando Valley just as the city was being transformed from a sunny agricultural outpost to one of the nation's metropolitan magnets. The Navarro orange groves had long since become shopping centers.

Miguel barely tolerated Malcolm Tennyson for marrying his daughter without even meeting the family, without going through the ritual of asking *pedir*, or acceptance. He blamed Malcolm for the years of estrangement, even for the all-too Anglo name he had given his daughter and grandchildren. Now he would have the opportunity to welcome a proper young man, one who understood the courtesies of age and position. Someday, Miguel could only hope, Isabel and their children would return to their Mexico City roots.

As a wedding gift for his granddaughter, Miguel purchased a two-acre property near Isabel's parents' San Fernando Valley estate. That's where the new couple set up housekeeping and planned to start a family. Andres completed his medical training and moved into residency. Isabel settled in to await the arrival of their first child. At five months, Isabel miscarried. She quickly became pregnant again. Four months later she miscarried again, this time requiring a hysterectomy.

The failed pregnancies took their toll on the marriage. So did Andres' long nights away in residency, his growing interest in surgery and a new residency in San Diego, which now meant he was away during the week, flying or driving home for weekends, and not all of those. The glow tarnished. The fairy tale faded into tedium for Isabel. Andres was too handsome, too vital, too easily aroused to remain alone when not at home. His extracurricular anatomy sessions became too apparent to be ignored. The divorce came just four years after the wedding. Not a divorce, really. The Catholic Church wouldn't permit it. But arrangements can be made, particularly with families as prominent and as generous to the Church as the Aragons and Navarros.

What can puncture daydreams? For Isabel, the sharp lances were the realization that she would never have children of her own and the end of a marriage she had once considered perfection. Her turmoil all the greater for the want-not serenity of earlier years. How to handle adversity when your mental immune system hasn't been reinforced by prior exposure? How to adapt to life in the valleys after so many years at the mountain top?

3

Dear Carmie:

I read your latest letter about all your new adventures in New York and at Lisagore Bankshares. So interesting and exciting. I know you will do killer work there. Your letters mean so much to me. They keep me from becoming a candidate for the psych ward. My life here is too dull to write about, even talk about. Just managing this big house, going to charity things with mother, and, can you believe it, she's even got me into a bridge club!

Any more I feel that my mind is a time-release instrument of sadness. I think I'm over the loss of my babies, but then I'm not. A cloud forms. Tears come like raindrops. It ends. I think I'm done. And I am, until the next storm. There's always a next storm. I didn't know the children. They didn't know me. No names for headstones. It's that way for much of life on earth, isn't it? All species have young. Many know they will die jumping up stream or burying eggs in sand. Or they kill those who are threats to their babies. I never understood the bond before I laid my own eggs. It's not a bond tied on both ends, though. How many bear cubs come home for mother's day after they grow up?

My own youth feels so distant. Now when I see a snowflake, or spring flowers or golden leaves, all I can think of is how transient. Life's so fleeting. I used to entertain myself with thoughts. Now my body feels idle while my thoughts run away so recklessly. I think of those acres of airplanes and ships at anchor no one wants or needs any more. Not that long ago shiny, desired, useful. Now just immobile, waiting for the scrap sentence. Disposability.

I can't believe I became useless to Andres. Well, maybe not useless, but devalued. We were the most important people in each other's lives. Now I'm the most important person in my life and I'm struggling to make sense of it. Why? You know, when I go to art galleries and museums I like to get up very close to a painting to see the brush strokes. It amazes me how anyone can be close enough to the canvass to make the most delicate of lines or dabs or squiggles and to understand how that will look to someone who observes the whole painting from ten feet away. I've been making those strokes up close in my own life and when I step back I see that the whole picture's a mess.

Oh, my, Carmie. I should wad this letter up and throw it away. When I step back and look at what I've written so far all I see is a lonesome, aimless old lady. I'll survive. I promise. But it helps me so much to talk with you. Don't give up on me.

I love you,

Tenny

Dear Tenny:

Not long ago a close friend of mine was killed in a car accident. As I sat in the church, listening to the memorial service, I felt myself choking up. Tears, yes. But more than that. It became harder to breath, harder to swallow. I had this sense of panic, almost to the point of running from the church. But then I asked myself, what am I feeling? Remorse that such a wonderful friend had lost her life at such a young age, of course. But more than that. I was feeling sorry for myself. Sorrow for the loss in my life as well as hers. No more last minute dinners with her. No more days shopping or going to fun places. I was feeling my own loss. She was gone, beyond feeling. It was my first real experience with death, and it was so hard to understand.

Now you have to understand your loss. I can imagine how horrible. Not just your own children but the prospect of not having others. Cry all you need to, but know what you are crying for. Yourself. And since it's about you, you can pull yourself out of it and move on.

The lesson here isn't one of melting snowflakes or mothballed ships. It's living the rest of your life as it can be lived, by you, a healthy, brilliant woman in her prime. Read this and put it up on a wall where you can read it often. It's from Dante's Inferno, and if you excuse the gender reference (they had a different idea of political correctness in the fourteenth century) the message fits:

Up on your feet, this is no time to tire,
The man who lies asleep will never waken fame,
And his desire and all his life slip past him as a dream,
And the traces of his memory fade from time,
Like smoke in air or ripples in a stream.

A few letters ago I suggested you go back to school. Your answer? I'll quote your own words: "Oh, I'm not a kid anymore. I'd be an old lady in those classes. I'm not sure I could handle it." Excuse me, but you and I are the same age and I'm not an old lady. Neither are you. Get a grip, Tenny. You can breeze right through those business courses. And at the other end you don't even have to worry about getting a job. Drop the Navarro name. Go back to being an Aragon. Last I heard there was a company by that name that had thousands of people on the payroll. That grandfather of yours still hires Aragons, you know.

I'd offer to come to L.A. and be with you, but you need to work this out for yourself, dear friend. I'm sure you will.

Love,

Carmie

Carmie was right, as usual. Brother Federico was still in executive training. Why not her? Adversity had veiled the obvious. Groupo Aragon did employ tens of thousands of people. Its interests reached into banking, mortgages, swaths of agriculture, communications, entertainment. It controlled much of Mexico's electric power generation and distribution. In many areas it was a virtual monopoly. Why not join Federico in the family business?

***

Tenny's return to USC's business school was a different experience than the partying of her former life. Not as frivolous. Actually more satisfying. There were classmates her age, women who also had married and divorced, or returned from the Peace Corps or military service, or those who just needed more age or savings. Undergraduate work led to a master's program in business finance. Within three years, Tenny walked down the graduation aisle, cloaked in the school's cardinal and gold regalia, diploma in hand.

But her plan to join Federico ended abruptly just before her graduation when he phoned to tell her he was leaving the company. It was a Friday afternoon. He had just informed Papa.

"Leaving? After a dozen years training to run the company?" She was incredulous.

"I've been called, Bell. I can't explain it, but it's something I must do."

"Called?"

"I'm joining the Jesuit order."

"You, a priest?"

"Yes," he quietly replied. "Me. I hope I am worthy of it."

"What's happened, Federico? What's happened to you? Have you thought this through?"

"It's not a matter for thought, Bell. It's a matter of mission. I've been called."

Within days Federico had a new address, the thirty-seven-acre Montserrat Jesuit Retreat House, north of Dallas, Texas. Federico had been accepted as a novitiate, the first step on what would likely be a multiyear journey toward becoming a Jesuit priest.

Miguel was shaken by Federico's abrupt departure. He had so carefully mapped Federico's future, not only to benefit his grandson, but to preserve the Aragon line, to continue Groupo Aragon as it should be continued, as an Aragon enterprise. He had even convinced Federico to drop the Tennyson name. Now, Federico was out the door. Gone.

Through another door walked another Aragon, Isabel. Suddenly an unexpected dilemma for Miguel. Federico was a bright young man, not particularly assertive, but very presentable to the outside world. Inside the organization he had shown a willingness to listen closely to long-time, experienced company managers, to accept their counsel, and to not interfere with operations that through the years had been extraordinarily successful. Isabel, however, Miguel's *pequeño tesoro*, his little treasure, was another matter. She was her mother's daughter, a bit rebellious growing up and even more so, he noticed, since the end of her marriage. Not only would she be a woman in what traditionally had been a man's executive world, but her willingness to not rock the boat could be a question, and most upsetting to harmonious operations. He had always envisioned Isabel in the proper role of wife, mother, guardian and manager of the family home. Now she was on his doorstep, asking for an executive role. Miguel fretted for days over this puzzle.

Finally, a decision. Isabel would join the wealth management team. Miguel had long hoped to add wealth management as a lucrative revenue stream, handling the portfolios of the nation's elite, steering them into investments beneficial to Aragon's broad range of products and services. None of his plans had yet succeeded. In wealth management, Isabel would not be exposed to existing Groupo Aragon organizations. She would be more or less independent, removed from potential conflicts with line managers. In a way he would be throwing his *pequeño tesoro* into the deep end of the pool. Maybe she would find a wealthy and well-connected husband there. Maybe she would succeed and build a practice independent of other company activities. Maybe she would fail or tire of the executive life. Yes, wealth management. A good solution.

Seven years had elapsed since the idolized princess wore a gold tiara and a necklace of flashing diamonds as she stood on the altar with Andres Navarro. Years in which she had survived a wrenching transition from rejected, infertile bride to now, at age twenty-eight, a woman embarking on a professional career. While the interval years had been difficult for her, they were a valuable prerequisite for hunting down and capturing rich prey. That's not a game best played with unrealistic illusions. Those who claim assets counted in more than seven figures are not dreamers, except, possibly, if they came by their wealth through inheritance. For most of the moneyed class, reality is packaged with every dollar or peso. Making money is one thing, keeping it another. Force fields go up to guard against the hungry hordes always at the gates with ideas for how to spend another's wealth. Isabel was signing on to participate in rough, often ruthless competition.

4

Isabel's first conquest was Rafael Celeste, a popular figure on the long-running Latin soap opera *Los Amantes*, The Lovers. Celeste played father to the show's female star, a beautiful businesswoman constantly embroiled in love and financial affairs requiring her father's money, counsel, and often his contacts with police officials and judges to extricate her from trouble. Celeste was in his mid-sixties, age appropriate for his fatherly role, needing little make-up magic. His younger years had been his partying years. The television show had settled him in one place, with a steady job and a secure family. It had made him a wealthy man. Celeste long since should have placed his millions into Groupo Aragon funds and investments. The soap opera aired on an Aragon television network. Celeste was often featured in Aragon entertainment magazines.

All of this gave Isabel considerable research to work with— the tapes of the television shows, the newspaper and magazine articles that featured him, the files from others at Groupo Aragon who had tried unsuccessfully to win his account. Isabel spent weeks preparing before she made her first move, an invitation for lunch. She was an Aragon, a difficult invitation for Celeste to refuse. Once in conversation, Celeste was impressed and flattered that Isabel was such a fan. She was familiar with all the players. She recalled many *Los Amantes* highlights, dividends from her recent binge watching of past episodes.

They met at Hotel Geneve's La Terraza restaurant, under its high glass atrium.

"I never drink at lunch or during the business day," she said. "But please, if you're inclined."

"Will you join me in some wine," he said.

"Perhaps a sip," she replied. "Please, you choose."

Through three courses and a bottle of fine French cabernet Isabel said nothing to disturb the sense that this meeting was anything but personal. Once she was drained of questions about *Los Amantes*, she moved the discussion to Celeste, his background, his plans, his family. She was interested. She was genuine. She was an admirer. She was grateful for his time. Would it be possible to come to the set some time to watch an episode in creation?

Wonderful. She would be thrilled. For so many celebrities, vanity and recognition move in tandem. Celeste was only too happy to talk about himself and to bake in the warmth of admiration. When the check came, Celeste made the honorable gesture of reaching for it.

"Please," he said, "This has been so enjoyable. Do me the honor of allowing me to host you."

Celeste fully expected her to decline his offer. Instead, she replied, "That's very gallant and generous of you. Thank you."

That answer was off script. Obviously she was in sales and trying to win his account. She selected the most expensive restaurant in Mexico for lunch, and stuck him with the bill. What's wrong with her? Doesn't she know this game? Celeste seethed silently as he reached for his wallet. Me, a simple actor, and the great Groupo Aragon can't afford lunch?

They walked together through the hotel's corridors, past its stained glass, its famed chandeliers, its dramatic, historic paintings. Isabel purposely remained close enough to Celeste to envelope him in her scent, enhanced by a few fresh dabs of Jean Patou's "Joy" fragrance. They each had car and driver waiting, and as they parted at the curb she pulled him close and left a discreet, moist kiss on his left cheek, complete with a trace of her red lips.

In a soft voice she whispered, "This has been so enjoyable for me and most generous of you. It means we must do it again soon, my treat, no arguments about it from you as this time. Next time when the check comes don't be so naughty as to argue. Behave, promise?"

Her look was coy and flirtatious. Their heads were just inches apart, almost touching. He was enchanted by this woman, her looks, her manner, her sweet scent. He knew he must accept, all sense of irritation over the cost of the meal quickly evaporated.

"Next Tuesday, 1:00 p.m. Right here. I insist. I'll make the reservation," she said, continuing to hold his arm by the elbow, daring him to decline. He didn't.

Isabel learned in her business school classes that when chasing executive level sales, statistically only 17 percent of sales calls result in a second meeting. Up to five meetings may be required to close a deal. By not paying for the first meeting she virtually assured herself another.

Celeste had Isabel on his mind between meetings. This clever, interesting, energetic woman. He looked forward to being with her again.

She was waiting for him in the hotel lobby, ready to greet him with a hug, a quick, father-daughter hug. He appreciated that it wasn't more suggestive. Rafael Celeste didn't want to be sexually seduced but knew he would have little resistance if that was her objective. His days of clandestine encounters were over. His confessions made. His conscience cleared. He and his wife had settled into a life of comfort, respectful of one another. Nevertheless...

She selected an even more expensive wine than they had consumed a week earlier and chatted idly about this week's episodes of *Las Amantes*. But his interest, and finally his questions, turned to her, to Isabel.

"So, let me ask, are you an American or a Mexican?"

"Do I have to choose?" she asked. "By birth I'm both. My Aragon roots are here, as you know. But I also feel very American, having been born in New York and grown up in Los Angeles."

"I didn't know you were born in New York."

She recreated the route of her life for him, as he quizzed her intently. Last week she had asked most of the questions, stroking his celebrity. Now she found the roles reversed. His curiosity was aroused. He had become the fan. Los Angeles. Hollywood. Tell me about it. What celebrities do you know?

"Now don't you forget," she told him over desert churros, "you promised me an invitation to one of your show's video tapings. When can we do that?"

"Next week, in fact. We're doing two shows each day, clearing time for the producers to work on another project. What day would be best?

"The end of the week, Thursday, Friday, either one. I'm very excited. I've never seen a show produced live."

"Well, it's not exactly live. We may do a number of takes of certain scenes. The editors put them together later. Making television programs or movies is a tedious business, often just a few frames at a time."

"Don't spoil my illusions. I can be a star-struck child. I'm amazed at actors and actresses, how you can become the characters on a script, and then completely turn yourselves into other characters with the next script."

"I don't have to do that. I can remain my plodding old self in program after program. I sometimes feel I am that man whose character I inhabit."

"You can't discourage me, Rafael. I'm in awe."

Isabel had secured a third meeting. She had yet to ask for the order. That was about to happen.

Friday, 1:00 p.m., the last of the week's ten-show marathon. Isabel was due on the set a half hour earlier, a seat for her arranged in the director's booth. Two hours before air time Isabel called Rafael.

"I'm heartbroken, Rafael. I can't leave our office. Aragon Investments is offering a private placement to our clients today, one of the most outstanding we've ever had. Our energy company's purchased a refinery near Tula and created a separate entity for it. It's just a remarkable opportunity and all of us are working with our clients to make sure they know about it and take orders before the investment closes."

All true. Unsaid, Isabel knew about this a week earlier. She strategically timed this call.

"I will miss you here, Isabel," said Rafael. "There will be other programs. Another time. But tell me, is this an investment that should interest me?"

"You? Oh, I'm so sorry, Rafael, this is a client-only offering."

"What if I become a client?"

She was silent for an appropriate interval.

"I don't know. I doubt it on this short notice. Are you really interested?

"Yes, I'm really interested."

"I'll try."

And so Rafael Celeste became Isabel's client. Within days he transferred his $10 million account to Aragon. Two months later, after Rafael had enjoyed a nice profit on his investment, Isabel finally kept her studio date. Rafael proudly introduced Isabel to other members of the cast and staff. She left with the likelihood of adding three more accounts.

These sales were quickly followed by more in Los Angeles: Gerard Daniels, a wealthy Los Angeles land developer, arranged through his son, a business school classmate of Isabel's; Wiley Corcoran, a movie producer she met at a Beverly Hills party, James Richards, a young computer hardware engineer, newly rich from the sale of his networking startup. Los Angeles was proving to be virgin territory for investments in Mexico, with distinct tax advantages, arranged by this charming lady representing a multibillion dollar old-line financial behemoth.

Contrary to Miguel's concerns that Isabel's gender would be a handicap in Latin countries, it was a major asset. Doors opened more easily for her than for her male competitors. Male resistance tends to melt readily in the presence of attractive women. Once in, her impressive knowledge, ideas and business savvy most often kept her there.

Isabel loved the freedom of the road, the challenge of the chase, the unpredictability of each new destination. Her first road romance was with Caesar Rosario, an executive with Cortez Agricola, one of Brazil's leading vendors of agricultural equipment. They met at a Ministry of Agriculture reception in Sao Paolo. Isabel had just signed a new account with an equipment dealer who suggested they celebrate at the ministry party. Introductions were made with Rosario, elegant and appealing in his red blazer, stark white open-necked shirt contrasting with his dark skin, jet-black hair, trimmed Van Dyke, and happy eyes.

"Señora Aragon, my respects," said Rosario, bowing slightly as they were introduced.

She extended her hand, and a warm smile in greeting.

"Will you be with us in Brazil for long?"

"I'm planning to leave in two days. Sao Paulo is so beautiful. I wish I could stay longer and see more of it."

"Please don't think it forward of me. But I so much enjoy showing our city to guests. If you are free tomorrow, I would be at your service as your guide and driver."

Isabel steered clear of romantic involvement with coworkers, clients, or anyone she felt might compromise her business activities. Rosario was a midlevel sales executive with a good income, but, as she quickly learned, a bank account level well below her minimum targets. That made him maximally attractive. She also quickly learned the Rosario was a lot of fun to be with.

Isabel had planned to leave Sao Paulo in two days, but for no particular reason. Her calendar was clear for the next week. Lunch with Caesar was delightful. His tour of the city was that of a practiced and entertaining enthusiast. By evening she had cancelled her flight to let Caesar teach her how to tango. She stayed for three more days. The affair lasted four months. It was the first of many during her five years traveling through Central and South

America. Five years in which she became a wealth management superstar for Groupo Aragon.

In her sixth year with the company, Papa Miguel suggested that it was time for Isabel to learn other aspects of the business. Mergers and acquisitions, like wealth management, existed in its own business universe, one deal at a time, with changing players. For Miguel, here was another opportunity to place Isabel in a role that did not involve direct participation in Groupo Aragon's ongoing business lines. Her first test would be in Chile. For years Miguel had been trying to get a foothold into Chile's financial markets. Now he had indications that Banco Temuco, a midlevel regional bank could be available.

Isabel flew home to Los Angeles to spend long hours with her father studying the banking business. Then she was in Mexico City, camped out with executives of Credit Aragon. Finally, she felt ready. Isabel rented an apartment in the city of Temuco, about 400 miles south of Santiago. There she disappeared for days into local libraries and museums, familiarizing herself with local history and Mapuche ethnic culture. The Mapuches, she learned, were among the few indigenous South American peoples who successfully resisted the Spanish conquest. Now Isabel, an Aragon, had arrived to attempt a takeover of their financial system.

Isabel moved in slowly, meeting key players, identifying those who would be decision makers, learning their interests, their strengths, their weaknesses. Through one careful step after another, she prepared them for an offer, assessed reaction, and finally, in an all-night session where she refused to break for food or sleep, she wore them down. A deal was struck.

Isabel had done it, and at what Miguel considered an astounding bargain price. Not only would Banco Temuco be a good investment, he already had designs on how to leverage the asset to reach much deeper into Chile's economy. His little treasure had done it brilliantly, and with guile and style. Perhaps he had been mistaken about keeping Isabel on the fringe of corporate activity. Yes, he thought, Isabel is ready for bigger things at Groupo Aragon.

Bank mergers take time. Complicated assets are involved. State and national regulators must review and approve. Temuco had become Isabel's life, her home for months with few breaks. She was ready to leave, and would, once the papers were signed. The target was tomorrow, five months after the first handshake agreement.

That meant that today Temuco's board room was shoulder-to-shoulder with bank executives, lawyers, accountants, staff, and monitoring government officials. Into this organized bedlam came Carlo, one of Isabel's assistants, with a message: "Call immediately." It was from her father. Her father was never in the line of her financial transactions. Miguel had kept Malcolm penned where he first placed him, managing Southern California Trust and Savings, a relatively minor holding in the Aragon universe. This had to be personal news, not business.

The urgency of the message left no doubt that the news would be unwelcome. Isabel said nothing. She gripped the desk, sat down and reached for a glass of water.

"Señora, are you ill?" It was Victor Saez, Temuco's executive vice president.

She looked up, grateful for an opening.

"Not ill, Victor, thank you for asking. But not much sleep lately and too little food. Too much time here, I guess, and not enough time in your good Andes air. If you don't mind, I'd like to leave for a while. I'll be more alert for it."

"Of course, señora. We will continue while you rest. Can I get you anything?"

"No, Carlo is here and I'll have him take me to my apartment."

As they walked to the elevator, Carlo whispered, "You look pale. Do you need a doctor?"

"No, I need to get back to my apartment as quickly as possible."

Finally in her room, she was able to call her father.

"It's Miguel," said Malcolm Tennyson. He died a few hours ago. Heart attack. It happened so suddenly. He asked his secretary to get him an aspirin. By the time she returned he was on the floor. He died before medical people could reach him."

Miguel. Papa Miguel. The light of her life. A bond she had had since before memory. The childhood home. This job. She owed him everything. And now she owed him her tears, which flowed instantly and liberally.

"Isabel."

"Isabel."

"Listen to me, Isabel."

Her father's urgency demanded an answer. After a long silence she finally managed to speak.

"How's mother?"

"In shock. It's not that you don't think about these possibilities for a man eighty-eight years old who works the way he does. But then it happens, and the loss doesn't seem real. And, Isabel, you know their history. Even so, she's in distress."

The tears continued. The voice barely did.

"So am I, father. So am I," she sobbed.

"Listen to me, Isabel. You're alone? We can talk?"

"Yes."

"I know what this means to you. To all of us. But you must hold yourself together. Fortunately, this happened in corporate headquarters. They can control the news there for a while. But not for long. By morning word will be out. You have to settle Temuco today."

"Today? Impossible. The government agents are still reviewing the documents. We still need to round up some directors to sign off. Today? It can't be today." Isabel was jarred back from grief.

"Today. Once word is out they will ask for a delay. Without Miguel they will want to change or kill the deal. This is one of the biggest deals Aragon has had in years. We can't afford to lose it. You know how fragile it all is."

"It's just money. More money. Can't we just grieve? My heart's breaking."

"It's not just money. It's my job and yours. They called me from headquarters to tell me Miguel had died and that you need to save the deal. Before his body's even cold. They're counting on this deal going through. I hate to think how they'll react if it doesn't."

"Who? Who's they? They sound heartless."

"Do it Isabel. I know you can. Make it happen today and grieve tomorrow."

And she did it, her sense of success tempered by the knowledge that withholding news of Miguel's death was borderline fraud and that the Temuco people whose confidence she had gained through months of patient cultivation, and would betray today would not trust her tomorrow, or ever again.

At 3:00 a.m., with the last papers signed and their transmission to Mexico City certified, she packed her bags, woke her driver, and without alerting her six-person Aragon support team, whose members were still unaware of Miguel's death, left Temuco forever.

5

In life, Miguel Aragon sat at the center of Mexico's wealth and influence. So now in death. His memorial service at the Metropolitan Cathedral stopped traffic in the business center of Mexico City while mourners, numbered in the thousands, filed past his coffin and sat for eulogies. The Metropolitan Cathedral, the largest in Latin America, dates to its consecration in 1656, a project of the conquistadors, built, no doubt, with help from funds provided by that century's Aragons. Now the latest of the Aragon patriarchs, Miguel, lay handsome and regal surrounded by white velvet in a casket molded of brushed bronze, his eyes closed, his face at peace, the perfect image of an Aragon elder.

For so many years Miguel's thoughts and actions were the fountainhead for the power and wealth of others. They loved him, feared him or hated him, but they could not ignore Miguel. Today was not a day for fear or hate, only love. No man had done more to strengthen Mexico's place in the global economy than Miguel Aragon, said Mexico's president. Mexico City's mayor described Miguel's good works, the donations to the city's poor, the city's culture, the parks and playgrounds. The bishop blessed Miguel as a great man and great patron, allowing the Church to expand its many works and extend its teachings. Entertainers who performed on the Aragon network and in its movies, sang, spoke, told endearing and colorful stories about him. It was a day to lift Miguel to the angels and to write his life's story into the enduring scrolls of his nation.

Malcolm and Maria Tennyson were there. So was Federico, fetched from his mission serving Mexico's small villages and communities. Aragons from distant places merged into what in earlier times would have been the Aragon court. It was a day of affirmation for the Aragon dynasty, the Aragon brand, both personal and business.

Retiring to the family compound, still in mourning dress, Isabel considered her future. She would continue working with Groupo Aragon, of course. She knew few of those who inhabited the higher floors of the company's headquarters. She would wait for the corporate hierarchy to sort itself out and then go where she was assigned. But Isabel's world had been a transient one for many years. Before resuming her work, she hoped now to take some time to be with her mother in Los Angeles, to comfort her, to adjust her life to the new reality.

As Isabel was making travel arrangements a messenger delivered a note from Miguel's closest Groupo Aragon associate, Javier Carmona. Could she meet with him tomorrow to discuss aspects of Miguel's will?

Javier Carmona had been with Groupo Aragon for twenty-five years, starting as one of Miguel Aragon's many staff attorneys. Through the years, employing legal skill and corporate wiles he rose to become chief counsel. During his early days at Aragon he had earned a degree in finance by attending night school. That proved a powerful asset for Miguel. In Javier Carmona, Miguel had an adept lawyer who also understood the balance sheets. As Miguel aged and spent less time with business matters, Carmona was handed more keys to the inner vaults of Groupo Aragon.

The executive floor, reached by its own private elevator, and accessed only after scrutiny by an armed member of the company's protection service, contained only two offices, one for Miguel and the other Carmona. The floor space between them was the domain of two veteran secretaries. At the opposite end of the executive floor was the corporate board room.

Carmona greeted Isabel with extravagant courtesy as she exited the private elevator.

"I am Javier Carmona," he said, with a slight bow. "It is an honor and pleasure to meet you at last. Your grandfather, Don Miguel, spoke of you with such affection and enthusiasm. I feel we already are friends."

"That's very kind of you, Señor Carmona. I'm only sorry our meeting is the result of such a sad occasion."

"My deepest condolences to you and your family. We here at the company have long felt we, too, were part of Miguel's family. All of us were so close. Of course, our loss and our grief cannot measure yours. Please have a seat. We have much to discuss."

Carmona touched his hand gently to Isabel's back and steered her into his richly paneled office. He motioned to Isabel to sit on a sofa opposite his, across a table already prepared with a silver coffee serving set and china cups.

"Let me go directly to our business," said Carmona. "Your grandfather has designated you as his principal heir. He has directed his estate to award you the greatest number of his ownership shares in the company. At current value we estimate those shares to be worth a billion U.S. dollars."

Isabel had never wanted for money. Her family already was wealthy by most standards. For a life already lived without financial limit or stress, the bequest was surprising and welcome, but she did not receive news of the inheritance as a staggering or life-changing announcement. In fact, numbers so large were hard for her to immediately absorb. What came next, however, stunned her.

"Señora, your grandfather always had hoped that your brother Federico would succeed him in the enterprises. Although of course Don Miguel respected God's will and he gave your brother his blessings, it was one of the greatest disappointments of his life when Federico left for the monastery. After you successfully secured the Temuco merger, your grandfather met with me to discuss your future with Groupo Aragon. He told me that he saw in you someone who could quickly rise to the top of the organization and, in fact, replace him, the position intended for Federico. I agreed and so, had he lived, your next assignment would have been here, with me, learning our most important markets and everything one must know to manage an enterprise as large and diverse as ours. In his will, Don Miguel arranged a path for you to one day replace him as the chief executive. And so, unless you have other plans, I am hopeful you will move back to Mexico City, work here for as many years as required to learn our business, and then, when you are prepared, return the Aragon name to the corporate leadership. At your age, you may look forward to decades as one of the most powerful business people in the world. This was your grandfather's wish."

While the significance of her financial inheritance didn't immediately rock Isabel's composure, news that she would be put on track to manage one of Latin America's largest and most powerful companies did. Her eyes widened, her mouth went dry. She leaned forward toward Carmona as if she missed something in the statement, searching the floor for words that dropped out of the sentence, and when reassembled would change Carmona's message. This was Federico's job being offered to her. It was always Federico's job. Never in all of her dreams had she coveted it or expected it to be hers.

"You are surprised, señora?" said Carmona.

Isabel nodded. "Shocked."

"Don't be. Don Miguel was a very practical man. He never permitted emotion to direct his decisions. He dreamed of an Aragon to replace him, but would not have considered you if he doubted your ability. You built our wealth management practice when no one before you could. You brought us Temuco under the most trying of circumstances. Don Miguel had confidence in you as well as love."

In her current job at Groupo Aragon, Isabel was ten rungs from the top of the ladder. Talented, experienced people filled so many executive positions. She knew so little about what they did or how they did it. Despite her vast store of self-confidence, she felt totally unsuited to be chief executive of Groupo Aragon. But this was Papa's wish, and his decision. Maybe she could rise to it.

In a daze, she nodded approval and gratitude to Javier Carmona for his friendship with her and with Papa for so many years.

Isabel returned to the Aragon home compound in Mexico City, past the compound's guards with their AK-47s, past the Tamayos and the Boteros and the Riveras, so familiar, all waiting to greet her, hanging as they always were when she was a child, in the long entry hall, past the portraits of notable Aragons. Mexican colonial history, family history. Proud family history.

She had to talk with Federico.

6

After completing his Jesuit training and taking his vows, Federico had disappeared into village Mexico. Few knew where to find him at any given time. Isabel and her family feared constantly for his safety. These were dangerous days and he traveled in a land of dangerous people. Drug cartels particularly, but also the politically corrupt and the paramilitary groups that seemed to abide no laws. And there was the disease, the hunger, the bandits who often preyed on unsuspecting travelers. These were the places Federico, son of wealth, chose for his mission.

Although earlier in the day Isabel had promised Carmona she would tell no one about their conversation, she knew she had to tell Federico. He was a priest after all. A priest who had walked away from the very opportunity now being presented to her. They met at dusk, strolling through the garden of the family's fortified compound. Isabel described her remarkable meeting with Carmona and asked for Federico's advice.

Federico stopped, turned, and to her surprise wrapped his arms around her as if comforting her for a grievous loss.

"Heavenly father," he said, words voiced with unmistakable agony. "Why must it come to this?"

Isabel, confused by Federico's reaction, said nothing. He locked arms with her and resumed walking at their garden pace.

"Bell, I have never told anyone why I left. I never planned to. But now, because of Papa's legacy for you, you need to know. I will tell you everything. Then you decide what you must do. I won't judge you, no matter what that decision is."

What followed was a story that, having heard, Isabel so much wanted to wish away, to not have heard at all.

"Groupo Aragon, our family company, the company that has provided you, me and others so much wealth, is a criminal enterprise."

"Please," she said, "let's not be melodramatic. She smiled at Federico, assuming he was teasing her as he often used to.

"No," he replied, "criminal is the appropriate word."

"I learned this slowly, over many years, doubting my own eyes, ears, judgment, all the while. I was the novice. Those I worked with were so experienced. They spoke and acted with so much knowledge. They treated me so kindly and with great respect. If there was a mistake in understanding it had to be mine.

"But it wasn't. As my responsibilities increased and my management portfolio expanded, I came to understand perfectly how Groupo Aragon made its money. My moment of certainty arrived when I was appointed assistant general manager for banking. I discovered that more than a thousand accounts that government regulators had flagged for suspicious activity had never been reviewed."

"That sounds like incompetence, not criminality," said Isabel.

"Planned incompetence. While other departments were staffed with skilled managers, banking was in the hands of inept cast-offs, the kind of people you would hire if inefficiency and disorder were your objectives. Not only did suspicious accounts go without review, billions of dollars and pesos in wire transfers went unmonitored during my time there. No one had any idea of the source or destination. The only possible conclusion was that our company was a safe portal where drug money could be washed and cleaned, corrupt officials could feel secure with their bribes, and huge sums could be hidden from tax authorities. I even discovered some accounts from other countries' despicable dictators who were looting their national treasuries."

Isabel stopped walking. She withdrew her arm from his and faced him.

"Surely you reported all of this."

"Yes. And here's what I was told: Pay no mind to it. This is normal business practice, not just at Aragon but at all banks."

"And Papa?"

"He would always reply the same, I'll look into it."

"Did you consider going to the authorities directly?"

"I did consider it, until I discovered they already knew. Some of the dark accounts were theirs."

Isabel sat down on a garden bench, hands folded, staring ahead at nothing in the twilight. Federico stood beside her, a foot on the bench, his forehead in his hands, the words increasingly difficult to come by, the enormity of his revelations wrenching him even now, years after submerging them in his conscience.

"It's not just our banking enterprises that are corrupt. Once my eyes were opened I saw that we made huge profits from ownership interests in industrial cotton production. You're aware that cotton is one of the worst offenders of child labor, throwing mere children into the fields for backbreaking work with little pay. We filed fraudulent reports about losses, allowing us to claim large government subsidies. We falsely swore on government affidavits that we conformed to all labor laws.

"Groupo Aragon holds a virtual monopoly on broadcast television. It paid little for the spectrum through long-term arrangements negotiated with government officials who we rewarded with ownership shares in Aragon. By manipulating power shortages though generating systems that Groupo Aragon owns, the company creates spikes in energy costs and profits illegally in trading markets. In fact, across the company's entire ownership universe—insurance, mortgages and corporate finance—I found no sector where legitimate business operations did not mask illegitimate practices.

"And so I struggled with all of this, not knowing what to do—until I learned about Groupo Aragon's secret support for the militias. In Guatemala, Honduras, El Salvador, Peru, Columbia, and elsewhere. While our families were living the life of social elites, our company was funneling money and arms to paramilitary groups throughout Central and South America, killing and torturing tens thousands of innocent people. Many priests and nuns who tried to stand in the way of injustice simply disappeared or were murdered.

"When I saw those files I knew I had to leave Groupo Aragon. To do it publicly and noisily would do no good. The authorities were too compromised. A public statement, even just a simple letter of resignation with the reasons for it would have cost father his job and mother a broken heart.

"And I certainly thought of you," dear Bell. "You would have had to choose loyalty to either me or Papa Miguel. You had lost two babies. You were divorcing Andres. How could I have done this to you? And for what purpose? No, it was best that I just disappear. I decided that though it would be a small act of penance, I would become a priest and return to the communities exploited by my family and try to save a life, or help raise awareness, or provide what solace I could to those who need it. Do you know, Bell, that nearly half of our people here in Mexico live on less than what in America would be $4 a day? They have no access to credit. In the villages they pay some of the highest rates in Mexico for everything—food, telephones, light, and heat for their homes. And they have so few options for healthcare and education. They need so much. I see this every day. It's my life's work. It's the most rewarding work I've ever done."

As the night darkened, a few lights appeared in the garden. Isabel wished they would go away. Federico's tale spread darkness through her mind and body. She wished no light. The world had turned black. She listened quietly, staring at the path, too weak to walk it. Could this story, this moment in her life not be a moment at all, but rather a dream borne of the sadness of losing the grandfather she loved?

Federico sat beside her and caressed her hand.

"I'm sorry, dear Bell. So sorry. I never…."

"If I had heard this from anyone but you, Federico….it would have been a fantasy."

More moments passed. She turned to him.

"What you're telling me happened years ago, Federico. Maybe things have changed since you left."

"Would that it be so. To relieve this weight. I once saw all of this from the executive offices. Now I see it from the villages. I share the results of this corruption with those I serve. The child labor, the high cost of electricity, the raids on land, the disappearance of good people. No, Bell, nothing's changed."

"What will I do, Federico? What can I do?

"Bell, you can accept the power they give you and try to change its course to a more benign or even more helpful one. You are strong, maybe strong enough to do that, but I genuinely doubt it. Had I been a better man, I might have tried. Would I have succeeded if I stayed? No. The culture is too strong. So many are compromised. I don't know how it can be changed. I just don't know how. As a woman in a man's world trying to upend power and fortune embedded in a hundred years of history?"

A long silence punctuated his doubt.

"Walk away and do other things. The world is open to you. You have the skills, the knowledge, the resources to walk nearly any path you choose—except the one you are on. The offer has been made to join them. If you refuse their offer you quickly become their enemy rather than their figurehead. To decline to run the ship means you are not one of them and they will always fear mutiny if you stay aboard. My departure was a shock to them.

They will be much more alert to you. They will push you off quickly unless you walk away first."

In all of her thirty-six years, Isabel Aragon had what most people would consider only a few bad days. Her miscarriages. Her divorce. Otherwise, what can go wrong in the life of an attractive, rich, very smart woman, raised in a cocoon of opulence? Learning that her beloved Papa was the architect and chief administrator of a corrupt enterprise that brought misery to so many others was beyond shocking. Otherworldly. If the shrubs in the garden began speaking to her she could not have been more disoriented.

Federico was not just her brother and close friend, but her north star, a priest and someone who had seen the enterprise from the inside and walked away from it. There could be no doubt that Federico spoke truth. Now she understood Papa's reluctance to employ her in the company's core business. Why had he changed his mind in the last days of his life? Did he think her cunning in making deals meant she would readily accept the rest of the company bargain of lie, cheat, and steal? Or did he see in her someone who might reform an enterprise he knew desperately needed transformation?

They left the bench and walked through the darkness for many more moments in deep silence.

"You and I share the same sense of right and wrong, Federico, but we're from different molds. You chose not to confront them. I believe I can. I say nothing now, I spend my time learning what they know and building alliances. And when I become chief executive I make the changes that must be made."

"They will kill you."

"Kill me?"

"Most certainly. You will have an untimely accident. Or fall mortally ill from some strange disease or condition, certified by legitimate medical authorities."

"They are that evil?"

"Evil? No. That's what makes this situation so impossible for us. "In most respects they are good people. They faithfully attend church. They send their children to the best schools. They contribute generously to worthy causes. For the most part they are shrewd and accomplished business people. But they all live within an evil system. For generations Groupo Aragon and other companies like them have paid off politicians and used their economic and political power to dislodge the weak from their possessions—all justified as common business practice. They create victims each day, and as in both the Aztec and Mayan cultures, losers suffer and often die.

"You heard the eulogies at the service. They were heartfelt. Papa was loved and respected because he was a valuable part of this system. The church was filled with winners, and Papa was truly a hero to them. The losers were not there. They could not afford the fine clothes, the cars and drivers, the big payoffs required to be in the pews all around us. If you were to try to change the culture of Groupo Aragon, you would be a threat to all those who were there to mourn. Yes, they would find a way to remove you. Then they would all pay homage at your funeral. The Aragon board is not making this offer to give you power. It's to be a face that helps mask the true nature of theirs."

Isabel pondered for a moment. "What if I were to confront them immediately, explain that I understand what's been happening, but that there's more to be gained by doing it honestly, and that they should know from the start what to expect?"

"They won't allow it."

They walked for moments more in silence.

"What can I do? I don't have all the options that were open to you, Federico."

"Meaning?"

"I can't even become a Jesuit priest."

7

Five days from her walk into darkness with Federico. Five days of personal anguish. Could she talk about this with her father? No. He had to be aware, or at least to suspect the truth. His head was down. He was doing his job. He and mother were living comfortable lives. Malcolm Tennyson was not one to raise ethical questions with Groupo Aragon. Certainly he had been in no position to confront Papa, his lifetime nemesis. Federico had never talked to father about it. Neither could she. She could talk with no one, only herself, in lonely hours when there was no distraction to divert her from the truth. On this, the fifth day, Groupo Aragon's board of directors was meeting. The introduction of Isabel Aragon was the first item on the board's agenda.

Now she sat facing the company's twelve directors, all men, each of them a major figure in Latin America's corporate world. Javier Carmona, ever gracious, introduced Isabel to the board.

"For those who do not personally know Señora Aragon Tennyson," said Carmona, "I want to commend her as a worthy heir to Don Miguel, who we all respected and loved as our own brother."

Heads around the table nodded and all rose as one in a gesture of respect. It was a room that reflected Miguel Aragon. Paintings by elite Latin artists marched across the walls, an attraction and intimidation for those whom Miguel wished to impress. The conference table was itself a work of art, fashioned by hand from rare Bolivian rosewood. The water pitchers were hammered silver from Taxco. Marble topped side tables stood in each corner, against Brazilian ebony wall panels. The board room and everything in it was museum quality.

Isabel had never been here. She was stunned at the opulence that surrounded her, unnerved by the commanding stature of the men who stood to greet her.

"As you are aware, gentlemen," Carmona continued when all were seated, "It is Don Miguel's wish that Señora Tennyson be prepared for Groupo management. We all owe much to Don

Miguel, and I am sure we all agree that we should respect his wishes."

Heads around the table nodded respectfully.

"Of course, señora has much to learn." He turned to her.

"All of us know of your great success in closing the Temuco merger in Chile last week, and we are most grateful for your skill in doing that in the most trying of circumstances. Now we are hopeful you can become familiar with our entire enterprise so that one day you may play a much larger role. But I have spoken too long. señora, please address our board."

Her moment had arrived and she was terrified. The impulse to run from the room nearly overcame her. Her next impulse was to speak meaningless banalities, to avoid confrontation, to be a nice girl and do what was expected. But an image of Federico flashed before her. He had been here. His choice was to accept the inevitable. And Papa? Papa could not have willed her, his little treasure, to become a criminal. He must have been counting on her to make the changes he knew needed to be made. Last night, alone with her thoughts, she had decided to try to alter this reality. It might take years. But if she was patient and recruited allies….

Isabel unfolded a sheet of paper.

"Gentlemen. With respect for your time, and to assure that my thoughts are conveyed to you the way I intend them to be, I have written a brief statement.

"Señor Carmona……" she began by naming each person at the table individually to establish a personal bond.

"My grandfather was a vital part of my life. He taught me much. He wanted so much for me to succeed. He was an example for me of how to live my life. He taught me to be honest and truthful. I am sure he would expect no less from me today.

"Those of you who helped build Groupo Aragon have created an enterprise central to the lives of hundreds of millions of people, in Mexico and throughout the Latin world. You all can be proud of the countless jobs you created and continue to maintain. The homes, the agricultural fields, the industries, the research, all that you've accomplished. Thanks to your management skills, your energy, and your creativity, Groupo Aragon is a Latin American success story like few others."

Heads nodded. The men at the table knew that flattery was not a negotiable asset, but in the hard world of business, its rarity makes it most welcome.

"These are positive accomplishments and strengths. I applaud you all for them."

She stopped to sip water from the crystal goblet before her. She breathed deeply. For a moment she closed her eyes. Then resumed.

"And because of such success, Groupo Aragon has the resources to accomplish much more.

"As we all know from our basic sciences, where there are positives there are negatives. And we all know from our day-to-day activities that Groupo Aragon has negatives. We have done and continue to do things that do not make us proud. I need not go into detail. You know more than I what I'm referring to.

"I am humbled that you have agreed to honor my grandfather's wish—that I be groomed for leadership. In my heart I believe I have the skills, the temperament, and the desire to do this job and to do it well. I accept that challenge with respect and gratitude. But I am not my grandfather. While I honor his memory I do not honor some of his practice. Our time is not his time. My generation is not his generation. My business standards are not his. Therefore, so there will be no mistake of my intentions, I will accept this responsibility with the understanding that Groupo Aragon will move in a new direction."

She had everyone's full attention now. Her listeners' faces became uniformly noncommittal and impassive. This was a board comprised of those who played for high stakes. They knew how to mask feelings, no matter how intense.

Isabel continued. "It is in our best interests as a company to have a just and dependable legal system, where businesses and individuals alike can count on enforceable contracts and a minimum of corruption. In the United States, a generally fair legal system is an asset to all business. The larger the business, the larger the gain. We should work to bring such a system here. I believe we all know what I'm speaking of.

"We control so many markets and can continue to do so in a fair marketplace. Bribes for contracts and political influence are not and should not be necessary. Corruption creates a trail through a dark forest filled with frightening possibilities. Groupo Aragon should be an acknowledged leader in ending these practices.

"Money laundering. Is it the legacy of Mexico and the grand Aragon name to be the conduit for drug cartels and brutal dictators and other criminals throughout the world? Do we need to make our money that way? If, to run a successful business, we need to violate laws and help others violate laws, there are big problems with the management of that business. If we don't, let's not.

"These are just some of my thoughts, gentlemen. I know you all to be gentlemen, honorable men. I ask nothing less for business done in Groupo Aragon's name. I accept my grandfather's destiny for me in that spirit."

The twelve men gathered around the conference table just stared at her, silently. Slowly, expressions formed. David Colon, director of banking and finance, betrayed a wry smile, lips turned up. Gerardo Aguirre, the board's vice chair and managing director, veteran of twenty years of Aragon combat and victories, revealed in eyelids that folded into narrow slits his anger at such impudence. Some heads turned to look at other heads, a slight twist of a neck, a cough and sudden glance. Isabel, expecting shock waves, held steady for them. She was determined to wait out the silence for a reaction.

It came from Javier Carmona.

"Señora," he said quietly, his voice at a volume and intensity no different from his introduction of her, with a matter-of-factness associated with the announcement of a lunch break.

"Señora," he repeated. You have given us much to consider and I promise you that we will. We now have a very long and detailed agenda of other matters. We thank you for your time and suggestions and after the board completes its business today I will be in contact to discuss our next steps. Please, let us all thank Señora Aragon Tennyson for her appearance with us today."

Carmona rose from his chair and began applauding. Others reluctantly followed his lead. Isabel wanted to talk more, to exchange views, to bring matters to a conclusion. But Carmona would not have it. In the gentlest of ways, he told her to get lost. It was an instruction she could not refuse.

***

She returned to the family compound in mental turmoil but pleased with herself for being true to her intentions. She spoke truth to some of the most powerful people in Mexico, ruthless, cunning people. Would they admire her for the guts she displayed in calling them out? Would they hate her for interfering with a longstanding game at which they were most proficient and clearly successful? Ground that had seemed so solid to her just a few days earlier now felt dangerously unstable. Her idyllic life was threatened. Her idol destroyed. The wealth all around her now appeared to be dripping with the sweat and misery and blood of her family's victims.

Two messages waited for her when she returned home. One was a request that she meet with Javier Carmona at 10:00 a.m. the next morning. The waves roiled in the wake of Isabel's meeting with the board had rippled quickly. The board apparently had lost no time reaching agreement about how to deal with her.

The second message was an envelope. Inside, on a silver chain, was a Saint Benedictine medal, worn not just by Roman Catholics but by those of many denominations to ward off evil and temptation. Isabel recognized it as Federico's. It was accompanied by a brief hand-written note from her brother. "God be with you. I will always be there for you, even if you never ask…" Federico had disappeared back into the land of Groupo Aragon's victims.

8

"Señora, so good to see you again. Thank you for being here on such short notice. I am certain that you would like to resolve questions about your future as quickly as possible, and that also is our wish for the stability of Groupo Aragon."

"Yes, certainly," Isabel responded. "I hope the members of the board accepted my comments in a positive spirit. That's what I intended."

"We all appreciated your candor. It's so much easier to do business when all parties are as forthright."

"I respect the achievements of the board members and look forward to working with them and learning from them."

Why not assume the best, thought Isabel.

"Ah, señora, that is what we must discuss. In your American baseball you have what are called veterans who have been playing the game for a long time and rookies who are new to the game, yes?"

"Yes, and you don't have to convince me, I'm a rookie."

"But yesterday you spoke to a group of veterans. A group that includes many who would be in a business hall of fame, if we had such an institution. You spoke in a way that was most disturbing, as a rookie."

"I certainly regret if any took offense. I meant none. I just didn't want to surprise anyone later with my views on how the business should be run."

"It was not an offense. It's very hard to offend people like us who have been through so many difficult and delicate business experiences. It was actually helpful. We all understood from your remarks that there would be too deep a divide between us to have a successful long-term relationship. It is much better that we know that now than later. We all appreciate that you have made that clear."

"I'm sorry to hear that."

"As are we. It would have been an honor to have had a member of the great Aragon family in leadership again."

"What do you mean, would have?"

"The members of the board have decided to terminate our relationship with you immediately, on cordial terms, of course, before any misunderstandings arise that might compromise the business later."

"But you can't do that. My grandfather's will…. you yourself said it was his wish."

"Forgive me, señora. At yesterday's meeting of the board I was reminded of an amendment to the will, signed and executed while I was traveling in China. Your grandfather used an outside counsel. The amendment provides that the board must ratify any decision for succession. At yesterday's meeting the board declined to ratify your status and instructed me to reach a termination agreement with you."

Federico anticipated this would be the most likely outcome. *They won't let you*, he had said. She had hoped for better but since it came as no surprise, she managed to maintain a rigid composure. She had overcome her weaknesses yesterday, confronting the entire board. She could certainly go one-on-one with Carmona.

"Javier, you have invented this barrier haven't you? You said nothing about this when we first spoke. There is no such addendum. I do not believe it and I will challenge legally. I will not be bullied."

"It hurts me, señora, that you believe I am dishonoring your grandfather and his trust. He's a man I loved and honored as I would my own brother. Yes, there is an addendum. Here's a copy."

Carmona had the document ready on his desk and handed it to her. As she scanned it he said, "It's all properly executed and registered. It was created by one of Mexico's leading law firms."

Isabel saw that this track had closed before she even left the building yesterday. She moved to another, one of conciliation.

"Javier, I've had time to study the business. And, yes, I've spoken with my brother. What I said yesterday, about being able to grow and profit and do that without exploiting the weak or skirting the law or making a mockery of ethical behavior, I believe that. I have no way of knowing what my grandfather faced in building Groupo Aragon. But I know today's business. You say one of my strengths would be to expand our enterprise into the United States. To do that, we would have to comply with much more rigorous ethical codes and legal restraints than you have in Mexico. Let's work together to migrate Groupo Aragon into being a good citizen rather than a corrupt one."

"But señora, we already are good citizens. In the last year alone we supported such causes as the nation's soccer team, the national opera, thousands of scholarships for bright young students to attend colleges anywhere in the world, and local causes in every state and community in Mexico. We are good citizens."

"We are a corrupt monopoly," Isabel pressed on, "We can change that. Everyone at the table yesterday is rich beyond any fortune they could possibly spend in their lifetime. Billions and billions of pesos are in Groupo Aragon's accounts just waiting to be distributed to those of us who privately own shares. Meanwhile we starve workers and grab their homes when they can't make a mortgage payment. As a monopoly we charge far more than we need to charge for services people can't live without. The reduction of profit by even a small amount could make huge differences in the lives of tens of millions of people. And we would have a healthier economy—more money to spend, better educated people, housed better, lower health costs.

Isabel paused, looking for a signal from Carmona's passive expression to see whether she was making an impression. There was none. He was the veteran. The pro. Probably the hall of famer.

She continued. "We have it in our power to reduce all the killings from the cartels and make a significant reduction in violence, lawlessness, the transport of illegal money. That's all I'm talking about, and it should neither upset you and the board nor disqualify me from a leadership role in this company."

Carmona retained his demeanor of cordiality. He offered her more coffee. He weighed his response carefully. She waited. The next move would be his.

"Señora, it is not for us to say what the culture of an entire nation or continent will be. We live in the time and the place where we find ourselves. There are fantasies and realities. Your grandfather operated extremely successfully in this world. Should you try to change this now, others would only fill that vacuum and most likely would do it with less concern for those you hope to help. If you value Don Miguel's memory, the good man that he was, the loving family patriarch, the bearer of all the things brought to you and your family, listen to those with far more experience and knowledge than you have. I am so sorry señora. I'm afraid there will be no possibility of the enterprise allowing you to participate in our management. You have told the directors of Groupo Aragon of your vision for the company. Now they have told you that your vision is not theirs. We will have to part ways."

Conciliation track ended, Isabel moved to round three.

"You should know that I will challenge this."

Carmona was silent for a moment, apparently in deep thought.

"Does that disturb you?" she asked.

"Forgive me, señora, I was just thinking, trying to recommend a law firm in Mexico substantial enough and courageous enough to accept a management control case against Groupo Aragon. So many firms would find conflicts with business they already do with us and with the companies of those who serve on our board."

"I'll find an American firm."

"Ah, yes, an American firm. They would cost you a great deal more, of course. I hope you have the resources to pay them."

"I'm rich. You told me that yourself. I'm worth a billion American dollars."

"You certainly are, as soon as we transfer the stock to you. Unfortunately, the employment agreement you signed with us years ago includes a provision that anything of value owed to an employee by the company will be frozen until any litigation between the company and the employee is resolved. It's a standard clause, for the company's protection. And of course it would be applied if you litigate. You certainly are free to make any claim you wish against the company. And once those issues are resolved we will release what's due to you. That may be in, what, three, five, ten years? The Mexican judicial system isn't known for its speed and efficiency."

Carmona's handling of her was relentlessly proper and cordial, with even the most dire threats positively framed. She was only now realizing how masterful an adversary he was. But she was not finished.

"Javier," I have contacts. I've been dealing with people of wealth for many years. I can afford to hire counsel. Eventually you will have to release my money. Everyone who works with me will know they will be paid."

"As you wish, Señora Tennyson. But before you go, it would be in your best interest, in your family's best interest, to know that we have been investigating many irregularities that seem to be connected with Southern California Trust and Savings, our bank that your dear father has so ably managed for many years."

That threat sent an instant chill up Isabel's back, and for the first time in the conversation she lost control.

"My father! He has nothing to do with this!"

"Of course he doesn't. I am just mentioning it as a friend, so it will not come as a surprise to you and your family."

"What type of......irregularities?" She spit out the word.

"Some missing funds. Possibly nothing. Perhaps clerical error. But we cannot be certain. It would be most unfortunate if your father, so close to retirement, were to be held responsible for any problems found by our examiners. Such things, you know, can lead to time in prison as well as dismissals."

Carmona had this card in his hand all along. She had never considered it. Ruthlessness to her had been an abstract concept. Now she saw its face. She had a lot to learn.

She just sat and stared at Carmona, who, with kindly eyes, didn't blink.

Hall of famer is all she could think of. Hall of famer. Game over. Rookie loses.

They understood one another. No more words needed to pass between them. But Carmona tried never to leave a defeated foe lying wounded and unattended after a negotiation. Angry losers were dangerous.

"Señora Tennyson. Because of the affection your grandfather held for you he left you a sizable portion of his own fortune. When all the papers are properly filed and money is transferred you will be one of the richest women in the entire world. You can do anything you want. You can buy yachts. You can have your own personal jet plane. You can buy your own island. You can buy your own bank and operate it any way you wish. You can give it all away if that's your choice. The one thing in this entire world you will not be able to do is have any position in authority with Groupo Aragon. Welcome your good fortune. Don't grieve for any loss.

"The enterprise will accept your resignation from your current position with regret and understanding after a proper mourning period. Your father's good name will be secure. Sizable donations will be made to the charities important to your mother in your grandfather's name. "Life will continue, and likely much better for you than before. We wish you only the best."

Her energy spent, understanding her defeat, the tight ball of determination that had been Isabel Aragon Tennyson unraveled into the cushions that had been her battle station. She looked at him for a silent moment, a look that simultaneously conveyed both admiration and disgust.

"Who will become the chief executive of Groupo Aragon," she asked, quietly, curiously.

Carmona stood, signaling that the meeting was over. He extended his hand. Reflexively she allowed him to help her rise, not a handshake, more of a splint for her broken spirit.

"Yesterday the board elected me to that position," said Carmona. "I will try to honor your dear grandfather, my best friend, Don Miguel, by managing Groupo Aragon just as he would."

Political

Years

9

For most, the bulging bank account that accompanied Isabel on her return to Los Angeles would have been life's defining experience. For Isabel, conflicted by feelings of love for and betrayal by her grandfather, and the tainted source of her new fortune, the money was not enough to cure her sense of defeat and loss, feelings that traveled with her from Mexico City and remained despite all remedies she used to get past the black days just endured. Loss of Papa Miguel, and the obliteration of his revered pedestal. Loss of self-confidence. She felt adrift. No goal to aim for. No job to go to. For the past six years her work had been her life. Her home was the 6,000-mile sea of air between Los Angeles and the southern coast of Chile, with ports of call in between. Fun, excitement, her ego polished with each new business and romantic conquest. Now it had ended, abruptly. In little more than a week, her triumph with the Banco Temuco deal had spiraled into Miguel's death, Federico's shocking revelations and, finally, her humiliating failure to secure the Aragon legacy Miguel had intended for her.

She filled the first weeks of her return with busy work, some necessary, like finding ways to secure and invest her new fortune, some frivolous, like replacing most of her furniture and dressing her kitchen in a happier shade of blue. She wanted her new world to look different than the painful one she was leaving behind. Though she kept herself occupied with mail, phone calls, family, nothing weakened her consuming sense of sorrow. Until she thought of Carmie. Once again, Carmie.

So many times it was Carmie she had turned to when they were both young and things went badly at home, or a boyfriend dumped her, or she just felt teenage blah. Carmie had helped her get past Andres and her miscarriages. Now the need for Carmie welled as an imperative. Once the thought entered her head there was no denying it. A phone call, a plane ticket, and within two days the old friends were together in New York City, sharing margaritas at the Gramercy Park Hotel bar, near Carmie's apartment.

While Tenny was becoming a force in Latin American finance, Carmie had been growing her own reputation on Wall Street as a trusted and perceptive financial analyst. Carmie knew enough about Groupo Aragon from street talk not to be surprised at Tenny's story. What did surprise her was the courage and naivety her friend showed trying to upend that corporate behemoth. She loved Tenny for it.

"You know of course," said Carmie, "Carmona was right."

"Not from you, too, Carmie!"

"No. Hear me out. Even if Carmona agreed to let you stay there and try to change the culture, your chances of doing it would be worse than zero. The other barracudas in the company would do you in. I fight turf and control battles every day, and that's right here in New York, where the rule book means more. If you hadn't lost to Carmona, it would have been to whoever's under him gunning for his job, or some competitor, or judge, or politician. It's the system. No. You have to pick fights you can win."

"What fights? I've got nothing now. No job. All my old business ties have been cut. It's like starting over with no direction, no place to go, nothing to hang onto."

Carmie jumped off her bar stool and circled her friend like she was a strange object in a curio shop.

"You don't know what to do? You don't know what to do? You have no direction? Your old life is over? Are you nuts or what? You don't have to live in someone else's corrupt world. Make your own world. A clean slate means no obligations to anyone but yourself. You're your own person, with all the money anyone could ever want. Put all of it to work—all of it, your money, your time, your experience, your energy, your brilliance, your dedication—all of it—doing something positive, not picking impossible fights.

"What should I do, set up my own foundation and give money to good causes? I've thought of that."

"Listen. You came up with an agenda for Aragon. It didn't work. Take it somewhere else, somewhere where it will. My friend, you were pretty unrealistic thinking you could change the entire Mexican business and political culture single handedly. Admit it. That was a foolish thing you did. Lovely, but foolish."

"Okay, maybe so. But then why did my grandfather write me into his will as a future company CEO? He knew as well as anyone that it was a corrupt enterprise. I'd like to think he wanted me there to clean it up."

"Could be. And I would cherish that thought. He may well have had a late-in-life conversion and after seeing you perform decided you'd be strong enough to clean up their act. That's really the way you should remember him."

"Oh, Carmie, I want to. I really want to. Federico has a darker view of it. He thinks Papa misread me. I pulled off so many deals using marginal ethics, Federico thinks Papa came to believe I was one of them and could be trusted to be a figurehead without rocking the boat. That's the life Papa apparently had planned for Federico."

"Miguel's motives don't matter now. Think kindly of him. It's easier for you. If he misjudged anything, it likely was how quickly his people would turn on you and run you out. What does matter is what comes next. Are you sure you don't want to use your money to lead a jet-set, glamorous life? No one would blame you. In fact, it's what most people would probably do if they struck it rich."

"No, Carmie, Federico inspired me. He's doing penance his way. I need to find my way."

"Well the place to start is in the real world."

"The real world?"

"You've been riding in first class and looking down at the world from 30,000 feet. What do you know about people who can't find jobs or who need three jobs to keep the lights on and food on the table? Do you know anyone like that? Can you name one person? One hour you've spent with them?"

"No, you're right. Not one."

"Do you know what it's like to run away from abusive husbands, with no money and no relatives or friends to take you in? Do you know what it's like to live every day looking over your shoulder hoping you won't get outed by your employer for being here illegally, or your husband or wife or kid won't run a red light and be hauled off to a relocation camp? All the time I see people writing big checks to their old alma maters, or hospital funds or other causes without having a clue where that money goes and what it goes for. But they feel good about it because it's quote, *charity*, unquote, and they get the tax write-off. Don't be one of those people. You're too good for that. One of your great talents is doing the research before you act. That's how you got so many clients when no one else in Aragon could. Now do it for yourself.

"If you want to use your money for the Aragon agenda, first do the research on what that agenda should be. Get down on the streets and get some experience learning what organizations do that help battered women, homeless people, hungry people, sick people, unemployed people, overemployed people. To fix problems, you have to understand them. You are what Carmona called you, a rookie. Become a journeyman. Maybe if you see these problems how they really are, in person, you may not want anything to do with them at all."

"Are you saying I should be like a Salvation Army volunteer for the rest of my life?"

"Well, if you want to become Mother Teresa for Los Angeles why not? My guess, knowing you, is that it won't take long for you to become more useful than just a soup kitchen volunteer. You'll figure it out. You're a smart girl. The point is, you have to start over somewhere. If you're not interested in a life of luxury and would rather spend time and big bucks helping people, get to know how people live and what they need and what would really help them."

Tenny stared into her margarita glass, her mind weighing her friend's advice. It made sense. That was a big key to her business success. Knowing. Being prepared. No winging it. What did she really know about life, other than how it's lived in the very narrow spectrum of her class of wealth and privilege and power? Federico had considered his move for years. He had weighed all his alternatives, dismissing many for reasons he could explain to himself and to her that awful night in the garden. He made a rational choice. Her reaction had been emotional, impetuous, not carefully considered or realistic.

She lifted her glass and licked salt from its rim.

"Okay, you're right, as usual. I buy it. Now what do I do? Walk into the closest food bank and volunteer?"

"In a way. Look. I've got an idea. For years I've been working with a group here in New York called New York Lights. It's sort of an umbrella organization for a lot of the groups that have food banks, shelters, charity distribution, things like that. We raise money, get management help and back them up so they can spend more of their donations on serving people, not administration. Move to New York and I'll introduce you to all the players. You'd fit in great here. And think of it, the two of us on the streets together raising hell like we used to. New York's a great city. It deserves us."

"I'd love that, Carmie. I'd love to spend more time with you. But my father's about to retire, mom's heart's a big concern for us and Miguel's death has been tough on her. I should stay close. Besides, I like living in Los Angeles. I've had two homes, really, Mexico City and L.A. I don't think I'm up for a third. After all those years of living on airplanes and hotels, I'm sort of desperate to just live in one place."

Carmie looked at her friend closely, tapped her fingers on the walnut bar top as if keying up alternatives.

"OK, how about this, then. We have a sister group in Los Angeles called L.A. Lights. Not as big or developed as the one we have here in New York, but it's really well run and mostly feeds the hungry. An old classmate of ours, Hal Thompson, remember him, from those awful statistics classes? He's a lawyer and he spends a lot of time helping this group. He's also in court a lot arguing for tenant rights. He's a real saint. Hook up with Hal. He knows all the players. You'll be a good team. I'll call him and set up a meeting. It's a way to get started."

10

"Tenny!"

No one but Carmie had used that name in years. Since college she had been Isabel, prowling Latin America and California wealth communities like a hungry feline. Her prey, big bank accounts. The wealth world knew her as Isabel Aragon Tennyson. Now, here was a voice from her past, startling her with its enthusiasm as she entered Starbucks. Carmie must have asked Hal to be particularly welcoming to her fragile friend. He beamed sunshine and embraced her.

Carmie had known Hal well in college, where she, like most young women in their circle, used sharp elbows against constant competition to dance with him. Tenny hadn't paid much attention to Hal. Hal had seemed rail thin to her then. Now he filled his suit as pleasantly as a Zegna model. He was clean shaven, a welcome change from all the beards and mustaches so ubiquitous in Latin America. They settled in over lattes.

"So tell me," she asked, "why am I here?"

"Good question," Hal replied. "Carmie says you can be anywhere you want doing anything you want. But I'd guess you're here because you want to do more than entertain yourself."

"Well, yes. Carmie thinks I don't know enough about how most people really live. She's right."

"Neither do I. I mean, I'm hardly an authority on people. But I've had a lot of experience with people near the bottom rungs."

"Homeless? Out of work?"

"Sure, but you'd be surprised how many need help who have jobs and homes."

"Like?"

"Just yesterday I got a bank to hold off foreclosing on a woman who works three jobs and it's barely enough to cover day care for her kids, along with her mortgage and the food for their table. Nearly every day I get a call from some group to help a woman whose husband beat her bloody and she ran from the house and needs protection. Things like that."

"And where's L.A. Lights fit in?"

"A bunch of us try to coordinate all the groups on this side of the divide. You know, the food banks, homeless shelters, rape crisis people, all that, to see if we can change things at wholesale."

"Wholesale?"

"Yeah, wholesale. Social service at retail is important, but there's never enough volunteers, and too little money. We're fighting some entrenched heavyweights and we need to bulk up."

"I'm not sure I understand."

"I think that's the answer to your question about why you're here. I'll show you. It's hard to understand if you just talk about it. Just tag along with me for a while. Go where I go. See what I see. It explains itself."

She took a last sip of latte, the last bite of her chocolate biscotti. This felt right. More than right. Here she was, in her mid-thirties tingling like an impressionable teenager at the prospect of living with the underclass. Hal was offering to guide her on an adventure. She nodded assent, trying as best she could to mask her excitement.

***

Her car phone rang as she drove home from meeting with Hal. Carmie.

"So, how'd it go?"

"Wow, you don't waste a minute, do you. I just left him."

'And…"

"Hal's going to show me the streets. That should help cure my 30,000 feet problem."

"Great. And what do you think of Hal?"

"Nice. Nice guy. He made me feel like he was glad to do this for me."

"Did he make you feel anything else?"

"Carmie! You're the one who had a crush on him, not me."

"Okay, okay. I'll ask you again in a few weeks, after you two have spent some time together."

11

Tenny and Hal met most days at Hal's law office in Studio City, a small enclave of Los Angeles just over the Hollywood Hills in the San Fernando Valley. Hal tried to whip through work for his paying clients during the morning hours, leaving clean up details for his two paralegals. Then it was on to wherever the day's pro bono work took them. Sometimes to L.A. Lights' store fronts helping to manage food service or clothing distribution. Other days they could be in court, fighting for a restraining order to stop an eviction. Or at a contentious city council committee meeting to plead for more money for a rape crisis shelter. This was the vortex that sucked up Hal's days, and now hers, turning her notions of help from abstract penance to a cause with human faces.

The Los Angeles Tenny returned to was home to about ten million people, where rivers of races and cultures converged. Los Angeles had become one of the most unequal places to live in the United States. Earnings, life expectancy and educational achievement all registered far higher for those living in prosperous and whiter beach and hill communities than in neighborhoods largely populated by Latinos and African Americans.

Until Hal, Tenny's life had been protected as carefully as if she lived inside an insulated rainbow. Unpleasantness not welcome. Now she was sharing streets where a warm cup of coffee, a cot for the night, a clean toilet, medication when needed—so many things taken for granted by those in her pre-Hal life, were daily uncertainties. Not for "groups," or "classes of people." But for those with faces, names, families, individual crises that defined their daily reality. Before, in Tenny's world, there had been safety, now there was just enough disorder to keep her on the edge of discomfort, occasionally even slipping into fright. She was traveling through space she had never known. She loved it.

To these encounters, Tenny brought an important asset Hal lacked, fluency in the Spanish language. She could understand what English-only speakers often missed, key details of a problem, the nuances of feeling. Slowly she was evolving into more than Hal's appendage, a development Hal welcomed. It meant that they could widen their reach.

One of the best ways to make money is to have money. With the right investments and little or no labor, money makes money through interest, dividends, rising land values and stock prices. Tenny had spent years managing the wealth of others. It gave her a valuable head start on how to manage her own. A billion dollars is a thousand million. Invested at 5 percent, that billion earns $50 million each year. Not all of her money was invested to produce interest. Some was used to buy real estate and undeveloped land for future appreciation. Some went into venture funds. More than she would admit found its way anonymously into local causes and support for individuals who came to her attention. Even with her generosity, even with her annual tax bill, her fortune continued to grow.

In Hal's world, her new world, she was Tenny Tennyson, volunteer. Presumed well-off divorcee or widow or single woman with a good heart and free time. No one knew of the Aragon connection, the deep Mexican roots, the bottomless wealth stored in her accounts. She was always in jeans, the non-designer variety, sweatshirts or something comparable, tennis shoes or walking shoes, and lightly made up. She cut an unremarkable figure. When they traveled it was in Hal's eight-year-old Ford sedan, not her silver 700 series BMW.

Months into their collaboration, Hal had a day-long court date in Long Beach, followed that evening by a neighborhood council meeting in East Los Angeles, a poor, densely populated, overwhelmingly Latino-centric corner of the city. That meant a lot of driving. Thirty miles from his office to Long Beach, another thirty back to pick up Tenny after the court session, and then twenty miles each way from Tenny's home to the East Los Angeles community center. It was 11:00 p.m. when they reached the driveway at Tenny's hillside home off of Beverly Glen Drive. He had never been here. She had never invited him, until now.

"Come in for a drink," she said. "Been quite a day for you."

"One for the road?" he smiled. "Sold."

"Let's sit in the living room," she said. She bent down, turned two knobs and a fire immediately sprang into life from the artificial gas logs in front of her. It was a chilly night. The warmth was welcome. Hal went where visitors to this home always were drawn first, to the floor to ceiling sliding glass doors separating the living room from the outdoor pool and patio, awash tonight in shades of blue and kinetic herring bone patterns designed by the pool's lights. Beyond the patio, the San Fernando Valley, an endless carpet of light, a transfixing sight, even to those who see it often. A landscape created by man, not nature.

"My home in Mexico City was on a hillside like this. As a little girl I would look down on the city's lights hours on end. I imagined so much that was happening inside all of those lights. Little girl thoughts. I guess that's why I bought this home. To recapture some of those feelings."

She settled onto the sofa facing the fire, legs curled up, drink in hand. She handed Hal his as he sat beside her, looking into the flames, the only light in the otherwise darkened room.

"Oh, that's good!" said Hal. Much better than I usually drink. What is it?"

"It's a rye. Dickel, from Tennessee. My favorite. And not expensive."

"Well, after today it's really welcome. I was more than ready for it. Thanks for asking me in."

They sat in silence for a few minutes, hypnotized by the erratic dance of flames.

"Actually, if you hadn't invited me in I was going to ask anyway. There's some business I'd like to talk about."

"Oh, Hal, just unwind. You've done so much today."

"Something you said tonight just clicked with me. Remember, during the talk about getting more cops on the streets in those neighborhoods you said I wish I had the power to just do it. I'd just put up the money and the cops would be there. I've been thinking about that driving you home. In a way, an indirect way, you already do have that power."

"Me? Wonder Woman! I had no idea!"

"Well not with a cape and a funny suit. But your money could pay for a political organization that could get the power."

"Where do you buy power?"

"Politics. Political organization."

"We already have friends in city hall and other places."

"This job's too big for just friends. Not people just willing to give us the time to hear our case and then think about it. It has to be people like us. People who will just do it because they believe in it. People who already are persuaded. People we put in power and can jerk right back out if we have to. We need a political organization.

"I'm not sure I understand. I don't know anything about politics. I've never voted. In fact, I've never even registered to vote."

"And that's it," he said, suddenly sitting up straight. "That's it. You're not alone. Think about it. If we could turn the thousands of people like you who work so hard as good cause volunteers into a political force, and lash in the labor people and environmental people and all the ethnic groups—Latinos, Japanese, Chinese, Koreans, blacks—what a force. We'd be unbeatable. We could elect anyone we wanted. We. I mean people like you and me, who think like you and me. We could run L.A. and most of the smaller cities in the county."

Tenny laughed. "Hal, you need another drink. "

He willingly handed her his glass for a refill.

"Yes, I do need another drink. That's good stuff. But hear me out. If we could register and mobilize all of our natural supporters, we could elect our people to the jobs that make policy and write the checks. Christ. That community we were in tonight needs a thousand more jobs. It needs a rec center for kids. Did you take a good look at those fire engines? Hand-me-downs. Class sizes there over thirty kids, 50 percent more than Beverly Hills. They need safe day care. They need everything. But they're not even fighting for it. "

"Why?"

"Why? Because we've trained them to beg for crumbs and then lick our fingers in gratitude if something, anything, good happens."

The outburst surprised her. She thought they were decompressing after a stressful day. Dancing fire. Excellent whiskey. Hal seemed in no mood to relax.

They sat quietly for a few moments. She wanted to respond but wasn't sure how.

He turned to her, smiled widely and shook his head.

"Sorry, Tenny. Didn't mean to rant on you."

"It's one of the things I admire most about you, Hal. You're doing all this because you really mean it. You don't just think it, you feel it."

He took a long sip of his drink. Then another.

"When you said tonight *if you had the power*. That was an eye opener for me. I've been thinking like a lawyer, handling individual cases. And I've been thinking like a lobbyist, trying to convince powerful people with arguments they might or might not buy, competing with other people with more money and more influence. But the key to getting what we want is political power. And if we package it right, we can get it."

Hal turned to face Tenny.

"Tenny, would you be willing to write a million dollar check to start a political action committee?"

"What's a political action committee, and what do I get for that kind of investment?"

"It's called a PAC, and it's a legal way for people to organize for political action. We'd use it to pull together all of our allies into a single political force. We'd put pressure on people in office and we'd elect our own slates. The payoff? Tens of millions, maybe hundreds of millions of dollars more from the city and county and federal government for all the causes we're working for."

"Sounds like a good investment. You figure out how to do it and make it work and I'm in. And if it's as good as you say I can twist a lot of other arms for more."

Hal leaned over, held the back of her head with one hand and kissed her cheek hard. The sudden act of affection startled her. He moved quickly between political calculations and gratitude and back again.

"We need a pro to create a strategy, a plan. We have to pull the groups together. We need to run real campaigns. And I know just the guy. Ben Sage. My best friend in high school. Now he's one of the best political strategists in the country. He works out of Washington. You'd really like him. He knows everything we don't about running campaigns. Ben Sage."

He hugged Tenny again, his brain afire with this transcendent idea, his body feeling the glow from two glasses of straight whiskey and now the heat radiating from this woman next him, lips close to his, arms returning his embrace, the scent of her hair.

Tenny needed no further stimulation. Hal's lips were just inches from hers. She dove into them, her lips wide open, devouring his tongue, running her hands wildly through his golden hair. Her sudden move pushed Hal back into the pillows. She hung on tightly, falling gently with him. She was so very hungry.

There would be other nights. The next three, in fact. Passion had erupted with too much force to be easily contained. As the days became weeks, the intensity ebbed, but didn't disappear. Naked body time, once introduced into the lives Tenny and Hal were sharing, would remain.

Many years earlier Tenny had fallen in love with Andres. For her, it was love as she always had imagined it. Andres became her life. Twice since then she had met men who not only set off sexual sparks but consumed her every thought. For a while. Those encounters peaked quickly and just as rapidly declined. She felt she had so much love in her, but that love came in brief bursts.

She had been there with Andres. She had little interest in revisiting the pain of a broken heart.

***

"Did you ever sleep with him?" asked Tenny.

"No," Carmie replied.

"Tell the truth. I won't be jealous."

"Never really came close. I might have if things were different. But outside of just having a good time at parties with lots of other people, we never connected where it could have happened. And since I've been in New York, my only contacts with him have been long-distance."

"Too bad."

"Are you bragging!"

"No, just stating a fact. Anyway, maybe he wasn't as good then as he is now."

"Do you love him? Is this going anywhere?"

"No. It's just here and now."

Actually, she did love Hal. She loved him for so many things. His dedication. His work ethic. His courage. His sensitivity to others. Now, she added to that list his exceptional performance in bed. But it was a love of mind and body, not of the heart. She was so thankful for that. Falling into romantic love with Hal would have come at the expense of the other bonds they had. Their work together gave her life meaning. She woke each day with great anticipation of new adventure or satisfying causes that new day would bring. For her, the arrangement was ideal. Her true love was her work.

Hal seemed not to want or need more either. No suggestions they move in together, or plan lives together. No words of love, except during those moments when such words are expected, when they pour forth on their own and evaporate with the last sighs on the pillow. In fact, Hal had a new true love, not Tenny, but politics.

12

In high school, Hal played power forward on the varsity basketball team, six foot one, all arms and legs, bone thin. A starter, not a star, but serviceable on a team that won more than it lost. Popular enough to run for student body president, not popular enough to win. Ben Sage had a different trajectory. He was the writer, the editor of the school paper, the quiet one usually found on the edges of the crowd, not in the spotlight.

Hal and Ben met as high school freshmen. One day Hal offered to give Ben a ride home from school on his Cushman motor scooter. Three blocks from Ben's house Ben began losing his grip and yelled for Hal to stop. Hal just laughed and accelerated faster. Ben tumbled off the scooter onto the hard asphalt, cartwheeling, scraping, bruising. That was the beginning of their friendship. Don't ask for an explanation why. They couldn't tell you. For the rest of their high school years they were best friends. Movies, double-dates, road trips. Then separation into their own life lanes.

Ben never doubted where his lane would lead. He would be a newspaper man, a journalist, an observer and chronicler of action, wherever the action was. Everything interested him, but no single interest so much that he wanted to build a silo around it and call it a career. Journalism could be anything. It was a mile wide and an inch deep. That suited Ben. It was his idea of a great lifestyle.

But as often happens with career plans, reality injects obstacles and choices seldom written into the original playbook. In Ben's case, the life-changing diversion came in the form of a friend running for mayor of Hawthorne, a forty-block indistinguishable rectangle of Los Angeles County that they call a separate city. Ben succumbed to his friend's plea to manage the campaign. Why not? It would be an interesting experience, helpful to Ben later in covering elections as a reporter. No one, including Ben, expected this campaign to win. But it did. And what an emotional high election night was. Ben had never felt anything like the rush. Not from alcohol or weed or even seeing his byline on newspaper stories. Others took notice of Ben. A county commissioner. A congressman. More wins. A proposal to join a political firm in Washington, D.C. More success. Now, on his own, a star in the narrow spectrum of stardom that attaches to the trade of electing candidates for public office. Ben's firm, Sage and Searer, was on the short list of most Democratic Party candidates in the United States who could afford professional consulting and management.

Despite Ben's other workload, he could not resist Hal's call to change the political dynamics of Los Angeles. Hal was one of his closest friends, Los Angeles his home base. With some rearrangement of his work schedule, Ben was able to respond to Hal's call before month's end. He brought with him to Los Angeles an arsenal of political weapons, including strong contacts with national labor and political leaders. He persuaded those contacts to lean hard on their local affiliates to enlist in Hal's new political creation. They called it "Lights on L.A.," or LOLA for short.

"I like it," said Ben. "Whatever Lola wants, Lola gets…you know, from *Damn Yankees*. We start with a winning image even before our first election."

Tenny wrote the big check she had promised and raided the wallets and purses of wealthy friends and business contacts. There's nothing like a war chest to make a political organization real. With money and a coalition of labor, environmental and ethnic groups under the tent, LOLA immediately became a power factor in Southern California politics.

Ben set up a LOLA office in the heart of the city's financial district, a brash show of force aimed at the local power structure. He imported his partner, Lee Searer, to recruit a veteran team of local researchers and organizers to manage operations.

Lee Searer was Ben's muse, the wonk who read the eight-page newsletters and hundred-page reports others just scanned, if at all; the researcher who could spot and develop the nuggets of information that would underlie campaign strategy, the theorist who could combine unrelated information into a powerful new way of looking at things. Lee was a refugee from academia, a former professor of American history at the University of North Dakota who met Ben during a campaign for the state's congressional seat. Lee loved the details, the demographics, the registration and turnout numbers, the polling crosstabs and data overlays. For Lee this all became discovery, and a platform for creativity.

Ben was the artful strategist. He would mold Lee's information and ideas into the messages that would control the campaign's narrative. Each campaign custom-made, many breaking new ground, deploying methods never before tried. You never knew what was coming at you from a Ben Sage campaign. It would be novel, hard to defend. It would be a campaign others would try to imitate. By then Ben would have moved on, attacking from new and unexpected directions. Ben began his career as a pencil pushing journalist, but slid seamlessly into electronic communication. He loved writing and directing radio and television commercials. He was a master at training candidates to make the most of their assets before crowds and cameras. Together, Ben Sage and Lee Searer were formidable.

Tenny was intrigued by all of the new political developments. She willingly underwrote and raised much of their costs. But politics was a world foreign to her. What she did know now, thanks to Hal, was the world of need, a world she had entered hoping to find a new life's purpose. Immersion had changed her. It was no longer about her but about them, those she encountered in her daily work. Those who never expected to be in a free soup line.

Families grateful for bundles of clothing. Children parked in temporary day care for parents who could neither pay nor do without their paychecks. As a charitable organization, L.A. Lights served a broad spectrum of the Los Angeles community. Undocumented immigrants were in the minority, but it was those cases that touched Tenny down to her Aragon roots.

Gloria was one. A sixty-year-old restaurant cook who glued patches of carpet on her shoes so she wouldn't leave tracks in the desert sand that border guards could follow. Gloria had returned to Mexico after ten years in Los Angeles to attend her father's funeral and had no legal way back. So she spent her meager life's savings to be smuggled across the border.

Fifteen-year-old Julio was another. In Sonora, he was threatened with death and the murder of his family if he didn't join a local drug gang. Father Federico Aragon shielded Julio for weeks until he could put him on a path to safe passage to the United States to live with relatives.

Most of the immigrant women who arrived at L.A. Lights had deserted Mexico after being victims of multiple physical attacks. Lawlessness ruled their daily lives. Bandits and militias would use the darkness of night to steal, rape, and murder.

Once, Federico wrote a letter to Tenny asking about a young woman named Delores who had come to him for protection, and whom he had helped with money, food, and the names of those who would cushion her in her flight to safety. Nothing had been heard from her since she left home. Her family was frantic. Tenny found Delores, in a white bag, with a red tag, in Arizona's Pima County medical examiner's office. Delores almost made it, but she had died of hypothermia. Her thin cotton clothing was no match for an exceptionally cold night during which she slept in hiding near the border.

For Tenny, many of those from the Latino community who came through her doors were victims of a system her own family had helped create. Through her contact with Federico, she knew not just why so many of the needy were here but what they had fled from and endured to get here. The flight from thugs hired by large land owners to quash peasant land protests, the scourge of disease casually treated for lack of local medical services, the search for opportunity for better lives than they and their families had ever known. Survivors shared their experiences with Tenny. But Tenny knew more than their stories. She knew the names and addresses and motives of many who contributed to such hardship and made flight, however treacherous and uprooting, an imperative. Tenny could see both the immediate problems and their antecedents. The whole, big, ugly picture.

Inevitably Tenny's past became current legend among the clients of L.A. Lights. The Aragon name was too well known. The Aragon tentacles too much feared. Yet many new arrivals owed their safe passage to the aid and advice of Father Federico, whom they regarded as a saint. Tenny, in her sweatshirts, jeans, comfortable shoes, and with her generosity of time and money, was approaching that status.

13

The economic engine driving the Los Angeles region is more diverse than most U.S. metropolitan areas. Manufacturing, international trade, finance, entertainment, tourism, and agriculture. Serving the region with water and power is itself a major industry. So is the expansion of offices, homes, highways and other infrastructure needs to keep up with century-long population growth. For many, that growth has been the source of enormous wealth, much of it generated by the labors of one of the lowest-paid work forces in the United States. Tenny joined L.A. Lights when business leaders were promoting more growth by touting Los Angeles as a low-wage alternative to unionized San Francisco.

L.A. Lights' mission was to help the victims of that economic divide. Hal organized LOLA to help close it.

Lee Searer quickly produced research documenting that tens of millions of public dollars had been invested in recent years to subsidize private projects such as hotels, sports venues, and industrial parks. In addition to actual cash outlays, taxpayers underwrote construction and maintenance of roads, ramps, and water and sewage systems to connect those projects and to advertise and promote them. Many private structures were built on public land ceded to developers or leased or sold at deeply discounted prices. Lee's research helped Ben create a short powerful mission statement for LOLA: "Public Dividends for Public Investments."

The research was a wake-up call for small business people who had been paying taxes but not sharing in the rewards. A coalition of small business owners was organized to fight for a more inclusive agenda. Other groups joined: clergy for economic justice, organized labor to fight for better pay and working conditions, environmental groups for land use and recreational payback in the form of parks, green energy and pollution control.

LOLA became the hub of many moving parts, carefully structured to pursue multiple agendas, mostly in a non-adversarial way—through the power of research and calls for equity. The effort was having success, but it still lacked the hefty punch Hal Thompson had envisioned. To do that, LOLA had to elect its own and instill the fear of political retribution in others. Hal and Ben scanned the political landscape for a suitable target, and found it in the form of Bert Wilmont.

Bert Wilmont was one of the key gatekeepers for the business power elite. Home-builder turned politician, Wilmont had chaired the Los Angeles City Council budget committee for the past eight years. Eight years of dramatic population growth but little change in the city's financial commitment to education, transportation, affordable housing, social services. Wilmont's tight fist had crushed many progressive plans. Wilmont had been easily re-elected three times. Now he seemed about to make it four. No candidate of substance had dared take the risk of running against him. That was the topic of this day's LOLA board meeting.

"Eight thousand votes, tops, would beat him in the Democratic Party primary," said Lee Searer. "Maybe seven thousand if the turnout's light. I've checked these numbers three ways. We're talking a ridiculously low bar for such an important council seat."

"Then why haven't we been able to recruit a candidate?" asked Ben.

"Fear," said Hal. "Everyone's afraid of Wilmont. Cross him and forget about ever getting a return phone call. If you want a future in L.A. politics or need anything from the city council, you don't challenge Bert Wilmont. Lee, how many volunteers can we count on if we compete in this district?"

"Around 130 have signed up. And there's maybe another 200 or so in the area, no more than a half-hour drive away."

"So, let's assume," said Hal, "only fifty volunteers working an average of four hours each week. That's two hundred hours with about five solid contacts an hour. A thousand contacts a week over ten weeks. Ten weeks, ten thousand personal contacts. We can do at least that many on the phones, too. Double that for many households with two or more people and we're talking forty thousand personal touches.

"Ken, how many union members in Wilmont's district?"

"About five hundred," said Ken Barkley, the AFL-CIO representative on the LOLA board.

"Tenny, with the right candidate, could you contribute or raise two-hundred thousand dollars for this campaign?"

"Sure. But who's the right candidate?"

"If no one else is willing to go for it, I will" said Hal.

All eyes around the table turned toward him. Never before had Hal been mentioned as a candidate for any office.

"It makes sense," said Ben. "Hal grew up in this district. He knows it well. He has no assets that would be at risk by challenging Wilmont. How much time can you spend on the streets, knocking on doors, Hal?"

"I could start tomorrow and do it nearly full-time."

"Realistically," said Ben, "I think Hal could cover two thousand individual doors in a ten-week campaign. Maybe more if we buy him an extra pair of good shoes."

"I've thought this through," said Hal. "Working with Ben and Lee's numbers, we can probably reach at least half of the likely voters in the district, at their door and by phone. And we can mail all the likely voters at least three times. With a two-hundred-thousand-dollar budget, we could pay people to deliver door hangers at the homes of target voters we don't reach with volunteers. Ads in the local papers are cheap. Wilmont's never raised more than fifty thousand for his campaigns. He won't this time, either, since he won't be expecting a tough race. He won't know he's in trouble until it's too late."

"It's risky," countered Lois Morales, representing United Latinos, one of LOLA's partner groups. "Lose and we're really shut out of anything we want from the council."

"Not necessarily," said Ben. "If we win, we're golden. If we come close, others on the council not as politically secure as Wilmont will get the message. To be a political power you have to exercise it, show it, make others fear it. Taking on Bert Wilmont is a gamble, but when you see how few votes we need to win, and you add up the resources we can throw at him and the value of the prize if we beat him, this campaign is ready-made for us."

"But what about you, Hal? Are you ready to be a candidate?" asked Seth Calley, the Democratic Party's district chairperson.

"I've watched that jackass up close for years," said Hal. "He'll chase a good idea down three flights of stairs to kill it. Lee's shown me the research from council votes, committee votes, newspaper and TV clips, conflict-of-interest stuff that no one's ever reported. I can use all of that to beat the shit out of that sonofabitch."

Tenny could feel the sizzle of excitement and opportunity arc around the table. The energy in the room was unlike anything she had experienced during her years of anticipation and success in wealth management. She savored the moment. She also sensed that Hal's life was about to undergo dramatic change, and with his, so was hers.

Whatever campaign skills Bert Wilmont brought to his first election had seriously eroded into complacency. For his past three campaigns, Wilmont had faced rag-tag, disorganized opposition. This time he was confronted with a well-funded campaign managed by a professional national agency using the latest computer-based data to power a field organization built on a database of likely voters. In the media, Wilmont was being forced to answer for votes and decisions he was hard-pressed to explain, but which served as grist for the creative media campaign being run relentlessly against him. Hal Thompson, a social service advocate with little prior name recognition, proved a telegenic contrast to Wilmont's dour demeanor. When the two went head to head at forums and debates, Hal held his own as a tough and informed challenger.

Organized by Sage and Searer's veteran teams, election day was worthy of a presidential voter turnout effort. Hal not only won a powerful seat on the council, but the victory stamped LOLA as the strongest political organization in Los Angeles County. The voiceless now would be heard. East Los Angeles would get not only more cops on the street, but also a new recreation center and low-cost day care. Before long, Hal would entice hundreds more good-paying jobs into this area of the city that desperately needed them.

14

Two years into his city council term there was a new Hal Thompson, a savvy politician, comfortable in the halls of power and the board rooms of the powerful. Hal was seldom seen now at the L.A. Lights office or other stops along his once familiar daily trail. It wasn't that he had abandoned his social activist roots. He was just growing new ones, as a creative force in Los Angeles politics, popular with the media and the public. Ben Sage's campaign expertise and Tenny's money allowed him to retain tight control of LOLA, and with it, a powerful lever for shaping city policy.

Tenny continued to live on both sides of the economic divide. During most days and many nights, she was a leader in the Los Angeles social service community, camping out in L.A. Lights headquarters and offices of affiliated organizations, donating and raising money, serving on boards, handling broad administrative jobs, and solving problems at the most personal level. Other days and other nights she was the wealthy heiress, socializing with moneyed friends, enjoying concerts and operas and art show openings, skiing, or traveling. She and Carmie made time for one another. They traveled together to sample Italy's wine and nightlife, and on a longer break they explored Japan and China.

As Tenny's role in L.A. Lights deepened, so did her mother's. Despite fragile health, Maria Tennyson was a frequent presence at the food banks and resale shops, insisting on volunteer duty. Estrangement between Tenny's mother and grandfather had framed a life for Tenny that spanned her Mexico City childhood and her family's exile to Los Angeles. Tenny had borne the tension, but she never understood its origin or the reason for its intensity.

"Why, mom? What was it between you and your father that made you go to New York as a young woman and made us leave Mexico?"

Tenny had never asked while Miguel lived. Whatever barrier there was between Maria and Miguel, she desperately wanted not to be part of it, not to mediate differences, neither to condemn nor defend. She loved them both and as long as their estrangement remained in a dimension beyond her own, she could share that love without guilt.

But now Miguel was gone, the Miguel who lived and the Miguel whose once pristine image had been warped beyond recognition. Questions begged for answers. Driving her mother to L.A. Lights for a morning's volunteer work, Tenny found the courage to ask.

For a while it seemed that her mother would not answer. Maria sat quietly, an aged woman with multiple physical infirmities, at a stage in life when events that once seemed defining can be jettisoned to lighten the load for whatever comes next.

"If he had died young," said Maria, finally, weighing her words carefully, "I would have loved him as a daughter should love a father. But it was as if he had died while knowing he was very much alive. Can you understand that, Isabel? He was alive, my father, but never my father."

"Many fathers travel and work nights and put careers ahead of family," Tenny said.

"Yes," said Maria. "and many children accept that. This was different and I was different. For Miguel, it was as if I did not exist. No interest in me. What I was doing. What I was feeling. I was an inanimate object. He cared more for those damn portraits on the wall. They were his life, his past, his legacy. I was nothing. I grew to hate them. I grew to hate him."

"You know, mom, I was kind of wild growing up. Maybe not as rebellious as you, running off to a different country. I can understand that. But when you and dad went back to Mexico City, Papa gave Federico and me so much time. Maybe he regretted not giving all that to you, too."

Maria disappeared into a world beyond words.

"Mom," said Tenny, after a few moments of silence, "Mom, are you okay?"

Her words came, reluctantly. That chapter of her life was long over, the scars buried deeper than words could excavate.

"After we returned," said Maria, "I learned some things. I sensed some things. Our home was beautiful. I love Mexico City. I had many friends there. But I learned…"

The silence returned. Maria clearly was being consumed by emotion. Sentences disjointed, unfinished.

More silence.

And then a complete thought.

"Miguel is gone. Let's pray his sins are forgiven and he's blessed by the Lord."

Maria knew. Somehow she knew. And knowing, she fled, leaving behind her son, Federico, to find his own escape. Maria's father was a criminal. She had consigned Federico as a victim. That decision, that past, was too painful, even now, for Maria to discuss.

Tenny said nothing more to disturb her mother. She had her answer.

***

Although Hal had moved on, Tenny found her life without him to be good and satisfying. She would talk to him occasionally, meet less often in person. Both kept full schedules, especially Hal, who wore his city council role like a new skin. Since their meetings had become rare events, Tenny was mildly surprised when Hal invited her to have lunch in his office. It had been months since their last contact.

When she arrived, another surprise, Ben Sage was also there to welcome her. Ben was seldom in Los Angeles since Hal's election to the city council. Campaigns across the United States kept him constantly on the road. But Tenny and Ben stayed connected by phone. Ben was not shy about asking her to contribute to whatever candidates and campaigns were current. She was a willing contributor. And their conversations spanned more topics than money. She enjoyed Ben's colorful stories of political combat and the people involved. Ben also was obsessed with scientific discovery. His journalist's mind could assemble nuggets of information from multiple sources and synthesize them into compelling visions. At any moment in any situation Ben might captivate listeners with what seemed like tales from the future.

"Think of it," Ben might say, "we've discovered the elements of life at the genetic and cellular level, and we're close to being able to move those genes and cells around to create whatever living thing we want and to stop whatever gets into our bodies to kill us. We've found god, and damned if it isn't us."

Another time he might focus on something as simple as a mushroom. "We're related to fungi, you know. Unlike most plants, fungi inhale oxygen, exhale carbon dioxide and get sick from the same kind of germs we do. Fungi are incredibly interesting. In fact, when you put them under a powerful microscope what you see is a sea of threadlike membranes. It looks like a cross section of the human brain."

He loved to inject what he considered fun facts into the most sober meetings. He used it as a tactic to lower tension or divert topics. At one especially contentious meeting Tenny attended, where a Sierra Club official was balking at joining the LOLA coalition, the official was about to walk out, saying all this was giving him a fierce headache.

"Did you know," Ben said, without missing a beat, "That until 1916 whisky and brandy were listed as scientifically approved medicines in the United States?" Ben opened a desk drawer, and pulled out a bottle of Jack Daniels. "Take a couple teaspoons of this," he said.

Now and then, not often, but often enough to concern her, Ben also could be sorrowful. Once she asked him about that, hoping to cheer him from whatever had him down. "In this business I'm entitled to have five bad hours a month," Ben said, laughing it off.

"Have you noticed it, Carmie?" she asked during their long flight home from Beijing. "Ben's such a good guy, but as much as he tries to hide it, sometimes I think he's also a sad guy, a lonely guy."

"Let me tell you about it," said Carmie. "It's not something Ben wants to discuss, ever. I learned about it from Hal. Ben was married once, happily, apparently. A woman by the name of Alma. They called her Almie. Ben and Almie had a daughter. Both were killed when a drunk driver slammed into their car. Ran a red light."

"How awful."

"Ben was traveling at the time, deep into a campaign. He's never been able to forgive himself for being away, not being there for them. As if that wasn't terrible enough, the other driver, an elderly woman, was politically well connected. Her driver's license was suspended for a year and she was put on some sort of probation, but no more than that. Ben wanted her tried for manslaughter. It never happened. "

"How long ago was this?"

"Not sure. Ten years maybe. I got to know Ben a few years back when he was working in a New York mayor's race. That's when I realized that after you dig through all of the poll numbers and thirty-second spots, you find one deep guy. Lots of layers you seldom see. Ben visits their graves a lot when he's in Washington. I know it sounds weird, but Hal says Ben still writes letters to Alma, I guess to keep her memory alive."

"Weird, yes. It also would be incredibly romantic if it wasn't so tragic. He needs to move on."

"I know. A few times since I've tried to draw Ben out about it, see if I could help. But he just seems to have buried his soul with Almie so he can keep being with her."

"Has he had professional help?"

Carmie shrugged. "Hal would know. I don't. I think winning campaigns is some therapy. Beating people he thinks use their money and status to bend the rules and hurt people I think is his revenge."

***

Hal had box lunches waiting in his office when Tenny arrived.

"Sorry about that loss in Texas," said Hal. Ben's candidate had just missed winning a primary election for Congress.

"A tough one," Ben conceded. I made a few mistakes."

"No one can be perfect all the time," consoled Tenny.

"No," said Ben. "In fact I just read that Kevlar, Super Glue, Post-It notes and photographs all came to us from lab blunders. Maybe I've just invented something wonderful."

"Well let's talk about creating something wonderful together," said Hal.

"Tenny, Pete Marcus told me in confidence the other day that he wouldn't be running for re-election."

"Marcus, the congressman?"

"Yes, CD 1. East L.A., Compton, Carson. Heavy Hispanic. He asked me to run for it."

"Really. Go to Washington? Are you going to do it?"

"No. I'm going to run for mayor."

She was stunned. Hal? Mayor? It had never occurred to her.

"Whoa. Pick me up off the floor. After only two years on the council, you're going to run for mayor? Do you think it's possible with your record of social action? Would the money people let you get away with it?"

"You know, I get invited these days to places they go. They still want things they used to get from Wilmont. I think I've convinced a fair number that it makes sense to have a mayor who's at home across all the interest groups—blacks, whites, Asians, Latinos. We're in a different place since the Rodney King riots. Even after all the years since then it's still tense out there, and not just for the cops. The business community really feels it when there's social unrest. I'm arguing that I'd be their best bet to lower the temperature, bring communities together. I think they trust me. We'll see."

"I've drawn up the game plan," said Ben. "In a five-or six-candidate primary, Hal needs about a hundred fifty thousand votes to come out on top. With his background in L.A. Lights, we can probably get half of that in the Latino community alone. If he wins the primary, he wins the general. Not a slam dunk, but worth a shot."

"Amazing," she said. "Mayor Hal. I never considered it."

Hal grabbed a straight backed chair, turned it around so the slats were facing Tenny and moved it directly in front of her, cage-like, not two feet away and sat facing her.

"Here's another thing you've never considered. We want you to run for that first district congressional seat."

Tenny looked at them both blankly.

"That's crazy. I'm no politician. Am I even eligible?"

"Of course you're eligible," said Ben. "You're an American citizen, born in the U.S.A. You'd be a lock to win it. The district is 43 percent Latino. After what you've been doing in that community we can clear the field for you. Little or no primary opposition. No Republican would come close."

"I'd run as a Democrat?"

"Of course. Aren't you registered as a Democrat?"

"Yes. I did it just a few years ago, first time I registered to vote, when we got into politics. But I've never paid much attention to politics, except around here. I don't know the first thing about Washington. Why would you want me to run?"

"To scoop up federal dollars," said Hal. "If I'm mayor I'm going to need you there to get more money for our projects. Simple as that. We're short-changed now because there's no one in the L.A. delegation who has your drive. They all take no for an answer. You wouldn't. You and I together could make everything we've done so far look like small change. We can transform L.A. and the whole area."

Tenny smiled and shook her head. "Get serious, you two. Me? A political candidate? Why don't you ask me to be a standup comic, or a tap dancer? It would make just as much sense."

Tenny clapped her hands and smiled at her own joke. Or what she considered a joke. But Hal and Ben were dead serious. Ben pressed on.

"You'll be great. Just be yourself. Walk the streets, shake hands, give a few speeches…"

"Speeches! I've never given speeches."

"Of course you have," said Ben. "You give speeches every day, but just to small groups. What do you think you've been doing these past years? Doing the same thing for politics is no different."

"Bull shit!"

"OK, there are some differences. But listen, I wouldn't even suggest this if I wasn't absolutely sure you'd win."

"And then I have to move to Washington? I don't want to move to Washington!"

"Not really. Just commute. Back and forth. A couple days a week."

"Ben! Don't mess with me."

"OK. But there's nothing wrong with that life. You'll be great at it. Nobody says no to you here, and they won't there. For the same time and effort, you'll be doing a lot more good for a lot more people."

"But what about L.A. Lights? I just walk out on them? What happens to it?"

It was Hal's turn.

"Tenny, you've built L.A. Lights into an incredible operation. You're helping more people than ever. Just as important, you've built a real organization. Very talented and committed people. That's what a great manager does. The simple fact is L.A. Lights will run just fine without you.

"In fact, if you deliver from Washington and I deliver from city hall, that organization will have way more help to give. Don't get me wrong, but you've outgrown day-to-day management of L.A. Lights. You came here to get real life experience. Few people in government have the understanding and background you have now. It's time to move on and use everything you've learned to get more done. That is, if you're still interested in this kind of life, helping people. No one would blame you if you moved on to other things. You've done so much already."

She had no defense against his reason for her leaving L.A. Lights. In fact, she had been mulling future moves herself. More and more asking herself "what's next?" Going to Washington, D.C., as a member of Congress was far from what she ever considered "next." To her, that seemed like an admonition spoken in tongues. But the more Hal and Ben wrapped her in their net of logic, the less remote it felt.

She stared at them both with a mock glare.

"And what will it cost me to give up a job I love and move to a city I've never wanted to live in?"

"Probably $500,000."

"Or put another way, a half million dollars!"

She turned to Hal with her arms outstretched. Tenny was feigning distaste for the idea, he could see that.

"Hal, do something. Say something."

He moved his straight backed chair even closer to her, their noses nearly touching. Eyes locked tightly on hers. One-time lover to one-time lover, mentor to student:

"Do it."

15

"Tell me what to do, Ben."

"What do you want to do?"

In a few hours she would officially file as a candidate. People would be asking questions. She didn't know what to say. In her anxious state of mind Ben's reply sounded sarcastic. Ben had pushed her into the race. She expected to be handled by this professional political handler.

"What kind of answer is that?"

"A serious answer," said Ben. "Some candidates need a lot of help. They freeze in front of crowds. Some have no idea why they're running, except to get elected. Some work well in small groups but not on big stages. Some make no eye contact. Others shake hands grudgingly or walk around with forced smiles. Being a candidate is an unnatural state of being.

"Most people I've worked with are just good people entering a totally foreign and unnatural world. But I've seen you in all kinds of situations, Tenny. You're great with people one-on-one. You know what people of this district need, and you have good ideas. You may be a bit shaky at first, but it won't matter. Hardly any media will cover you this early. Make your mistakes and learn from them. Pick your topics. Talk from your head and your heart. I'll come up with a schedule for public appearances. For the first week or so I'll go to most of them with you. I'll take notes and we can talk after. My team will manage all the details like organization, media hand-holding, bookkeeping, scheduling, all that. Just be the candidate. I trust you. Trust yourself."

During the first days of the campaign Tenny was on the street visiting key community leaders and delivering two or three speeches a day in living rooms and public spaces. At night, she and Ben would meet for dinner for what he called the download, carefully assessing everything about her. He had advice on what she wore, how she walked, where she looked when she shook a hand. He annotated her speeches, making suggestions on how to tighten them up, where to leave room for applause, reordering speech topics to build to more emotional endings.

By design, during the campaign's first days Ben scheduled Tenny to be in familiar, comfortable places with encouraging friends. Even then, for Tenny, it was unfamiliar territory, asking for help and support rather than delivering it. She was self-conscious, a bit embarrassed, often unsure of what to say or how to say it. It didn't matter to those she met. They were her people, ready to hit the pavements for her, offering suggestions and advice. Never before a creature of politics she had no concept of politically correct limits. If it was on her mind, it was on her tongue and expelled with great intensity through her lips. What she said gave voice to the collective thought of tens of thousands of people in her congressional district, messages she understood well after years of working the streets of Los Angeles' forgotten. Whatever she said, no matter how long it took to say it, her listeners always wanted more. They had never heard it said so well before, if ever. Their hunger to be recognized for who they were was insatiable.

As campaign weeks bled into months, Tenny evolved into a campaign phenomenon. One of the nation's richest people campaigning to represent some of the poorest, with large crowds cheering her on. Of all the candidates in all of the Los Angeles area's congressional races, she was the most quotable. Television cameras were her constant companion, drawn to her because her events were good theater. Her scripts came from her own memory, drawn from realities lived, not position papers read. Her prescriptions for change had been forming through the years. Now, she could visualize them as programs for how things could be. Her campaign was transforming her, and her own self-image, irrevocably, from Isabel to Tenny.

Meanwhile, in the mayor's race, ideas that only a few years earlier might have been considered revolutionary were being discussed as mainstream options—so far had Hal moved the debate during his time on the council. His speeches and public appearances were augmented by Ben's media, setting the campaign agenda for all the candidates. Hal preached a gospel of stronger regional development propelled by better distribution of growth's rewards. New investments in rapid transit, living wages, publicly supported day care and kindergarten paid for by a fairer balance in the local tax structure. Hal's was a platform designed to appeal both to those who favored more developmental growth for Los Angeles and to those who had been left behind in sharing the benefits from past area growth. He didn't assess blame or promote rancor over how the economy became so skewed toward the wealthy in the first place. The pushback from the city's economic elite against this one-time pro bono street lawyer was more tepid than in past campaigns by insurgent candidates.

Hal's primary day victory in municipal elections was not assured until all the votes were counted, and recounted. Two months later, in the congressional primaries, Tenny cruised to victory and became Congresswoman Tenny Tennyson.

16

"Just call me Fish, everyone else does."

Tenny and Sheila Fishburne bonded immediately. Two high-energy divorced women on similar missions. Fish's mother was the daughter of a whaling boat captain from Barrow, America's northernmost community, well north of the Arctic Circle. Her father went to Barrow from Indianapolis to teach English. What he assumed would be a year's lark lasted a lifetime. Fish, like Tenny, was a product of two worlds.

Fish was picture-perfect for Alaska tourism brochures. Tall, slim, athletic. The hiker. The hunter. The all-around outdoorswoman. Savvy enough to hold her own with the oil moguls, politically agile enough to get elected as a Democrat in a state that elects mostly Republicans.

As congressional newbies, Tenny and Fish clung together through the initiation months, finding paths through corridors they'd never before tread, sharing thoughts about fellow members of often indeterminate logic and motive. Their new class was female-centric. Of twenty-six new Democratic members of the House, seventeen were women. Many beat long odds to get here and had no idea how long it would last, certainly not a lifetime. They were in a hurry.

Fish and Tenny organized "Great Cooks and Tough Cookies," thirty-three women, a once-a-week lunch group to pool their influence. "After all," said Fish, "one of the most successful groups like this ever assembled was organized by Richard Nixon as a young congressman, the Marching and Chowder Club. Two members of that group, Nixon and Gerald Ford, became presidents."

The women used their weight of numbers plus extraordinary gifts of persuasion to achieve multiple victories. While Fish was burrowing in with good results, securing her seat in Alaska's politically tough soil, Tenny was carting big wins back to Los Angeles, raising her stature not only in Southern California, but statewide. She staffed her Washington and Los Angeles offices with workers from L.A. Lights, people who knew the district she represented. She knew her district, too, really knew it. Carmie had once pointed out that her view of life was from a first class seat in a jet 30,000 feet above reality. For five years leading to her election Tenny had been schooled in reality, her classrooms were homes, schools, work places, police stations, trial courts, food stamp offices, union halls, and day-care, rape-crisis, and immigration centers. It had been a crash course. Now it was paying off, both retail and wholesale, as Hal had once described this business of helping people in need. Her staff was expert in solving individual problems. She and Hal were the wholesalers, compiling lists of big ticket items to bring back for entire communities. Though there were more senior members representing other Los Angeles area districts, she was Hal's main conduit. She was vocal, tough, popular with the media, secure from campaign opposition, and, not to be dismissed, the largest political donor and best fund-raiser in the delegation.

Beyond the bread, butter and bacon issues, Tenny fought fiercely for Latino rights and immigration reform. She enjoyed little success, but to the Latino community she was a champion, much in-demand for her fiery speeches, respected for her heritage. A Tenny speech inevitably had the political faithful on their feet. The promise of such an appearance guaranteed its sponsors a sold-out house.

And she had one more priority.

"I'm sort of in awe at how fast you've taken to all this," said Carmie.

She and Tenny were lunching in the congressional members' dining room. Many other members of Congress stopped by to greet Tenny and be introduced to Carmie. Tenny had only a short window for lunch. She was a member of the Banking Committee, and was on tap to introduce a piece of legislation at their 1:30 committee meeting.

"To tell you the truth, so am I. I think it's all the work I did in wealth management. You know, that's just sales with higher priced products. That's what I do here, mostly. Picking targets, selling ideas, wearing people down until they do what I want."

"I'm so happy and proud for you, Tenny. I just never dreamed you would be a politician, of all things. Why on earth did you even agree to run?"

"Well, Hal made a pretty persuasive case that we could work together and get a lot done. But I'll tell you, Carmie, and only you. It finally occurred to me that in Congress I might be able to do something about Aragon and all the other Mexican companies like them."

"Change Aragon, a Mexican company, from the U.S. Congress? Unlikely."

"Not as unlikely as you might think. A lot of business goes on between the U.S. and Mexico. Not just trade, but treaties, law enforcement, money changing. I once thought I might be able to work my way up the management ladder at Aragon and recruit allies and change the culture there. Well, now I think I can work my way up the political ladder here and really have an impact on what goes on in Mexico."

"You're still holding a grudge after all these years?"

"Not a grudge. It's no different than what I wanted to do from inside the company. Only now I know what I'm talking about. I've seen the human wreckage. I'm going to do my best to change it there and keep it from being imported here.

"But you are still holding a grudge. I can tell. You're planning to get even with Javier Carmona, aren't you?"

"And the whole rotten, corrupt crowd. I've done my research on this one, Carmie. I'm not a rookie anymore."

***

While Tenny did not forget or forgive what she had learned about Groupo Aragon, neither did Javier Carmona lose sight of her.

"In the event you had not noticed, Miguel's little girl has become a big player in the United States government," Carmona informed members of the Groupo Aragon board shortly after Tenny's election to Congress.

"Many strange people serve in their government," replied banking director David Colon. "At least now she knows she can buy influence, something she warned was an awful thing for us to do." The room erupted in laughter.

Carmona was not smiling. "I don't like it. This woman did not go quietly. Her ties with us are too personal, too historic. If she continues to gain political power she could be a threat to us."

"From the United States? How would that be possible?" asked Colon.

"How is it possible that a woman, who by blood and bearing is one of us, got elected to the United States Congress at all? It's extraordinary. And we cannot afford to lose sight of her. We have made her an enemy. She could become a dangerous one."

17

For three congressional terms, six years, Tenny owned her congressional seat. No one dared challenge her. Her popularity, her money, her success serving the district dissuaded anyone, Republican or Democrat, from trying to oust her. It might have lasted forever had it not been for Grant Hamel's overactive libido.

Hamel, a Democrat, was serving his fifth year as U.S. senator from California when rumors began circulating about his frequent visits to a pleasure palace near Reno. The rumors became a scandal when the *Sacramento Bulletin* published photos of Hamel entering and exiting the Beauty Farm, a well-known fee-for-sex establishment. Not just once, but on multiple occasions.

What made it worse was that those dates coincided with official committee trips for hearings on nuclear waste disposal and mass transit issues, all paid for at government expense. A Nevada hearing had been cancelled because Hamel reported he was ill—on a day photos showed him at the Beauty Farm.

Hamel fought back, apologized, offered himself for counseling and embarked on a well-trod trail of apologia. All this might have worked, despite his crashing poll numbers. It might have worked, had not the *Los Angeles Courier* published copies of the credit card receipts Hamel used to pay for Beauty Farm services. The public could have forgiven yet another married man straying onto a prostitute's reservation. But paying for it with a credit card? To get mileage points? The balance tipped against him, and Hamel resigned, leaving the Senate seat open for the governor to fill until the next election, just eighteen months distant.

The governor who would make that appointment was Harold Thompson.

While Tenny was having success in Congress, Hal had been building his own reputation as mayor of Los Angeles. Power is addictive, and Hal had inhaled it deeply. His public face remained that of a progressive reformer. With much less attention, he was also finding ways to see that oil, agriculture, and other industries with deep financial roots in California came into his debt. Personally engaging as ever, Hal became a fixture on the state's social A-list circuit. During one spin around that circuit he met and married Sally Pounds, the daughter of L. Irving Pounds, whose media holdings included dozens of California newspapers and broadcast properties.

Five years after his surprise election as mayor, Hal ran for governor. While progressives were now suspicious, his years of ground-level work for their movement continued to pay residual dividends. Ben was able to build a statewide organization from the base of the original LOLA movement in Los Angeles. Hal tapped into a deep well of campaign money through Tenny and through Irving Pounds and his influence. The state's oligarchs had learned to trust Hal as mayor. Many were willing to take a chance on him as governor.

Now, a year into this powerful new role in Sacramento, it was Hal's lot to appoint a U.S. senator who would fill out Hamel's term until the next election.

Ben Sage had no doubt who that should be.

"Tenny, of course. She's the most popular political figure in California next to you. The Latino community will be thrilled. Women will be grateful. When she needs to run on her own next year, she'll be a strong contender. San Francisco is reliably Democratic. Tenny won't have a problem winning the L.A. area vote. No matter who the Republicans nominate, she'll win. And it doesn't hurt that she can finance her own campaign."

Hal wasn't so sure.

"I've been getting pushback from the chamber, growers, and just about everybody. Mainly the banks. They'd go nuts. She's become a wild card. She makes them really nervous, more than anybody else. If I appoint her, I'll have a lot of explaining to do, especially with my own father-in-law."

"Well if you name someone those guys want, your own numbers will take a hit. There's no one else as popular as Tenny or with her name recognition. With the right candidate, the Republicans could take that seat next year."

"Does she even want it? I know she likes being in the House. I haven't heard from her."

"Then ask her. If she says no you're off the hook with all the groups that support her. If she takes it she's a winner. With her on next year's ticket she's probably worth a few more seats in the state legislature, maybe enough for a super majority."

Tenny had been ambushed into her first race for the U.S. House. Now that she was here, in Washington, seeing how power and influence was exercised, wielding a bit of it herself, she wasn't immune to the itch for more. A Senate seat, a national stage. Heavier weapons. All very attractive. Nevertheless, she was not expecting a call from Hal. She knew it was a tough choice for him.

Their past relationship would be red meat for the opposition. Could she handle it? Could Hal? Tenny had won election to the House on her own. The Senate seat would be a gift from a former lover. If the Republicans ran an effective campaign it could bring them both down. Then there was Hal's family to think of. Hal's wife would have to answer the other woman questions through the whole campaign, in public and in private, to all of her friends. Irving Pounds would have to answer for it to everyone he maneuvered into supporting Hal's campaign for governor. Pounds' newspapers regularly took Tenny apart in editorials. Pounds would be furious if Hal appointed her. No, she didn't expect Hal to call.

But he did. "My first choice," he said.

"I hope you have others," she countered. "You know the downside as well as I do. You'd be committing political suicide and setting yourself up for divorce." Then she spent ten minutes outlining all the credible reasons to avoid walking into such a political tar pit.

As she talked, Hal's thoughts turned back to their first meeting in that Starbucks. He, the idealistic lawyer, practicing alone, struggling to pay his rent, for what—to do things for people he knew needed his help. And Tenny, this wildly rich heiress, with a powerful motivation to get involved, and hardly a clue as to what she'd be getting into. Those were good days and good days together. Their lives had diverged but the memory of it was not so easily erased. On a political level, Tenny was right—she should be the last person he would appoint to the open U.S. Senate seat from California. On a potential performance level, no one else was in her league.

"Tenny," he finally said, "I'm appointing you to the Senate seat. Will you take it?"

The connection went silent as she took a number of deep breaths.

"Yes, Hal. Heaven help us both. I will."

18

Moving from the U.S. House to the Senate meant not just more office space, larger staff, a change of address. It would be a move from a small stage to one of the world's largest and most significant. Now she would be representing not just the 700,000 people in her congressional district, but the nearly 40 million people living in the most populous state in the United States. There were more Californians than there were Canadians.

California's economy, measured in GDP, was larger than most other countries'. Significantly, and most meaningful for Tenny, she was now representing a state economy twice the size of Mexico's. Her decision to accept the Senate seat had been tempered by personal relations, hers and Hal's. Now she was coming to terms with how radical a scale-up this would be.

After getting a yes from Tenny, Hal called Reed Guess, the Democratic Senate majority leader to alert him. It was the decision Guess was hoping for. Tenny's policy views were aligned with his. She would be a strong ally, if they could get her through the next campaign without being pulverized into unrecognizable parts by what promised to be a meat grinder of an election.

"Congratulations, I've just heard the news." The call surprised her. Hal asked her to tell no one until he could set up the announcement properly. But here was Reed Guess, phoning just moments later. "I've got a private office in the Capitol, away from the majority office," said Guess. "Can you meet me there in say, half an hour?"

Senator Guess understood the importance of the California Senate seat to his reign as majority leader, and how fierce the battle would be to hold it in next year's election. Tenny was filling an unexpired term. She would have barely more than a year to build a statewide following. If most California voters knew of Isabel Tennyson at all, they knew her for what much of the California media termed her radical ideas, her rich-girl background, her intense support for immigration reform.

Connecticut had elected Reed Guess as a war hero, a Silver Star winner, a young Marine lieutenant who saved his unit with minimal casualties after it was surrounded in Iraq. In an act of supreme courage, he had picked up a live grenade and thrown it back just before it detonated. Many lives were saved at the cost of Reed Guess's left hand and vision in his left eye. He entered the Senate, much like Tenny, with a progressive agenda and a fighting spirit, quickly rising to become Democratic leader. He had not only a compelling personal story, but also a strong platform presence. Marine erect and body fit, an aura of command developed in officer's training school that didn't fade in civilian life, a handsome family and clearly spoken ideas on what government could and should be. Guess also had designs on the White House. From the day he was sworn in as Connecticut's U.S. senator, he began laying the groundwork for a future run for president.

Tenny took to Reed Guess immediately. Why not? He was her kind of senator. Smart. Quick. Ideologically on the same page. And now, even before her appointment was announced, he was offering her any committee assignment she wanted and all the support he could provide to keep the seat next year.

"OK, now that we've done the expected," said Guess, "let's get to know each other."

They settled in for another half hour, discovering mutual fondness for American Indian art and textiles, pre-Columbian artifacts, ancient Peruvian weavings. Guess showed her photos of his wife and daughters. He invited her to go sailing with the family. He was so personal, so genuine, so interesting. She hoped her meeting with Guess was a sample of how her life would be in the Senate environment, more collegial and congenial than in the 435-member House. That would make her new life so much more pleasant than the one she was leaving. If not, she knew how to handle herself in open combat.

***

At 6:00 p.m. on a summer's evening, the Big Fish restaurant on Highway 1 in Rehoboth Beach, near the southern tip of Delaware, swims with summer holiday patrons. The Big Fish is cavernous, its walls alive with huge swordfish, marlin, and tuna, none in motion, all caught close to the Delaware shore and frozen in time for restaurant patrons. The centerpiece is a 715-pound blue marlin. Each year, a few miles south in Ocean City, Maryland, millions of dollars in prize money attracts anglers who bet on an underwater lottery, that the heaviest marlin will accept their offering of a squid snack on a J hook. Through the summer, the strip of shoreline connecting Delaware and Maryland is scented by coconut body lotion and the pervasive aroma of fresh fish on hot coals.

Lewes, Delaware is just north of Rehoboth. It's one of the oldest settlements in the United States, once a small slice of Holland. From Washington, it's three hours by car, an hour by Ben's red and white Piper Cherokee 280. Lewes is Ben's refuge. The single engine Cherokee is his preferred means of getting there. Lewes is where Ben vents to release the tensions of campaigns, where he tries to think big thoughts and avoid small thinkers. Ben has a home in Lewes, overlooking Delaware Bay, with a long stretch of unobstructed beach for walking, doing mind dumps of the present, digging deeper to bury the past, and adding words to his personal journal, one he's been keeping for years. His early entries were about them, helping to fill the airless space he occupied without them. Now he took dictation from whatever inspiration whispered to him when he had time to open his journal. He was no longer alone when he could write notes to himself.

In Washington, D.C., Ben maintained a studio apartment, large enough for his few changes of clothes, his computer and printer, and basic kitchen tools should he decide to eat at home and alone. He's rarely there.

Tonight he's at the Big Fish with Lee Searer. They flew here earlier, above the traffic snakes that curl to summer beach weekends from Washington, Baltimore, Philadelphia and points between.

"Okay, now we have her. What are we going to with her?"

Ben had just picked up their two martinis from the long bar managed tonight by Alena and Laura, two young women whose mixing and pouring skills were performance art, virtuosos of their trade, magnets for locals, welcome company for long-absent visitors.

Ben had pushed hard for Tenny's Senate appointment. It would be up to Ben and Lee to help her keep that seat in next year's election. The primary election was less than a year away. The general election sixteen months. The appointment was announced earlier that Saturday morning, timed to make the Sunday papers and Sunday California talk shows.

"This can be pretty messy," said Lee.

Ben grunted as he took a long first sip from his drink. "Very."

"You drew the big picture for both of them before they decided?"

"Yes. And maybe a little no. I really wanted her there. She'll be great. I may have understated how hard it'll be to be to keep her."

"Understated? You wanted to make sure we got the account?"

Yes, Ben wanted the account. Sage and Searer was a business. A very successful business in a very competitive service industry. To survive, marketing skills had to be on a par with political skills. And, often, fee collection skills from defeated candidates.

"We've done worse to get accounts. Sure. Why not? It's statewide California. You saw how much we made on Hal Thompson's governor campaign. This could be as big or bigger. How often do Republicans get a chance to pick up a California Senate seat? They'll be all over it. Spend their last dollar if they think they have a chance."

They made room on the table for the steamed shrimp.

"Here's what I'm thinking. She's a natural at being a candidate. She can write a check tomorrow. Let's start the campaign right away."

"Not a full-blown campaign?"

"No, and not one that's obviously political. Let's buy into all the cable channels reaching places that aren't slap-happy Democratic dependable. Statewide. Overload where they've never heard of her. Make her as familiar as Oprah. Get her on every day, maybe five minute blocks, same stations, same programs. Some people watch "The Price Is Right" every day of the week, like it's their job. They'll see her hundreds of times before we ever get to the real campaign. What is there between now and next November?"

Ben stopped to count on his fingers.

"Sixteen months times four weeks, what's that? Sixty-four weeks. Times five times a week. That's three hundred twenty time slots on each individual program. Different programs for sports shows than game shows or movies. We target her programs and messages."

"A lot of production. A lot of money."

"But not expensive production. Nothing that makes it look produced. No wild graphics or big set pieces. Just her. Sometimes in the Senate studio. Sometimes around Washington. Every time she goes to California we get a camera on her. She talks right to camera, right to the people watching."

"And the message?"

"The central message is her, Tenny, her character. Someone you like and trust. Someone who's smart and dedicated. She's real. She meets with real people in identifiable places. Let her talk, whatever she wants to say. She's so damn good at it. We just give her a subject that we want to hit, or one she wants to talk about, and let her run with it. So personal, it would be like getting naked in front of the camera. Over time making her unforgettable. With cable's reach, by next November maybe 20, 25 percent feel like they're on a first-name basis with her, thinking of her as their friend Tenny."

"I like it. We'd need to put on a separate crew, just for that."

"Right, and a million feet of videotape to index and store."

"And a ton of research to give her fresh material."

"Right."

"Worth it. If you think you really 'know' someone you're more likely to get mad at the attacker than believe the attack."

"That's my point," said Ben. "The best way to insulate her is for Tenny to do it herself, first-person. You see enough of her and she really comes through as strong and genuine. If they don't know her they may believe all the crap."

Lee nodded, finished his martini and took the last shrimp off the common plate.

"They'll be onto this sex thing soon," said Lee. "How about going on offense instead of playing defense? Let's do a big appointment ceremony. She goes to Sacramento, he hugs her, she hugs him, Hal's wife hugs them both. The daughters hug her legs, sort of welcoming their new aunt. They all go to San Diego and L.A. and San Francisco together, get on the front pages and television news. We get some press yo-yo to ask about the sex thing and they all shut him up and make him look like an ass. Makes it harder for the political press to do it again. The Republicans would have to carry the whole load with paid commercials."

"I like it," said Ben. "I'll see if I can get Hal to sell it to his wife."

"If his wife buys in, it may stop her father from going crazy attacking Tenny with those newspapers of his."

"If we do this right we might be able to win this campaign before it even starts by convincing any Republican heavyweight he'd be toast if he challenged Tenny."

Ben had ordered rock fish, a local specialty. Lee had a thick slab of Alaska halibut. Both dishes came steaming. The partners' appetites were now ready to receive them.

"Did you know," said Ben, "Earth is the only known planet where fire can burn. Everywhere else there's not enough oxygen."

19

For seven years as a member of the U.S. House, Tenny had aggressively tilled a small plot of ground. One congressional district, the poorest in Los Angeles, home to many jobless and with a catalog of needs beyond the resources of those living there to satisfy on their own. Tenny's job was to help narrow the gap between need and aspiration. That job wasn't done. It might never be. But now it was for others to try.

As a senator she surveyed an entirely new landscape of possibilities. She was like a tiger suddenly released from a cage into new habitat. Fertile soil for ideas and attention, unlimited prey to feed her appetite for reform and retribution. She needed only a few moments to get her new bearings, and then she pounced.

Henry Deacon was her first hire. Deacon, PhD in economics from Wharton, eight years on Wall Street, six more at the Securities and Exchange Commission, three aggressive years as staff director for the Senate Banking Committee. Deacon would be her chief of staff. She let him hand pick two legislative assistants who would specialize in bank regulations, hedge and equity fund operations, and other stops along the big money trail. She would enter combat with the money changers with claws sharp and fangs at the ready.

Her next hire was Rita Gonzales, long-time director of Our Goal Is Justice, one of the most important groups in the immigration reform movement. This was a fight they had to win, she told Rita. Conventional, unconventional, whatever was needed. We'll be there. She unhooked Rita from a leash with one instruction: "Get it done."

The close personal friendship that blossomed between Tenny and Reed Guess, her majority leader, didn't deter her from crashing Senate tradition. Within three weeks of her appointment, Tenny gave her first major Senate floor speech, a withering attack on the U.S. financial system, the people who manage it, and the government regulators whom she accused of weak oversight and a culture of coziness with those they were responsible for monitoring. Even her fellow senators took the lash for timidity in the face of raw financial power. Prescriptions for change? She listed a dozen and promised far more. Tenny had no intention of being a back bencher. Not now. Not ever. Reed Guess more than once during those early weeks whispered private counsel of temperance. "Sorry," she responded. "I'm a full-frontal attack person. You will just have to clean up after me."

Tenny's maiden Senate speech mobilized a vast constituency of political activists and reform-minded economists and writers. Within hours she was receiving interview requests and speech invitations. She accepted all she could. Experience in Los Angeles taught her that it takes a rampaging wall of public opinion to break down barriers of financial interest.

For a time, it seemed that Tenny's rocketing voter approval ratings would discourage other formidable political figures from challenging her. But the lure of a full six-year U.S. Senate term representing California was too enticing. Tenny's statewide base of support was still new, fragile, and untested.

***

Nineteen hundred miles southwest of Washington, D.C., Javier Carmona was stunned at Tenny's elevation to the United States Senate, a much more powerful role with infinite possibilities for dangerous mischief. Now that she had identified her targets with her first Senate speech, he knew what must be done.

Foregoing travel on a Groupo Aragon private plane, too easy to recognize, he arranged a charter to the border city of Mexicali piloted by trusted men who were paid well to have short memories. Carmona's long-time top security aide, Bernard Soto, waited at the ramp with a nondescript Ford SUV. The destination, a private hilltop compound, thirty miles south of Mexicali's city center. There, Carmona met with a small group to plan what he would call his "Legacy Project." Its goal would be not to create a legacy, but to end one.

***

Kip Dowling, the Republican congressman from San Diego, had come within eight percentage points of defeating Hal Thompson in the state's most recent campaign for governor. Eight points is not close as contested elections go, but political ambition needs little encouragement to reseed itself. Dowling's ego was being nourished from two separate sources. The national Republican Party believed it had a chance to regain a Senate majority. A rare open seat in California could not be conceded. From the money side, Dowling was visited by a trusted long-time banking industry friend who promised that campaign money would be available, a lot of it, whatever was needed.

A few hours before the filing deadline, Dowling showed up at the secretary of state's office to announce he would run against

Senator Tennyson. And he immediately signaled the type of campaign it would be.

"You've all heard the saying that politics makes strange bedfellows," Dowling told the media. "Well this year we're going to test whether California voters enjoy having a governor and a senator who actually are bedfellows. I think voters will find that both strange and unacceptable."

It came as no surprise that Hal and Tenny's past would be injected into their political future. But the intensity of that effort was beyond anything they had expected. Unflattering photos of Hal and Tenny in their social service days soon arrived at news desks of every publication and television station in California. YouTube and other Web sites were flooded with video clips and photos artfully Photoshopped and edited to create the impression of—whatever the viewer's mind could imagine. Some leaving little to the imagination. One particularly popular scene was two naked bodies in bed, with Tenny and Hal's photos attached and dialogue balloons over their heads.

Hal: I love screwing you.

Tenny: Now let's get back to screwing the people.

And so on. Coarse stuff. Gross stuff. Stuff designed to leave lasting images of a naked Tenny, a promiscuous Tenny, a corrupt Tenny willing to use her body and her money to grasp political power.

Another image: "Tenny" and "Hal" half-clothed in a cheesy motel room after sex. Starry-eyed Tenny, looking much older than her years, handing Hal a stack of hundred dollar bills.

Tenny: "Damn you're good, and worth whatever you charge."

Photocopies of Tenny's contributions to LOLA and Hal's political campaigns added to the unseemly picture.

And it wasn't all just sex.

L.A. Lights was accused of being something of an underground railroad for drug pushers and dangerous cartel members. Dowling's campaign matched criminal records with some who were helped at L.A. Lights when Tenny was prominent there. Two men who turned to L.A. Lights for meals and beds and were later arrested by federal marshals told the media that L.A. Lights was a well-known haven for people like themselves trying to evade criminal charges in Mexico. Dowling demanded investigations by state and federal enforcement agencies.

Sex and crime. For a while during the campaign, these were the only two campaign issues the media cared about.

Leading the media charge were publications owned by L. Irving Pounds, Hal's father-in-law. In deference to his daughter, and despite the heat and ridicule Pounds endured for it from his friends and fellow business elites, Pounds had endorsed Hal for governor. No one would accuse Pounds of betraying the business community this time. His media attacks on Tenny took on the armor of a holy crusade. Daughter Sally had agreed to join the road show announcing Tenny's appointment as a way to soften future attacks. Ben and Lee's strategy seemed to work well at the time. The photos of them all together, Tenny with Hal and Sally, were upbeat and charming. But against the backdrop of the political attacks that followed, the images just added more spice to the story. The worst was the cartoon of the three of them in a bed under the caption "My turn!"

Sally was mortified. For a while she buried herself in child and home management. As the campaign intensified, she and the children spent more and more time anywhere but in California.

The money being spent against Tenny was extraordinary, even for California, a state familiar with table stakes political spending. Most of it was funneled through dark money groups technically independent of Dowling's campaign committee. More than once Tenny had to dip deeply into her own fortune to keep pace.

Tenny under siege. It was an entirely new political experience for her. Maddening, hurtful, embarrassing. But all of the positive early media had worked to make Tenny a familiar and trusted figure to millions of California voters. In personal campaigning she was proving to be strong and resilient. The attacks hit her hard as Tenny, but she did not seem to flinch as the Candidate. Her immigration reform speeches and media had solidified the Latino vote beyond any majority ever seen in California polling. Her economic reform intensity increased as election day drew closer. It was a magnet for independents, campaign volunteers, and rally crowds, and it was a stark contrast to an opposition campaign built largely, not on issues, but on attacks on her character. A year's worth of advance positive media, the media campaign designed by Ben and Lee over martinis at Rehoboth, Delaware's Big Fish restaurant, was proving worth the $50 million that campaign had cost. As a result of it, the attacks she was enduring proved counter-productive to its attackers, riling voters who felt they knew Tenny well enough to reject the charges. Dowling's negative numbers increased as voters redirected their anger to Dowling for subjecting her to a gutter-level campaign.

This was both puzzling and disheartening for the small group meeting in Palm Springs to plan the final weeks' push to defeat her. Top Republican figures from Washington and Sacramento were there. So were representatives of many of the industry groups that felt threatened by her senatorial power.

Cal Burns, their polling guru, was fielding new numbers daily. "She's where she's been for weeks," said Burns. "We got her down to fifty-three percent, down ten from where she started but now we've flat-lined at fifty-three and can't get Kip above forty-three."

"There must be some weakness we can play to," said Reese Rollins, lead consultant for Kip Dowling's campaign. "Give us something to work with."

"Sex isn't working," said Burns. "As many people think it's romantic as think it's awful. And the more you hit her on that L.A. Lights thing, the more people see she spent years as Mother Teresa. But she did hang onto her Mexican passport until she got into politics. Tie her back to that Aragon company she worked with. Maybe she never really left. Maybe she's been secretly working with them to get business away from American companies. Maybe it's a jobs thing. Any good research on that?"

Rollins turned to Sam Moncrief, the chief lobbyist for California's banking industry and ad hoc leader of the industry's campaign to defeat Tenny. The money flow through Moncrief

y duck. But most of the time I don't think they follow m

you know who they are?"

uld be anyone. The cartels. The Mexican government
en the bishop is just checking up on me."

shook her head and closed her eyes.

hopeless," Federico. "No one follows you because
to do you good. You've been at this life so many year
d a church or a mission somewhere else. Come to the
es. I'm sure they can use you somewhere other than
from village to village. I mean it. Not a day goes by
t worry for you."

turned his attention to the bowl of vegetable soup and
him. He had the look of someone who did not eat often
when food was available. His robe hung from him with
support. He was not a large man. In Jesuit dress he
horter than his five foot seven frame. His brown hair
coarse, was now mostly memory.

ld you I was being watched, it was for your safety

noticed it after your election last November. I
ly. Maybe in January, February. And I didn't see it
man in a village I was visiting. I was staying with
ew days. He mentioned it. Padre, he said, who is
wing you all day? I wouldn't have known. Why
ho suspects that they are being followed? But
an told me, I did pay attention. And there was
e. I don't know if he was trying to hide or was
surprised, of course. So I decided the next day
if I could be of service to him. Many are too
as gone the next day."

again?"

e. Once I actually did speak with my shadow.
anything I could do for him. No, padre, he
o walk with me? I asked. No, padre, he said

had been virtually bottomless. Experienced political operatives had never seen a gusher like the one Moncrief controlled.

Now Moncrief imperceptibly shook his head to Rollins. The issue might have promise, but the campaign couldn't go there. Only Moncrief and a few others knew the money gusher's source. There were hints that it was Aragon money. No proof, of course. Moncrief picked up the money in cash from an associate in a San Bernardino bank, who said his contact was someone in San Diego. Across the border was Tijuana Nacionale and its regular delivery of pesos for dollars exchange. Beyond that, who knows. And for this purpose, better not to know. Without doubt, someone in Mexico wanted to defeat Senator Tennyson so badly that he had a wide-open check book and an enormous free flow of pesos to back it up. Best not to turn the spotlight there.

Reese Rollins got the signal from Moncrief.

"I don't think so, Cal" he said to his pollster. "What else have we got?"

***

Ben's Journal Entry
Almie

I celebrated Tenny's election by treating myself to a day at Santa Anita. Santa Anita is such a beautiful race track. The horses are magnificent. I could stare at them for hours in the paddock. Like royalty, which in the horse world they are. Fast horses get bred to fast horses to make faster horses. Horses bred to run longer distances come from horses with distance pedigrees. It's a science and art and it really works.

Since Tenny's campaign just ended I had her on my mind while I was watching these bloodline products today and thought of hers. Centuries of royalty. It works in horses. Does it in people? That's the way the world used to work. Once a king always a king. Until they bred some idiot who blew away the family jewels. How to explain Tenny? Is there some divine right about her? Aragons rule! When I think of all the people in California I know who would give their birthright to be a U.S. Senator. They live the dream with every breath, every word, every action. Now, here's Tenny. Just a few years from even knowing what Congress is. Never registered. Never voted. Whoosh, she circles the field and beats them all home.

Of course we had to enter her into the race. That's because she looked like the best choice. But the way she did it. Once Hal appointed her she flew out of the gate like no one I've ever trained. The Republicans threw everything they could think of at her. Nearly every other candidate I've worked with would have been blown away if they were hit with all the nasty stuff, backed by unlimited money. It hurt. It cut. It brought her down a bit. But all her positives overcame their negatives. She just attracts and inspires disciples like some kind of mythical goddess. And for someone who's never done this before…I watched her get stronger as the going got tougher.

On my bedroom wall now I keep a photo of Secretariat winning the Belmont stakes. He won by thirty lengths or more, like he was in a different race than the horses chasing him, horses that were the best in their generation. He made them look like pack mules. What I love about the photo is that Secretariat's front legs are extended as far front as nature allows. His hind legs are so far back they're almost out of the picture. Three of his hoofs are off the ground. He's flying. Just flying. The ultimate competitor. Straining every muscle to win.

Somehow, Tenny does the same thing to people, voters, in elections. But if I had a picture of her doing it she wouldn't be straining. For her it's effortless. Natural. What kind of bloodlines create such a person? I read Kirstin Downey's book about Queen Isabella, the book called the Warrior Queen. Are we looking at a bookend here? Half a millennium later? It's scary.

Love, forever (mean it!)
Ben

20

The night streets of Zona Dorada in Tampico, Mexico once were alive with young people heading to popular bars and travelers searching handicraft stalls for exotic bargains. That was before the murderous gangs decided to compete for control of this port city. Now, one takes quick steps through the dark, else they risk kidnap

or worse. Tourists keep their distance. Ma
are gone, leaving their colonial mansions
or burn.

The priest and the woman having
only six in the Fiesta Inn coffee shop
Staff leaned against walls or made or
There was little to do, few to serve,
ways to spend one's life.

The woman was United St
Tennyson. It would have been ex
the hotel, where she was staying
she was dining, to recognize her
Unremarkable black slacks, a
warm May night, a simple, be
odds were higher for her con
Aragon. His mission had ta
Tonight he was here to meet

Tenny did not check out
in Mexico City before fly
would return to Mexico C
as a member of a U.S. S
arms traffic illegally cro
Tomorrow the group
border with Mexican
to talk with Federico.
had said something t'
need to risk being ch
out" so that she co
the most violent c'

"Were you fol'
"I can never
follow me every
floor or miss n
"I'm seriou
"So am I.
to hide that

and the
at all."
"Do
"It c
Maybe ev
Tenny
"You'r
they want
already. Fi
United Sta
wandering
when I don
Federico
bread before
or very much
little structura
seemed even s
once thick and
"When I to
Bell, not mine.
"My safety?
"Yes. I first
don't know exac
myself. A young
his family for a f
that person follo
would I know? W
after this young m
a man following m
just careless. I was
I would just go ask
shy to ask. But he w
"And it happene
"Many times sinc
I asked if there was
said. Would you like

again. May I ask why you follow me? I asked. I am being paid to follow you. By whom? I can't say, he said. And what is it you hope to learn? I asked. I don't know, he said. When they ask me what you did while I was watching, I tell them. Who asks you? I can't tell you, he said."

"How extraordinary."

"Yes. My followers seem to be simple people. Not dangerous at all, and I believe they have little idea why they follow me. But they need the money and it seems a harmless occupation."

"It sounds like someone is paying these people not actually to watch you or get information, but just to let you know you're being watched."

"Or they want you to know I'm being watched. And that's why I told you. I am nothing to them. But you are important. If your enemies are paying people to watch me, they may be sending you a warning."

"Then you are in danger."

"I'm in more danger from the idle bandit or militia gang or disease or the drunken husband. These things I am conscious of every day and I take precautions. I mean no harm to anyone. But what you are doing is certainly a threat to powerful people."

Since her election, and with the prospect of six more years in the U.S. Senate, Tenny had reloaded for combat with the bankers, brokers, and others from Wall Street who had been her campaign foils. She had promised voters she would fight for change, and she meant it. The seed of mission had matured since that awful night learning from Federico the truth about Groupo Aragon. New branches sprouted with every new casualty of class warfare who walked through the doors of L.A. Lights. Federico had his mission. She had hers.

"Help as you can," Federico would counsel. "Help as you can. Dear Bell, you can only change things for the times, not the eternities. For eternities, the money changers have walked the earth and mostly ruled. They were in the temple distressing our Lord. Our own ancestors in Castile and Aragon could do no more than the purses of the wealthy would permit. It was the bankers and merchants of Venice and Genoa and elsewhere who held the strings to those purses. Use what power you have to achieve the possible. Don't squander it on unlikely quests."

Federico had taken Jesuit vows of forgiveness. Not Tenny.

"Isabella defeated the bankers, Federico. Columbus returned riches beyond anyone's dreams. She was able to cut those strings on the royal purse and turn warring provinces into a rich and powerful Spain. She wasn't timid. Oh, I'm sorry, you know I meant 'timid' as no reflection on you. You are anything but timid. It's personal bravery that allows you to do what you do. Power is to be used. Our family has used its power to crush people. I intend to use whatever power I have to cut cords of bondage and in a way free the serfs of our time."

They had had these talks before. Many times. But not like this. With Federico possibly becoming a target as a result of what she saw as her mission in Washington, D.C. This conversation had been too disturbing. She had little appetite for food.

"Come with me, Federico. Tomorrow. Come with me to Mexico City. I can't give up my work, and you needn't give up yours. You've helped so many here. Others need help in other, safer places."

"We can't run from callings and be at peace, Bell. Look, tonight we are in one of the most dangerous cities in all of Mexico. But we're secure because we are careful. We don't tempt danger. If I were to wind up in a shallow grave somewhere I would be of no good to anyone—me, you, our people, or the Church. I have no intention of leaving this world until the Lord says it's my proper time. I have what you might call good survival skills and a network of those who look after me.

"For my mission, I know my dangers, my risks. If you consider it your mission to threaten some of the richest and most powerful people in this world, you must be aware of yours."

White House Years

21

About 10,000 people each year are diagnosed with tumors in their pituitary gland. As cancers go, pituitary brain cancer is one of the least deadly. Most are benign. Statistically, 60 to 90 percent of those diagnosed with pituitary brain cancer are still alive ten years after diagnosis.

The tumor found next to Reed Guess's brain tested malignant. A surgical team at Bethesda Naval Hospital probed through his sinus cavity deep above the back of his throat and removed the pituitary gland immediately behind it, a routine procedure. Whether all the cancerous cells were removed with the tumor could not be guaranteed. These things take time and frequent, close medical monitoring.

Guess could have continued his campaign for president with a reasonable chance of living through one, or possibly even two terms in the White House. The Iowa caucuses and New Hampshire primaries were just four months away. He led all the polls against his only serious challenger, Virginia Senator Roderick Theodore Rusher, champion of what could be called the conservative wing of the Democratic Party. The Republican primary was a stampede of eighteen candidates with no clear favorite. Guess had better odds of becoming president than he did of being cut down by brain cancer before he could serve.

But election campaigns are seldom as rational as cold statistics. A candidate with a brain cancer diagnosis is a candidate facing a billion dollar wall of press scrutiny, and a politically organized death watch. Guess recognized that immediate widespread sympathy and prayers for his condition would quickly be redirected into more critical channels. He had to abandon his campaign.

Managing the Guess campaign's strategy and organization was Susan Cipriani, a political veteran and rival of Sage and Searer at the top rung of Democratic Party candidate politics. For the past three years, she had built the organization that would make Reed Guess president. For the past three nights she had been at the hospital with Guess and his family sharing their anguish, and the campaign's undoing. This morning, sleep deprived, powered by endless rounds of caffeine, but tightly focused on her mission, Cipriani appeared at the Georgetown office of Sage and Searer.

"It's true," she confided in Ben and Lee, "Senator Guess is withdrawing from the presidential campaign. You know how close he's been with Senator Tennyson in the five years she's been here. Their styles are different, but they agree on just about everything important. Rather than just fold up everything we've built for this presidential campaign, Reed wants to turn it all over to Senator Tennyson and try to convince her to run instead. I can keep the Guess campaign intact so you won't be starting in first gear. We've built a great group. Transition wouldn't be a problem since both Guess and Tennyson are on the same page when it comes to issues and outlook."

"Has he talked with her?"

"Not yet. It's up to you. You two know her better than anyone else in the campaign world. She's not likely to agree unless you both are aboard. And as a practical matter, you'd know how to adjust what we've built for Reed to her style and strengths. I'd like to stay involved, but I can't win her trust for this or manage her anywhere near as effectively as you guys could. Not in the short time before the primaries begin. So the question is—three questions, really. Can she handle a presidential campaign? Would you encourage her to get into it? And if she does, can you pretty much devote all your time to making this work?"

"You mean handling a Tennyson for President campaign with your people like it's our own?" asked Lee.

"Yes. With the organization we've already built and whatever help you want from me."

Tenny for president? It wasn't the first time the possibility had been considered. In the days after her election to the Senate, that idea had bounced through the writings of a number of well-known political columnists and commentators. A brief boomlet to draft her even resulted in an internet petition. Tenny quickly squelched all of that by announcing her support for Reed Guess.

She was the first Democratic senator to endorse Guess and never wavered. Ben was certain that she had never seriously considered running for president herself. Would she now?

"Yes," said Ben. "She's ready. She may not know it yet, but she's ready."

"And you?"

"We're in if she is," said Ben. "And we'd want you with us, Susan. Have Senator Guess make the call."

Three hours later Ben was in Tenny's Senate office.

"You're in on this, too?" Tenny greeted him.

"Not the instigator, but, yes, an advocate."

"How on earth do you think I can win? A so-called far-out liberal in a nation of centrists? A Latina at a time we're gridlocked over immigration?"

As she spoke, Tenny rose from behind her desk and walked to where Ben was standing.

"Wall Street's worst nightmare at a time when they can spend unlimited secret campaign money? A divorced woman whose former husband is god-knows-where doing god-knows-what? A single woman who hasn't exactly lived the life of a saint? Talk about a mountain to climb. Reed might have made it because he's a war hero with a beautiful family and a more restrained way of pushing issues. Me?" She poked a finger into Ben's chest for further exclamation. "I'm a walking political disaster!"

Ben smiled, captured her extended arm, reeled her into a hug and kissed her on the cheek. She rapped him on the forehead playfully with her knuckles and broke free.

"I'm not kidding, Ben. How do you think I can win?"

Ben settled down in a chair and motioned her to sit next to him.

"I didn't say you would win. I'm not sure you can. But I'm sure you should run."

"What are you talking about?"

"Look, win and you're president. Lose and you still have two years left in your term as senator. You're beating your brains out trying to get immigration reform and change the financial system. And for all your work, and speeches and crowds and enthusiasm, what's actually happened to change things? Nothing. You run for president and you elevate these issues to the biggest stage in the world. You make your case to tens of millions who haven't heard it. You win and you actually change the world. You lose and you've got a much bigger constituency for change than you could ever create as a senator. If you don't get into the primary, we get Rusher as our candidate and maybe as president. Even worse, we could get a Republican. Everything you've worked for goes backward."

She turned from him and paced a few circles around the center of her office.

"Damn you, Ben. You always make the most ridiculous ideas sound almost sensible when you're trying to get me to run for something. But why me? There's lots of others."

"Really? Who? Who else would raise a billion dollars for the campaign this close to the first primaries? Who else would put together an organization as strong as the one Reed has now? That organization folds if you don't run."

She paced a couple of laps more. Ben didn't push. He allowed her space for silence.

"But how do I win it? I've got all the vulnerabilities I just told you about. Admit it."

"How do you win it? Damned if I know. Susan Cipriani just blew my mind a few hours ago. Now I'm here blowing yours. You agree to run. I'll figure out how to elect you."

"Get out of here you trouble-maker. I'll think about it. I need to talk to a few people with more common sense than you. I need some time."

"You don't have much before the window closes and the Guess team begins scattering. Everything else gets a lot tougher."

**

Her first call, as always, was to Carmie, whose career had moved to the penthouse level of the Wall Street elite.

"Carmie, they're pushing me hard to run for president. What do you think?"

"Well," said Carmie, "I personally know eighteen of my fellow banker friends who would jump off the Brooklyn Bridge if you take over the White House. In my small world, your picture is on dart boards in every executive suite."

"But what do you think?"

"Me? I'd immediately take a leave of absence, or quit my job if they made me, and knock on doors for your campaign. And if you win, I'd be golden because I likely would be one of just three people on all of Wall Street whose phone calls you'd take. I'd be in high demand."

"And if I lose?"

"Then you and I would start a socially conscious venture fund and get even more rich than you already are. Or, even better, we'd just travel the world together breaking hearts and getting into trouble. That's how we started out as I remember."

"Hey, come on. This is serious. Do you think I could win?"

"Of course. The country's ready for Madam Hot. You're fiery, passionate. They'd love you. A lot of people already do."

While she was talking with Carmie, the call came in from Hal. "The governor's on the line," said the voice from Sacramento.

"Tenny," said Hal, "Ben's running a big campaign to get you into the race and I'm shilling for him. He wouldn't let me off the phone until I promised to call you."

"Well, my friend, you've done your duty. Now you have to say no more."

"But I do have more to say. Two words. The same two words I said when I asked you to run for Congress: *Do it*. You win California hands down. Washington, Oregon, Nevada, New Mexico, Colorado, maybe even Arizona. Then you take all of the states Obama won twice."

"Hal. Honestly. You know me better than almost anyone. Can I do this? Forget the numbers. Can I be what people see in a president? I'm totally different than anyone else in the history books. And if I win, what kind of leader would I be? I know myself pretty well and I'm not going to change much. I have so little tolerance for idiots. I'm more a lone wolf than good manager of people and things. When I start being eaten alive by ducks pecking on my ankles there's no telling what I might do or say. And I'm talking here about generals and admirals and leaders of other countries."

"Agreed. You're likely to screw up royally. But someone's going to get elected and whoever that is just as likely to screw up. Better that it's you."

"I just talked with Carmie. She says Wall Street would do everything it could to stop me."

"Sure they would. You know I'm pretty cozy with a lot of those types. They're terrified of you out here in California and still think I lost my mind when I appointed you. Expect the worst from them. But this isn't their year. In fact, the harder they push against you the better off you'll be. It just makes you more credible."

"Why don't you run? You could beat Rusher and get elected more easily than I could."

"Well, now that you mention it, I did spend some time last year testing whether I should. When I looked at getting in it was pretty clear I'd split support with Reed Guess and almost guarantee that Rusher would win the nomination. So I backed off. That's why I never asked you to support me or raise money for me. But while I was trying to make that decision I seriously had to ask myself whether this was what I wanted to do with the rest of my life, and I got some really good answers. I have a great family situation. I've never made much money, but after I leave office I can make a ton, and have time to enjoy it. By the time I heard about Reed's cancer, I'd drifted really far away from wanting to run for president. But even if I did want it, let's be real. You're way more popular than I am. You have natural support groups everywhere, women and Latino, that I don't have. And you can write a check for your whole campaign if it comes to that. I'd start off late with an empty bank account. The fact is, I just don't want to do it anymore. But I want you to. I really want you to. You can beat Rusher. And you, me, the whole country needs to beat Rusher."

"Hal, you left something out. What about us? We both saw how ugly that got in the Senate campaign. What was ugly then is bound to be horrible if I run now."

"I can handle my end of it. Can you handle yours?"

"I don't want you to get hurt. The Senate campaign was so hard on Sally and your kids."

"The only way I can be hurt now is if you don't run. Anyway, I've got my answer ready when the media quizzes me about us."

"And what's that?"

"I didn't appoint you to the U.S. Senate because you were good in bed. You just paid me more than any other candidate."

"Goddamn it, Hal," Despite herself she couldn't help laughing out loud.

Tenny moved on.

Fish was still a member of the U.S. House, winning re-election every two years and rising in influence. Republicans held the majority, but Fish was able to avoid the worst of political partisanship. She had friends in both parties. Alaska's an exotic destination and Fish was a valuable conduit for arranging trips there for congressional business, and often the hunting and fishing side trips that came with them.

"Of course you should be president," said Fish. "Why do you think we organized Great Cooks and Tough Cookies? Remember? Our version of Nixon's old Marching and Chowder Society? The whole idea was to elect you president."

"You bull-shitter! I thought the idea was to elect *you*."

"California has a lot more votes than Alaska, my dear. Besides, you can't pry me from Alaska. It's an ugly job, but someone has to do it. Best that it's you."

"So, will you carry Alaska for me?"

"Not a chance. But I promise you this. I'll be first in line with my hand out after you get elected."

Tenny had been trying all afternoon to locate Federico. Now he was on the line.

"Federico, where did I find you?"

"In Medina. Bell, I'm so very pleased to hear from you."

"You are well?"

"Quite well, my dear. I think of you often."

"Federico, I'm seriously thinking of running for president of the United States."

"Then my prayers have been answered. I've often thought that such a possibility existed. What a treasure that would be for so many people in the United States and everywhere. Someone with both a head and a heart and the power to make a difference."

"Federico, you're the only one who can really understand this. If I run, it would be because I feel the same obligation you do to make things right after what our family business has done. I can't change what's past but maybe I can do something about what's ahead."

"You've already done much good, Bell. Everyone here knows about you. You inspire people with hope. I'm so very proud of you, Bell."

"All my years as a small girl I heard from Papa that Aragons were different than most people. Leaders. Born to rule. He didn't use the word aristocrat much, but that's what he meant. We were a class apart. I believed that as a girl, then didn't believe it after you told me the truth."

"It's not the blood of ages, Bell. It's the good heart God gave you and the good sense to use it properly."

"Federico, you've always been my mentor, my wise adviser. Should I do this? Should I run for president?"

"Your taking the time to call me is the answer. You know the answer. You know you should."

"If I get elected Federico, you and I together will visit with Pope Francis. Would it be out of order for me to ask for his autograph? I am such a fan."

"Most certainly. First we will ask for his blessings. If you win you will need all the blessings he commands, in writing."

***

While Tenny made these and other calls, calls were moving the other way, into her U.S. Senate office. Word that she was jumping into the presidential race was filtering out. The political spotlight of Washington was being focused on her third-floor office in the Senate's Dirksen building.

Henry Deacon, her Senate chief of staff, saw that she was off the phone and felt it was time for a talk.

"Deacon, I think I'm going to go for it."

She didn't have to define "it" for Deacon.

"You know what this means. You have to keep the Senate operation going as if I'm here even though for most of the next twelve months I won't be."

"When do we tell the staff?"

"I guess that's a question for Ben. It needs to fit whatever schedule he's got for us. I'd better see him now."

"Well he's not far away. He dropped by about a half hour ago and said he'd be in the coffee shop waiting for your call."

In a few minutes Ben was there. It was just the two of them.

"Ben. I'm scared."

"Then you'll do it?"

"I'm in. Now what? And don't answer the way you did after talking me into running for Congress."

"What did I say then?"

"You said, what would you like to do? Right now I'd like to crawl into bed and pull the covers over my head."

22

Was the United States in a collective mood to turn the White House over to a president deeply rooted in Mexican culture? Barack Obama had been born in the United States and raised by an American mother and American grandparents, yet he endured years of grief from millions who could not reconcile his Kenyan father to his U.S. nationality. Tenny's Mexican roots went much deeper. Her attachment to her Mexican family was much stronger.

She was more politically vulnerable on the citizenship question than Obama ever was.

Conventional wisdom would say to mask your vulnerabilities. Announce your candidacy in Iowa or New Hampshire or somewhere with a sea of supporters and leave it to the opposition to call attention to your potential weaknesses. But Ben knew political prejudice all too well. He'd been in countless campaigns working for women and minority candidates where polls failed to show hidden resistance. A published ten-point lead a week before election could shrink to a cliff-hanger on election night. Few express their prejudice aloud or on poll questionnaires. In the privacy of the polling booth, though....these issues could not be finessed. They had to be met up front with enough drama to change perception.

For that drama, Ben and Lee selected a most improbable site to launch Tenny's campaign, a contrarian gambit given Tenny's Mexican roots and immigration's political sensitivity. She would announce at the Alamo. The Alamo, shrine to Davey Crocket, Jim Bowie, and other iconic historic figures who died fighting the Mexican army in a battle central to the annexation of Texas from Mexico.

"People will think we've lost our minds," said Lee.

"Do you?"

"No. I think it's one of the best ideas you've ever had. But we need to explain it and make sure the media understands what the Alamo was all about. The Alamo was about a fight for Texas independence. But at the time, Santa Ana had become a dictator in Mexico. He'd overthrown a democratic government and was trying to consolidate power in all the Mexican states. So this wasn't just an us-against-them war. Mexicans were also fighting Santa Ana in lots of places. It wasn't just Americans against Mexicans. It was freedom-loving people on both sides of the border fighting against dictatorship."

"Good. Very good. Common purpose between Americans and Mexicans. Not adversaries. Strong points for the media and her speech."

"And don't forget," said Lee, "the Alamo garrison was begging for reinforcements. Authority in the form of Sam Houston's government didn't see the Alamo as defensible or the fight worth fighting, so they just let Bowie and Crocket and the others hang out to dry."

"And die."

"Yes. Patriots abandoned by their own team."

"Another good point to make. We take care of our own, no matter where, no matter what."

"That's why your idea of launching at the Alamo is brilliant," said Lee. "Handled right it makes points most Americans can agree with, and helps erase the sense of difference."

"Brilliant, or lucky guess?"

"Does it matter?"

The advance team had only two weeks to make arrangements with the Alamo Foundation and to set up the stage, recruit high-profile speakers, work through details with city officials, contract for buses to bring in supporters, and publicize the event widely and well enough to draw a crowd that looked respectable in the next day's media. Susan Cipriani had built a strong organization for Reed Guess. It seamlessly wheeled into service for Isabel Tennyson. Despite the short notice and hurried planning, a sea of humanity poured into San Antonio. Traffic came to a standstill on nearby Interstate 37. San Antonio was accustomed to large street crowds, but this one's size and enthusiasm would be considered a new high-water mark in Texas presidential politics. Downtown San Antonio was all but shut down during the hours of Tenny's campaign launch. Hotels and motels were sold out despite all of the chartered buses bringing supporters on day trips. Tenny fans rode all-night buses from as far away as California.

Tenny had served nearly seven years in the U.S. House, more than five in the Senate. Her career and popularity had been built on a platform of frequent and passionate speeches. She and the speaker's platform were hardly strangers. But this was her debut as a presidential candidate. It would be the largest live audience she ever faced. Having the Alamo as a backdrop, with all its emotional symbolism, was risky enough. Compounding the risk was the one of first impressions. A weak, even a so-so performance could suffocate the campaign and her entire future political career with poor reviews even before it was out of its cradle.

Senators and governors, movie stars and other celebrity supporters had preceded her to the microphone. Bands had serenaded the crowd. Everything said to feed supporters hungry for rapturous adjectives drew rounds of cheers and thunderous applause. The bigger the buildup the higher the expectations. As she awaited her turn at the microphone, her anxiety level rose in tandem with those expectations.

Then it was time. She marched confidently onto the makeshift stage, a curtain of American and Texas flags draped behind her. Tenny's outward appearance masked her growing inner terror. Her throat turned dry. Her confidence drained. She walked into an ovation lasting fully seven minutes while hands were thrust at her for touching, children were raised up to camera level by beaming parents, and chants of *Tenny, Tenny, Tenny* echoed for literally a mile around. The bedlam stunned her. The outpouring brought tears. When it was finally time to speak, her eyes were so misted from emotion that the teleprompter ready to guide her through her prepared speech was a washy blur. She tried to focus but could not read the words. The longer she remained silent, the more silent the crowd became.

Spontaneously, since it was the only thing she could think to do in her emotional state, she turned to an American flag and began, "I…"

"…pledge…"

The words came slowly, each with its own space.

"…allegiance…"

"…to the flag…"

"…of the United…"

"…States of America…"

As she continued, others joined in, at her pace.

"…and to the Republic, for which it stands…"

By now 100,000 were with her.

"…one nation, …"

"…under God, …"

"…indivisible, …

"…with liberty…"

"…and justice…"

She hesitated, and raised both arms to the crowd.

"…for all."

And she repeated.

"for All."

She was regaining her voice.

"For all," she said again.

This time the crowd joined her.

"For All!" she all but shouted.

And the crowd shouted back.

She had not intended to lead the pledge of allegiance when she took the stage. It was a desperate handle that kept her from making a blithering fool of herself. Neither did she intend to sing. But the song came so naturally after the pledge. A rich soprano honed in church choirs through her teens.

"This is my country,

"Land of my birth,"

Quick to respond, the band fell in quietly with her.

"This is my country,

"Grandest on earth."

Once again the crowd lit up as a monumental chorus.

"I pledge thee my allegiance, America, the bold.

"For this is my country, to have and to hold."

The crowd cheered wildly again as the verse ended. But Tenny wasn't through. As silence resumed, she sang the second verse.

"This is my country, land of my CHOICE."

Immediately seizing the political significance of that line, the crowd once again erupted. When she could, Tenny continued.

"This is my country, hear my proud voice."

"I pledge thee my allegiance, America, the bold.

"For this is MY country, to have and to hold!"

Tenny's impromptu opening and the crowd's response became one of the most watched clips ever on YouTube. It dominated evening newscasts and next day headlines. Ben and Lee watched this unfold from behind a curtain to the left of the stage.

"A knockout in the first round," said Lee.

Ben, amazed beyond belief at the brilliant spontaneity of this reluctant candidate, could just stare ahead, trying to etch the scene permanently into memory, a golden addition to a full basket of life experiences. Tenny's brilliant opening perfectly set up the speech he had written for her.

"Greetings, my fellow Americans,"

The crowd responded with a roar.

"Saludos, mis compatriotas americanas."

The roar was even louder.

"I am here to begin a campaign which with your help will result in my becoming president of the United States."

(Applause and cheers lasting 2 minutes and 33 seconds.)

"And we begin on hallowed ground. Ground where so many brave Americans died. Why did they die? Because those living in Texas at the time would not tolerate losing their freedom to a Mexican dictator who had robbed that very freedom from the Mexican people. The Alamo heroes fought and died to be free and independent. As president of the United States I will do everything in my power to preserve and protect those freedoms and to extend those freedoms to all those who live without them."

(Applause and cheering lasting 1 minute and 23 seconds.)

"Why else did those brave Americans die within the walls of the Alamo? Because others did not come to their defense. They could've had help and reinforcements. They should have had help and reinforcements. But they were left to fight this battle alone, two hundred against thousands. As president of the United States when it is necessary to place our brave military in harm's way, they will not be abandoned. When we have to fight, we will. And those who we ask to fight our battles will never be abandoned. Not during the battle, or after the battle is won, or after they return home to a grateful nation. That is my pledge."

(Applause and cheering lasting 1 minutes 46 seconds.)

"Let me tell you some things about myself—before others do.

(Laughter.)

"I was born Isabel Aragon, named for Queen Isabella of Spain. Isabella bought Christopher Columbus's cruise ticket to this new world. Isabella was married to King Ferdinand Aragon, and so, yes, my friends it was my ancestors who helped make Columbus possible. That makes me an American don't you agree?"

(Round of laughter and applause.)

"Here's another thing that makes me an American. I was born in New York City and have the birth certificate to prove it."

(Extended laughter and applause.)

"I'm proud of my family's heritage. It's a heritage that made possible emigration to this continent of so many others from Spain, and France and England, and Germany and Italy and Russia and China and Japan and Korea and Vietnam and Ireland and just about every country in the world."

(Applause.)

"This is a big part of the exceptionalism we all feel for our great country. We live what we preach. So many cultures and talents temper our steel. So many cultures keep our national heart healthy and our achievements the wonder of the world."

(Applause.)

"For many years I worked in the neighborhoods of Los Angeles. I helped the jobless find jobs. I worked to get living wages for those who had jobs. I helped care for the sick and elderly and those who could not care for themselves. I helped feed the hungry and transport those who could not otherwise visit doctors or stores, or attend schools or visit loved ones. Many of those I helped were U.S. citizens. Many were not. Many were of my own Hispanic or Latino heritage. Many were not. But they all had this in common. They were decent, loving, family-oriented, law-biding human beings who asked for little except for the opportunity to work, to educate themselves and their children, to get medical assistance when needed, and to retire, when the time came, without being hungry or homeless or to die untimely deaths for lack of money to pay for care. And for those who need such help, if I become your president, I will not just say nice words on their behalf, I will move heaven and earth to bridge the gap from hopelessness to opportunity."

(Applause and cheers.)

"Liberty and justice for all! For all!"

(Crowd joins in.)

"For ALL!"

(Cheers and extended applause.)

"I've also spent years of my life with those who never had to worry about a meal, or a job, or a car, or the visit to a doctor. I managed the wealth of the wealthy. I suggested investments. I helped them buy businesses. I arranged for them to get huge loans. I directed them toward ways to save money on their taxes. I was successful in a business called 'wealth management.' Most of that wealth was honestly earned by those who had creative ideas, who worked hard, who managed enterprises well, and who invested wisely in growing businesses that created good paying jobs and strengthened their communities. This is the positive side of our economic system, the best economic system ever created to provide ladders of opportunity. "

(Applause and cheers.)

"But the rungs on that ladder are growing wider apart. And too many at the top are trying to pull the ladder up behind them so others can't reach it. They're not paying their just share to maintain our communities. They're not paying their workers just wages for what they do and produce. They corrupt our political process with their wealth. I know them. I've worked where they work and know who they are, and I promise you this: As your president, I will treat honest business fairly and with all the support and encouragement we can provide to keep our economy healthy and growing. But dishonest tax evasion, financial intimidation, and business practices that devastate homes, neighborhoods, communities, industries, and that prey on workers, I will go after with no quarter."

(Applause and cheers.)

"I'm a great believer in shareholder value. And I'm also a great believer in worker value, community value, family value, retirement value. Right now, our value system is dangerously out of balance, too richly rewarding the wrong things, starving living standards and opportunity for everyone else. We are better than this. We can do better than this. We will do better than this!"

(Applause begins to grow as she speaks.)

"This is America for all. For ALL! For ALL!!!"

(Thunderous roars of approval.)

For ten more minutes Tenny outlined what she had done while a member of the U.S. House and U.S. Senate to show that her words today were the culmination of years of action. She neatly interlaced policy with anecdotes from her years in Los Angeles and her extended family in Mexico. She closed with this:

"My brother, Federico, has dedicated his life to helping others as a Jesuit priest. I am so very proud of Federico. He could be sharing in the family wealth and living the life you see in glossy magazines. Many call him crazy to be living and working in poor Mexican villages rather than in a penthouse in New York or the beaches of the Costa del Sol. Federico is not with me here today because today he is in the Mexican village of Batopilas, one of Mexico's poorest, waiting to assist with the birth of twins due to be born there any moment. He will help the midwives and bless the newborns.

"Federico has chosen a life of service. And so have I. A different line of work than the priesthood, but the same goals: Helping people to make the most of the lives God has blessed them with. Free of fear. Free of hunger. Free to enjoy what our own U.S. Constitution mandates for all of us, 'the blessings of liberty for ourselves and our posterity.'

"For Federico, for our children, for those who find every day an unnecessary struggle, for all who ask only for opportunity for a fair chance to live their lives to the fullest of their capability and ambition, I ask for your support to be the next president of the United States."

23

Officially, it's the World Economic Forum. For most it's simply known as "Davos," the idyllic Swiss mountain retreat where the world's rich and powerful assemble each January to play, plot, and deal. Among the 2,500 or so with official name tags are many who don't really need them, immediately recognizable world leaders, entertainment celebrities, and captains of industry, finance, and commerce.

The media focus always divides between the official program of speeches and workshops and the epic drunken after dark socializing. But, as with most conference activity, whether the price of admission is $100,000 or $100, the real action is generally off site, in hotels and other venues where cards can be dealt beyond the eyes of those who don't play for such stakes.

This year, Davos predated the Iowa presidential caucuses by two weeks, a collision of timing much on the minds of all who disembarked from their private jets. A select few found invitations to a private discussion of the U.S. political situation waiting for them when they checked into their hotels and villas. The invitation came not from an American, but a Mexican: Javier Carmona, CEO of Groupo Aragon, one of the largest conglomerates in Latin America, and for many, a major partner in sizeable finance, energy, agricultural and other pursuits. Carmona was a man you could not ignore.

Jack Hurley couldn't ignore him, even though Hurley ran Blue Bancorps, one of the four largest financial giants in the United States. Neither could Pete Garner, CEO of Texas Global Oil. Irving Pounds was there. He was one of the few who knew that Carmona was the source of tens of millions of dollars spent in the unsuccessful campaign to defeat Senator Tennyson when she ran for election years earlier. There were four others in the invited group. Rene Delgado, like Carmona, leader of one of Mexico's largest business conglomerates; Carlos Mungia, former president of El Salvador, known to be one of the 100 richest people in the world; Kurt Bass, executive director of the Swiss equivalent of the American Bankers Association; and Bassam Zaman, an under-the-radar figure known to be close to the Saudi royal family and a conduit for many high-level deals in the wide arc of the oil rich Middle East.

Carmona had chosen his invitees carefully, for their wealth, influence, and the vast army of intelligence operatives and political power they controlled.

"Be assured, gentlemen," Carmona said, "we are together without ears from the outside. My security people have carefully swept this villa. We may all speak freely."

"About what?" asked Blue Bancorps' Jack Hurley. "It's nice to see all of you, but looking around, I'm not sure what for and why us." Hurley was blunt and manically protective of his time. He ran a behemoth with a market cap of more than $200 billion and a quarter of million employees. Hurley was a man without time or energy to waste.

"Let me get quickly to the point," said Carmona. "I've asked you here to discuss Señora Tennyson, a woman who could well become president of the United States unless measures are taken to stop her. I have particular insight into this lady, since many years ago she worked for me and I was forced to dismiss her from our enterprise, even though Aragon was built by her family and she was one of our largest shareholders."

"Twenty years ago, wasn't it?" said Pete Garner. Not still holding a grudge, are you, Carmona?"

"It's not the past that concerns me. She did no damage. But what happened long ago still matters, and all of you need to know why. She was not just an employee who was fired. Not just the granddaughter of Miguel Aragon. In his will Miguel specified that she should be groomed to be Aragon's chief executive. And with respect to Don Miguel, we would have honored his wishes. In fact, having an American face as CEO would have been quite useful for us to compete with U.S. companies."

"Glad it didn't work out then," Hurley smiled.

"Think about this," Carmona went on, undeterred. "She was offered one of the most important positions in international business. And what did she do? She came to our board, the first board meeting after Miguel's death, really just to be introduced so we could start her executive training program, and she demanded that Groupo Aragon totally change the ways we do business. Demands of the kind none of us could ever agree to. Ever. The board, of course, rejected them and we found ways to remove her from our organization."

"What kind of demands?" asked Kurt Bass.

"The kind you and others in Swiss banking are feeling this very day. Demands to disclose depositor files, and to minutely track the flow of money. Demands you in America see from her since she became a senator, to remove your investment business from your banking business, to criminalize simple errors in business judgment. We all see how she would close benefits we all enjoy from our energy businesses. "

"Well, we certainly know her," said Hurley. That's why we did everything we could to try to defeat her when she ran for the Senate. It was just bad luck and poor timing that we didn't. But this isn't the first liberal Democrat we've had to deal with as senator. And we feel pretty confident we could keep control if she becomes president. We have a lot of experience taming them down."

"This is a lady you think you can tame? I don't think so," said Carmona. "Let me tell you something. "Señora Tennyson has a role model from our ancient past. It was a Mayan princess by the name of Ix Wak Chan Ajaw. In the ancient city of Naachtun, which is now within Guatemala, there's a huge statute of Ix Wak Chan Ajaw, in full battle gear, standing on the back of her conquered victim. This warrior princess was ruthless with all her enemies. Many of the cities she conquered were burned to the ground. We're only now uncovering them and discovering how powerful and vicious she was with any who stood in her way."

"Interesting," said Hurley, growing agitated by the conversation. "What's the point?"

"The point is this," said Carmona. "Don Miguel told me about this to assure me that Señora Tennyson's choice of role models when she was young meant that she would have what we might call the killer instinct needed to run Groupo Aragon. He was right about her killer instinct, but he seriously misjudged whom she would find the enemy.

"We're the enemy, my friends. All of us. Anyone and everyone with wealth. If we don't stop her she will torch us all. You, me, and the entire class of people we associate with. She will go after all of us like no one ever has. I'm warning you, not just to save you, but because we at Aragon have similar interests. If she destroys your markets she destroys ours."

"So what do you suggest, Carmona?" said Pete Garner. "We're supporting Rod Rusher in the Democratic primaries. And if she beats us there, which is unlikely, we'll do everything we can to beat her in November. Our people tell us she'll be out by March, April at the latest. She got in late and has no experience running for president. The first thing she did as a candidate was pull that damn fool stunt at the Alamo that likely will kill her chances with a lot of voters. Personally, I don't see the threat."

Irving Pounds had been listening to all this. He was wealthy, but not in the league of others sitting around the room. Carmona had asked him to come for a reason. Pounds understood the reason.

"Gentlemen," he said. "Five years ago, after my fool son-in-law appointed her to the Senate, I sat in a room just like this with many of what I consider the smartest, most successful people in California, and I argued just like you're arguing, that she could not win a statewide election and that, no matter, we had all the resources we needed to keep her under control. How wrong we all were. We savaged her in her election campaign. Savaged her. She beat us, and has spent the past five years savaging us. I don't know about any Mayan princesses. I think of her as our own Margaret Thatcher, but on the wrong side. Don't take this threat lightly."

"So what do you want us to do?" said Hurley.

"Destroy her," said Carmona.

"Destroy her? Meaning…?"

"Take her down politically. We can't let her succeed. I've asked you here because you have all the resources you need to ruin her for good. Money, access to media. Research. Legislative traps. Everything. And whatever else you need, Bassam, Kurt, Rene, all of us and others would provide. Nothing is more important."

Hurley and Garner were both surprised and impressed at Carmona's intensity.

"You've made your point," said Garner. "We'll see what we can do."

With that the meeting ended.

Hurley and Garner stopped for a minute on the curb outside the villa, before getting into their separate cars.

"What do you make of all that, Jack?" asked Garner.

"Family feuds," said Hurley. "Irving Pounds and his daughter. And for the Mexicans it must be some kind of a clan thing."

24

Despite the money and resources his corporate allies poured into his campaign, Roderick Rusher could not overcome what many perceived as a cardboard personality. Momentum created at the Alamo carried Tenny to big wins in Iowa and New Hampshire. Roderick Rusher hoped southern state primaries would stop the accelerating landslide. He carried South Carolina and Arkansas, but he could not recover after losses in North Carolina and Tennessee. He was out after Florida. By April, Tenny was the consensus nominee.

The traditional business community was in panic. Rusher was their guy, the one who they bet on heavily to win the nomination. When it became obvious that Rusher would fall short they convinced him to concede gracefully, throw his support behind Tenny and try to use his influence for appointments and policy if she won. It wasn't an easy sell. Rusher had spent his adult life building toward this year's run for the White House. It was there, within reach, and then snatched away by the most implausible of circumstances. The opportunity of a lifetime was gone. He would have no more lifetimes. Decades of planning, working, compromising, would wash up on a barren shoal. It was not easy for him to accept. Harder still for him to pretend to be sporting about it.

The Republican field began with eighteen candidates, but by April it was clear that the winner would be either Senator Dorie McHenry from Michigan or Senator Chet Freeman from Oklahoma, neither of whom could count on enough delegates to nail down the nomination. The intraparty battle between the far right and the not-so-far right would continue right up to the convention, sapping financial strength and encouraging attacks that would prove ugly in the general election for whomever emerged.

All of this looked to be setting the table for a November walkaway for Tenny. But the Republicans proved resilient. The league of billionaires who had financed the various GOP candidate campaigns through the primaries were not about to back a predictably lost cause in the general election. The party's presidential candidate had to be competitive if for no other reason than to save Republicans lower on the ballot and to keep majorities in Congress.

After three ballots made it clear that neither McHenry and Freeman could gain enough delegates to win the nomination, wealthy patrons engineered a third choice, Jake Larson, governor of Wyoming. Larson hadn't run the obstacle course of primaries and caucuses, but he had received Wyoming's favorite son delegate votes, plus a scattering of others. Technically, he was a candidate, and the deeper the McHenry and Freeman feud sunk into an abyss of rancor, the more appealing Larson looked as a serious alternative. People said of Larson that he was right wing without being fright wing. He would prove a charismatic new face for a public weary of those who had been campaigning for nearly two years.

Larson's running mate was Lucy Bravo. Like Tenny, Bravo came from a Latin background. She was chair of the House Ways and Means Committee, solid on conservative issues, and a woman who played her politics as tough as a pro football nose guard. Bravo and Tenny knew one another from their days butting heads when Tenny served in the House. Bruising fights. Passionate differences. Bravo was clearly on the ticket to break some bones.

"Not good," said Ben as he watched the birth of the Larson-Bravo ticket on television. "The bastards worked some magic to turn disaster into a pretty attractive alternative."

Democrats would convene next week. The heat was on to counter a saleable Republican ticket with one of their own. Tenny's first choice for vice president was her old friend from Alaska, Sheila Fishburne, now a senior Democrat with a solid record of accomplishment but a very low public profile.

"We'd be great together," said Tenny. "We're on the same page with most things. I could trust her always to back me up."

"Can't do it," said Ben. "Two women. Two westerners. Two progressives. She adds nothing. Maybe she carries Alaska's three votes, maybe not."

Tenny was determined, but finally the full force of outside opinion came down hard on her. Reed Guess weighed in. So did Susan Cipriani, Reed's campaign manager who played such an important role in Tenny's own nomination. Finally, Fish herself convinced Tenny it wouldn't work. "You're almost there," said Fish. "Don't go for a moonshot."

The battle for Fish consumed valuable days. Now they were on the eve of the convention. A decision had to be made. Ben and the core strategy group poured over poll research to match potential names with battleground state electoral votes. One name kept rising to the top of the list. At first they dismissed it out of hand, until its logic became overwhelming.

"Rod Rusher? Not on your life! We don't agree on anything! I hate the bastard and everything he stands for…and everything he doesn't stand for. No way. Go back and get me someone else. Anyone else."

Tenny was adamant. She was also sleep deprived, tired of living the life of pointless convention parties, meetings, inane questions—the gauntlet that faces any nominee in the weeks, days and hours between when the nomination is secure and finally affirmed on the convention floor. Her inexhaustible stamina had been severely tested. Her patience with minutia always had a shallow threshold. They had to wear her down further to get her to agree to a Tennyson-Rusher ticket.

All the internal polls showed that the general election would be too close for comfort. Except when Rusher was added to the ticket. Just as Tenny could trace her family back to the rulers of Spain, Rusher's family tree was rooted with Virginia settlers who worked with Thomas Jefferson to create the Virginia Declaration of Rights, precursor to the Declaration of Independence. Ben saw in a Tennyson-Rusher ticket the elements of an America-for-All campaign, historic figures uniting the Anglo and Hispanic colonies and interests. Powerful messages. Powerful media possibilities. With Rusher they were likely to carry Virginia and they also could be more competitive in North Carolina and Georgia. Pennsylvania was a more comfortable prospect. They couldn't ignore Rusher. Rusher's many years in the U.S. Senate also helped Democrats in key competitive Senate races.

Tenny wasn't the only one needing convincing. Rusher wasn't thrilled about it, either. Her agenda was not his. But his patrons urged him to take it on and help influence their cause from the inside. After all, they argued, she might lose and being a good soldier now could make him the front runner next time.

Despite all the reservations, on the convention's closing night Isabel Aragon Tennyson and Roderick Rusher stood side-by-side fielding the blizzard of balloons and confetti that rained down from the arena's roof, the unity ticket that would carry the party's hopes into the general election. It would be the first and only time that Tenny and Rusher would ever hold hands and link arms with the pretense of being a team.

Powered by an enormous war chest, Republicans ran a replay of the sex and crime charges that dogged Tenny during her campaign for the U.S. Senate. These proved to be red meat issues for reliable Republican voters but failed to move independents.

Too improbable. Too scurrilous. Not believable. As in the California Senate race, efforts to bring down Tenny through sex and crime allegations proved more backlash than asset to the opposition. Too liberal? It didn't seem to matter. Voters were ready for new and different. Too Latina? By campaign's end voters had a much stronger sense of Tenny as a person—a fighter, a likeable, competent advocate for their interests. Rusher proved valuable to the cause, particularly in Virginia and other southern states where he was known and respected. Once on the ticket, Rusher campaigned as he always had—hard, and to win.

In November, Tennyson-Rusher carried 300 electoral votes. Isabel Aragon Tennyson would be the next president of the United States.

***

Almie

Even in our earliest days together, when paying the electric bill was a problem and our books came from the second-hand shop you told me that someday I would elect a president. Not once did you say that, but who knows how often. So often that I began believing it. I didn't love you because you believed in me. But I loved knowing that you did and that you were so willing to eat of out cans trying to get me there.

Well, we're there, Almie. President Isabel Tennyson. You would approve. I've never felt compromised in all the years I've worked with her. She's genuine, nothing artificial about her. She knows herself and why she ran and what she wants to do.

I'll never forget that day you were with me in Santa Cruz and saw the poster for that candidate for sheriff, Peter Demma. Work to help the country be a place where someone can win with a poster like this, you said. I grabbed the poster off of a phone pole and kept it all these years.

Moves with creative imagination
Powered by love and devotion
Guided by inner lights of awareness
Through the darkness of fear and suspicion
Toward beauty and joy
Beyond the images of life and death

Peter Demma lost, even in Santa Cruz, even at the height of the tribe movement there. I doubt anyone could win today with this message. But I've used it ever since to measure candidates. You would be surprised, or maybe not, at how many I've rejected because they were such ill fits. But Tenny comes close, and to think she's now president, with all that power to use her creative imagination, love, and devotion. For what purpose? We never know, do we? Good intentions are seldom enough. Reality is what we live, not what we expect.

We know so little. Even what makes up most of the universe, what we call dark energy, that's all around us, moving through us, we have no clue what it is. I've always thought that of you, Almie. What I feel and what I say. Words are poor agents. Are you part of the matter we still don't understand? You continue to pass through me, even though we've lost touch.

Love always,
(mean it)
Ben

25

January of the presidential inaugural year is a time like no other in Washington, D.C. Elaborate platforms are constructed next to the Capitol building and the White House. Parade grandstands line Pennsylvania Avenue, constricting sidewalks. Bunting hangs from hotels and offices. Throughout the city, people nervously check weather reports and generally find that January 20 almost always will turn up bone-chilling. Historic records show that for twenty-five days in January average temperatures are at freezing or below. But January is also the driest month of the year in Washington, averaging about three inches of precipitation, usually snow. Will it snow during inaugural ceremonies or the inaugural parade? Even without snow, will the wind be so conspicuous as to drive its way through the wools and furs and microfibers deployed against it?

Ronald Reagan's first inaugural was the warmest on record, 55 degrees. His second was the coldest, 7 degrees Fahrenheit, so cold the ceremony had to be moved indoors. The weather gods can be real pranksters. They interrupted George W. Bush's plan to use the George Washington Bible. Too risky to transport that day because of snow and high winds. Eight inches of snow greeted John F. Kennedy on his inaugural day. Army flamethrowers had to be used to clear the path for the parade.

Forecasts for the inauguration of President-elect Tennyson did not look promising. Relatively warm at somewhere between 35 and 40 degrees, and sunny. But in keeping with her high-voltage personality, the winds would be whipping hard—up to twenty miles per hour. Those lining the parade route or waiting four hours on the Mall for the swearing-in ceremonies would have to be hearty of spirit and creative in dress. Ski masks would be frowned upon.

For weeks, Tenny had been living in Blair House, a stately brick townhouse complex directly across Pennsylvania Avenue from the White House, assembled through the years by the U.S. government as safe quarters for visiting heads of state, former presidents and other dignitaries, and now the president-elect. While platforms were being constructed and plans were being made on the outside for the inaugural events, Tenny was inside Blair House working with staff to assemble her cabinet and to decide on those who would help create policy and manage the federal government. Carmie was Tenny's first choice to take the job of secretary of the treasury, but Carmie had other ideas.

"Let's start with this," said Carmie. "I am in no way qualified for that job. Just because I'm a big deal on Wall Street doesn't mean I have a background in everything touched by money."

"Then bring in people around you who know what you don't. The biggest thing we have to do is get the financial system under control. The banks. The credit system. All the ways the big asses are gaming taxes. We've got to put the brakes on all that. I need a treasury secretary who sees it the way I see it. I can't worry about having a person who just says, 'Yes, Madam President. Right away, Madam President.' And then finds ways with his equity-fund buddies to undermine me."

"You could trust me as Carmie your friend and policy soul-mate. But you wouldn't be able to trust Carmie to be the wise and knowledgeable counselor who could beat this crowd at their own game. Believe me, there are thousands of ways I could be danced around until in all sincerity and trust, I'd be giving you bad advice. And here's the second problem. Everyone who matters knows I'm not qualified. They would tear me apart at confirmation hearings. They'd use me to question your judgment and whether you were up to the job."

"But Carmie, I need you with me."

"Then make me commerce secretary. Nobody really cares who becomes commerce secretary. I'd slide through confirmation easily. Make Phil Stein treasury secretary. Phil and I are buddies. He's got credentials up the wazoo. The last few years at Harvard, he's sounded more academic than political, but believe me, Phil's one of us. He and I worked together on that European Union trade deal and I learned to love the guy. What's great about Phil is that he's not a loudmouth. No bull horns or bull shit. No grandstanding. But impressive as hell, respected everywhere. When the policy war starts, the Masters of the Universe will never know what hit them. Phil knows his stuff and would be such an unexpected choice. And best of all, I'm pretty sure he's a registered Republican."

"Republican? You want me to appoint a Republican to the most important job in the cabinet?"

"Don't you love it? He'd get minimal opposition from the Republicans. The Democrats will squirm, but they can't refuse your first appointment. The public will see you reaching across the aisle to end gridlock. And you'll get a reformer as ferocious about it as we are. Tenny, one thing about us, you and I always have had fun together, no matter what. Consider it just another in our lifelong girlie pranks. I can't wait until I'm at the New York Economic Club lunch where Phil first announces that he favors a return of Glass-Steagall, which I know for a fact he does."

Tenny pressed her friend Fish to take over the Interior Department. But Sheila Fishburne said she was perfectly happy being in Congress.

"Here's what you don't know about the Interior job," said Fish. "I'd have to defend land and resource policy that Alaskans hate. Nothing personal, but I'd much rather stay in Congress and fight you, and at the same time, of course, drop by now and then for a late-night nip so we can figure out how you can give me what I want."

Would Hal join her in Washington?

"And give up running one of the biggest countries in the world? Our GDP's bigger than India's, Canada's, Spain's. I should be invited to those G whatever meetings your economic people put together. Tell you what, Tenny. You win a second term and then appoint me ambassador to Paris or London. Sally would love that. She'd preside at all those formal dinners like a queen."

Although many of Tenny's closest friends were demurring appointments, she was finding strong talent compatible with her planned policy battlegrounds over the next few years. Most who agreed to enter her cabinet and other top jobs shared her sense of excitement and her passion.

Two nights before inaugural day, a visitor slipped quietly into Blair House, late, near midnight. The rest of the household was asleep, except for those whose job it was to stay awake, alert, armed and trained to treat with aggressive ingratitude any uninvited guest who might spoil the tranquility of the evening.

This visitor, however, was invited and expected. The guardians at the gate checked his credentials, escorted him to what would be his bedroom for the following four nights and bid him good evening. Then the front desk phoned the sleeping president-elect as instructed. She awoke quickly, splashed water on her face to wash away remaining elements of dream, donned a terry cloth robe over her night gown and hurried to the visitor's door. He answered promptly. She threw her arms around him in an embrace so complete and so forceful it could have lasted forever.

"Federico. Federico." She kept repeating. "Oh, God, how I've missed you."

Federico returned her embrace. He kissed her forehead, a gesture he had performed so often in his lifetime, on so many occasions, for many people. No occasion fraught with more meaning and significance than the pending inauguration of his sister as president of the United States.

Federico escorted her into his room, kissed the tears that had found their way down her cheeks, and said softly, "Bell, dear Bell, surely you must be tired. I'm so sorry to be here this late. You were so kind to send an airplane for me. But then there was a mechanical problem, and weather…."

"It doesn't matter. You're here now. You're hungry, I know. I'll order food. I can do that you know."

They smiled at one another, a thousand thoughts racing at byte speed through their minds, flashes of his life and hers, such different voyages.

"Tomorrow is soon enough. We will have time to talk then."

"No, I no longer belong to myself, Federico. I belong to a thousand people demanding my time. But they leave me alone now. This is our time. We'll eat, we'll drink, we'll talk now. Until dawn if we want. No one will interrupt us."

Four years had passed since Tenny and Federico met in Tampico, Mexico, drawn together by concerns that someone, for some reason, was following Federico's travels. Nothing had changed since then. More often than not, someone was watching Federico. Many of those Federico had ministered were asked the nature of their contact, what was said, what was promised. Federico was told of these encounters but had little concern. His work was to bless births, minister to the dying, teach children, renew faith in the faithful. He found sources of food when it was needed, provided medical assistance as he could, shared helpful information to villagers and did all that could be expected of a traveling Jesuit priest. In time, Tenny's fears for him subsided, but not his for her.

"I don't want to spoil this wonderful occasion, Bell. You should know, though, that people have been asking questions about you. Not just curiosity questions. Questions such as exact dates you traveled to one city or another working for the Aragon company, or as a member of the United States Congress. Who you met with. Even sexual encounters. These all began soon after your election in November."

"Who's asking? What people?"

"I'm trying to find the source. It's alarming, but some I believe are tied to the cartels."

"Drug cartels?"

"Yes, drugs and more."

"More?"

"The gun trade. Pay-offs to border officials. Assassinations. The worst people possible."

"How do you know this?"

"After all my years of travel, Bell, I have many friends, many people who care about me and my safety. More than once I have been alerted to leave places that were about to become violent. Many criminals still respect the Church and my robes. They protect me. They talk to me."

"Why would they be looking for things about me? The election's over. I've won."

"Maybe they fear what you will do now."

"I'll tell you one thing I plan to do, Federico. I plan to spend much time in Mexico. I plan to become as known and popular in Mexico as in the United States. And with my influence, I plan to push the Mexican government to make the kinds of reforms that you and I have talked about for so many years. And I am going to restore the family's good name."

"What a wonderful plan. You already are so very respected where I travel. Everyone asks me about you. But about that good name, Bell, don't consider us orphans of a great family that died before our eyes. Papa Miguel told that great family story to us so often, and with such feeling. But it's not true."

"Not true! How can you say that?"

"I've done my own research during these past few years. Queen Isabella had people burned to death for failure to convert to Christianity. She expelled all Jews from Spain, most leaving behind all their possessions. It was a fifteenth-century holocaust. As for King Ferdinand, he was even worse. A liar, a thief. He promised Isabella on her death bed he would never marry again, but months later he did. He promised he would help his daughter assume the throne but then plotted to have her confined as mad. No, Ferdinand of Aragon should be no one's role model. You, however, dear Bell, now have power such as Isabella and Ferdinand never dreamed. You will be a wise and humane ruler. But do it for now, for the living, not for the ghosts of the past."

***

The next day, four blocks west of Blair House another meeting, another reunion of sorts. Blue Bankcorps' CEO Jack Hurley entered Javier Carmona's suite at the Ritz Carlton hotel. Both were in Washington to attend the inaugural.

"A cordial?" Carmona, displayed a bottle of Dalmore 21, which Hurley immediately recognized as one of the world's most desirable Scotch whiskeys.

"Not usually an afternoon drinker," said a grateful Hurley. "But for Dalmore I'll make an exception."

"Good. To your health and continued good business fortune."

"I guess whether we have continued good fortune depends on the new lady in the White House. Sorry I doubted you when you warned us. She's tough."

"So now we must take a bit more extreme measures to destroy her popularity with the people and your Congress. "You have ways to influence members of Congress and the American media?"

"Yes, of course. Through our own people, through the association, the chamber. We spend millions at it and are really good at it."

"Very good. Then we will have to open channels between us. I will designate one of our most trusted people as a contact on my side. We will need one on yours. I'm also in touch with those we met with at Davos and others. Among us we will have a campaign that makes the very popular President Tennyson quickly a very unpopular and disgraced idol. If we do our work well, we can defeat her. If we do it very well, maybe we can see the last of her before her four years in office are over. We certainly cannot allow her to win re-election."

"Can you fill me in on what you have on her?"

"It's best that I don't say now. But let me assure you, you provide a way to make the stories known and to insure that members of your Congress interfere with her success. I will arrange the scandals."

26

While not all Tenny's prescriptions for future policy were popular, her intensity advancing them was. The country was aching for strong leadership. Now it stood before them in the person of a woman whose eyes glowed with energy seeking an outlet, a lightning bolt ready to touch down, a passion that flooded stages wherever she appeared.

Years earlier, after arriving in Congress where "why do they call you Tenny?" was a predictable, pervasive question, Isabel Aragon Tennyson decided to learn more about Alfred Lord Tennyson, the Victorian era poet whose name she shared. She was surprised that many of his words could have been hers. And she began using them.

Tennyson's "Charge of the Light Brigade," particularly its opening passage:

> Half a league, half a league,
> Half a league onward,
> All in the valley of death
> Rode the six hundred.
> "Forward, the Light Brigade!
> "Charge for the guns!" he said:

> Into the valley of death
> Rode the six hundred.

Another Tennyson favorite was the closing line from Ulysses: "To strive, to seek, to find, and not to yield."

The hot breath of her campaign had swirled the political winds of national opinion in her direction, sweeping up Democratic Party candidates who otherwise might have been left behind. When the final votes were counted, the Democrats controlled the Senate. The House remained in Republican hands, but reduced to just a slim five-vote majority. Not only had the Republicans lost dozens of House seats, those who lost were mostly right-wing zealots who for years had been obstacles to compromise. Twenty-two of the Republicans who survived represented districts that gave Tenny comfortable vote majorities. Those members could not afford to be total obstructionists. To extend their own political careers, many Republicans would have incentive to work with the new White House and the Democrats in Congress.

Tenny rode into office with an economy surging and world conflicts becalmed after a run of tempestuous years. This allowed her a wider range of focus. She had big plans to convert this good fortune into a fast start. As soon as the final blue state reported its election returns, sealing her victory, Tenny switched off her political circuits. She disappeared behind a wall of Secret Service protection and into a vortex of transitional issues and top-level team selections.

Ben had not seen Tenny since the raucous election night party in Los Angeles. That's when she claimed her victory from a platform at the fifty-yard line of Pasadena's Rose Bowl. More than 100,000 filled the stadium. Outside, hundreds of thousands more watched on giant Jumbotrons. Ben wanted no job, no part of the transition effort. He was neither surprised nor offended that his candidate had abruptly become inaccessible after more than a year of constant mind melds with her. He was impressed by the quality of the people Tenny was appointing and by the policy initiatives taking shape. What concerned him was the thin political depth in her appointments, a lack of interest in keeping the political organization together or transferring that organization's assets and still-potent voter reach to the Democratic National Committee.

On inaugural eve, for one last time, they assembled at Blair House, the key campaign staff, state managers, top fund-raisers, and others who had just donated a year of their lives to helping President Tennyson take up residence at the White House. Ben knew this would give him a rare chance to spend a few moments alone with Tenny. His carefully rehearsed warning went like this:

"The first few weeks and months are critical. The longer you can keep the glow of the campaign burning, the deeper the impression it makes. It fortifies you for later, when you put your popularity to the test with inevitable contentious policy battles. For those battles, you need campaigns as well-planned and executed as the one that elected you. Bill Clinton and Barack Obama both took nasty hits their first year because they dropped their guard."

Tenny listened to Ben's advice then grabbed his arm and escorted him into a small office away from the rest of the party.

"Ben," she said, "I ran and got elected to do things. I hope we manage to do a lot of things, but I'll judge myself by just two. The first year we get immigration. It's way too personal for me to fail. Whatever it takes, we're going to get it. And when that's done, we're going to break up the capitalist system we have now."

"Break up the capitalist system?"

"I'm aiming high, Ben. The whole financial system's become rotten and it's rotting the political system. We've got to get control of it before it tears the country apart."

"Well we beat them at the election game this year despite …."

She didn't let him finish. Tenny was a passionate woman, and her passion was clearly aroused.

"Ben, rigging elections, media monopolies, control of the regulators, hiding from taxes, all of that. Worst of all, turning the public against their own government and convincing way too many people that government's a problem, not a resource.

"Do you know what we're becoming? We're becoming a nation of customers and shareholders, not citizens. Think of the danger in that. It's all based on money, not community, not pride. If business does it, it's good. If government does it, it's bad. Why pay taxes since government just wastes it and screws things up. Business should run everything—the schools, the health system, the Social Security system, all the utilities, the airports, the FAA, the national parks. Just get out of the way and let the markets— oh, those efficient markets—decide what's best.

"How long since you've gone through the visitor's center at the Capitol? Or the National Archives, or the memorials to Lincoln and Jefferson and FDR and MLK on the Mall? I took dozens of groups from California around personally when I was in Congress. You look at the exhibits and see the movies and it all makes you incredibly proud. Common good. Common purpose. No matter how many times I'd go to those memorials and exhibits, or just see them, I'd choke up. I still do. Not only because I believe in our common purpose, because I'm so concerned we're losing it.

"I've lived a good share of my life where democracy doesn't work right. I used to look past it because I was okay. Not my problem. But then my brother Federico opened my eyes and I saw it was my problem. And then I had an experience I may tell you about some time that showed me what happens when economic power gets out of control. And then I worked those years in L.A. with Hal and on my own and saw things every day that made me ask why? This is personal for me, too, just like immigration. I'm putting together a plan to stop what happened in Mexico from happening here. We're a nation of citizens, not customers or shareholders."

Ben looked at her curiously. This was a Tenny he had never seen. Sure she was a fireball in campaigns and a terror in Congress. But all that focused on specific issues. Immigration. Health. Housing. Now he realized that this woman had set her sights on something far more ambitious: to change the national culture, or more accurately, to return the culture to those times seen mostly in war and national disaster when something else emerged, a sense of self, of place, participation, custodians of a revolution, where people think and act together for common good and purpose.

"What you're talking about, Madam President, is a campaign against nearly every entrenched powerful institution in the country. Not to be disrespectful, but you can't hope to win a campaign like that by winging it. We have the advantage of time. We should use it to recruit, to plan to organize. "

She had been semi-pacing as she spoke, agitated and exhilarated, both emotions powering her legs, arms, voice. Now she stepped right up to Ben and embraced him, hard.

"I love you, Ben. I really do. You're brilliant. You're decent. You're honorable. I'm proud to have been with you these past years."

She kissed him on the lips and then backed away, holding one of his hands.

"I did everything you told me to do during the campaign. When to wake up, when to go bed. When to smile and when to feign concern. I read your words as my own in speeches. I even gagged on Rusher. We did everything except have sex. Physical sex, that is. Mentally we bonded as tightly as two people can. I was on your turf. You were the expert. And you were right. I wouldn't have won without you. Hell, I wouldn't even have run for Congress, the Senate, or president if you hadn't set it all up and been so convincing.

"But now the political campaign's over. My days of partisan political elections are over. I'll do anything for you. Just ask. But what you're suggesting I see as a huge distraction from where I am now. "

"But, Madam President, it doesn't have to be…"

She cut him off in mid-thought.

"For Christ's sake, quit calling me that. For the rest of the world I'm Madam President. And I'll insist on that. For you I'm Tenny. I'll insist on that, too. Now I have to get back to the others or they'll think we are having sex in here. Ben, your work is done. Relax, read, travel, write books. Help more good people get elected or stay elected. If I run into trouble I'll call you, but for now, and I hope forever, I'm out of the political pool."

"No you're not," said Ben. "You're in the very deepest end of it, where more hungry predators than even you can imagine live and stalk and feed."

Ben smiled at her. A smile of genuine warmth and affection. He understood her better than most. In all her life she had rarely been denied. Now, with all the weapons available to her in the most powerful office on Earth, she saw no reason why that winning streak should end. You had to admire her sense of purpose. Her confidence. You also had to fear, really fear, her lack of experience with defeat.

***

President Tennyson's first months in office would be compared by historians with President Franklin Roosevelt's first hundred days, an explosion of compressed demand for change. No one doubted that immigration reform would be first up. The surprise was how quickly it became her first major legislative success. With Democrats back in control of the Senate, Reed Guess, in remission from cancer, returned as majority leader. He managed to steer an immigration bill through the Senate eighty-eight days after Tenny took office. The Republican-controlled House finally caved when Democrats agreed to a more onerous and expensive border control plan than the White House had recommended. The result was a bill barely different than the one George W. Bush had submitted during his presidency or the one the Senate had passed during the Obama years. Three months into her White House term, President Tennyson signed the new National Security Immigration Act, sending the decades-old battle into the courts, a battleground where opponents promised they would contest it for years.

Embittered by their legislative loss on immigration, and in an effort to calm their furious base of supporters, House Republicans revived Obamacare repeal. What followed was one of the most surprising cases of legislative jujitsu in U.S. history. Democrats allowed the repeal bill to come to the floor. Then, with the support of all House Democrats and fifteen Republicans, they amended the bill to delete the eligibility age for Medicare. Then they voted to repeal Obamacare. Within days the Senate passed the House bill and it was on the president's desk. The effect: a universal single-payer healthcare system built on extended Medicare would be phased in over a five-year period. It was a stunning development, totally unexpected. A strategy that post-mortems would reveal was hatched in the White House.

Next came an omnibus bill with money to subsidize day care for most lower- and middle-income families, thirty days of paid parental leave, and federal grants for two years of college or occupational training. All paid for by taxing high-speed financial transactions.

The Tennyson-Guess team was proving formidable in the Senate. In the House, Sheila Fishburne had risen into the party leadership and was the White House's most reliable pipeline for House Republican leadership plans. For Tenny, these were golden days. She came to office believing she could make good things happen, and they were happening. You could feel the excitement at every staff and cabinet meeting.

Tenny decided that now, after a frenetic, successful first eight months in office, it was time to reveal to Reed Guess the most ambitious plans of her presidency. With little outside attention, she had been meeting privately with Phil Stein, her treasury secretary, Carmie, her commerce secretary, and an ad hoc selection of experts in economics, finance, banking, housing, and community development. Tenny ran for president with a mission to perform major surgery on the nation's economic system. Her working group was formulating plans for accomplishing that mission. Reed Guess and their other allies in Congress were going to have to make it happen. Now it was time to tell him that.

They met for dinner at the White House, the two of them, privately, on a stormy night in early September, just before Congress returned from its annual August recess. Guess had been monitoring his cancer closely. His condition remained stable, his energy level high, his mind as sharp as ever.

"You and I," said Tenny, "are going to do something that will change the course of United States history forever, or, at least the next fifty, maybe hundred years."

"Haven't we already?" said Guess. "Immigration, healthcare, all the help for middle-income families. We've blown through a big part of the agenda."

"All good stuff. But think of what we haven't done. The money crowd still calls the shots. The economic system is still dangerously out of balance, most people are still desperately insecure about their futures, the country is still way behind in all kinds of development where we should be leading—like education and transportation."

And then she unwrapped her vision. An omnibus bill, the America's Future Act, a centerpiece for righting so many things that are wrong. The act would bring the financial system under control with a twenty-first century version of Glass Steagall, regulating hedge and equity funds and stopping banks from playing in the stock casino with the public's money. Anti-trust laws would be strengthened to restore competition among the richest and most important U.S. industries—banking, communications, airlines and others. Executive pay limits would be tightened and enforced. Worker participation on management boards would be mandated, the way they do it in Germany and elsewhere.

The reform would include the largest infrastructure building and repair effort since creation of the original interstate highway program. Accelerated conversion away from fossil fuels, integrated road sensors, battery stations, rail. A major overhaul of U.S. urban areas that would include technology rich schools and communications, housing built with new low cost materials, long-needed repair to water and sewer systems.

At the personal level, a much higher minimum wage would be guaranteed, social security would become a real pension program, not just a safety net. AmeriCorps and the Peace Corps would be expanded to provide wider pathways to education, job training, and jobs of last resort. Everyone who wants to work would find it in public service.

Postal banking, land trusts for low-cost housing, coops for small businesses, all would be encouraged. Just as Uber, Airbnb, Amazon, and others are changing how we shop and get around, the government would promote new and innovative ways to end poverty and unemployment, promote education and health, and restore America's assets and its faith in itself.

The dinner table was too small for Tenny's passion. She stood, as the evangelist she was, pacing back and forth, hands slicing through air for emphasis, voice rising and falling. And finally, as if to close the deal, she pulled her chair close to Guess, eyes fixed on his eyes, knuckles rapping the maple dining room table.

Guess leaned back in his chair, thoughtfully weighing his words before responding.

"All of this in one package?"

"Yes, one bill to sell. One sweeping vision of the future."

"And to pay for it?"

"I've had Phil Stein and others working on that. They've come up with a really strong package. People who make money from money pay the same tax rate as people who work for pay checks. We put a cap on total deductions, a minimum tax on foreign earnings, a tiny new tax on high-speed stock transactions. A small increase in the gas tax. Then we combine it all with making companies pay tax on the trillions in profits they're hoarding overseas, and crack down on the hidden billions like the ones the Panama Papers showed us. And we're there. If it doesn't work out to the last dollar, we make the case that all the work and construction and development that the America's Future Act would create would generate self-sustaining revenue."

Guess closed his eyes. "Good God, Madam President, think of what you're asking. I'm trying to visualize the power that will descend on us if we try this."

"Don't you agree with it?"

"Of course, I do. Every last public policy goal on your list, I agree with it all. But to try to do it all at once? Guaranteeing that every powerful interest in the world will join forces to fight us? It's so audacious. It's like launching a nonmilitary World War Three."

"And you need to be my Eisenhower."

As a senator, Tenny earned a reputation as an impatient firebrand, disrespectful of age and seniority, and with little understanding of legislative history and nuances. She was no less impatient as president. Reed Guess and other supporters tried to tame her touch when she pushed against inflated egos. Guess had what she lacked, a collegial style that bridged the political aisle. He was always popular with senators in his own party. His war injuries, his cancer, the courage he displayed in handling his unpredictable future and his voluntary withdrawal from the presidential race, earned him even more respect. Guess said he would keep his Senate seat and leadership role until his Senate term ended, or his body told him it was time to go home and die.

Tenny was now asking him to direct a legislative war that if successful could change life on the planet. If they failed, it could be the end of her presidency, along with the political futures of many of those who supported her. Guess was in a place he never expected to be. He felt his days on earth were limited. The cause was worthy. She intended to pursue it with or without him. He knew that without him she would fail. With him she had a chance.

"I'll get our leadership together with your working group," said Guess. "Let's see what we can put together."

***

Isabel Aragon Tennyson entered the White House with rock star celebrity. Twelve months later, her image was frayed around the edges but less than one might expect, given the intensity of the issues that crossed the legislative battleground since her inaugural. The public still liked President Tennyson, and liked the idea that Congress was actually taking care of business that had been warehoused for far too long. Her first year in the White House forged an unbroken chain of legislative success with little negative impact on her popularity. It was understandable why Tenny assumed that chain would remain strong, and why she failed to sense the forces that would soon bring her presidency to the edge of destruction.

27

In January of her second year, the State of the Union speech became the launch platform for the America's Future Act. It was a stunning concept, one plan, one piece of legislation to address the broad sweep of legacy issues facing the country. Her professional team had designed a plan solid enough to withstand the intense scrutiny of impartial experts. While many powerful interests would be losers, many others would benefit, enough to insure a deep reservoir of allies. Opening night was a hit. The show ran for weeks to positive reviews. Then, as the early wave of enthusiasm dissipated, the forces aligned to reject the America's Future Act merged with those determined to bring down President Tennyson.

Autocrats can say "do it" and it's done. Plutocrats can throw enough money at it and it's done. The U.S. form of representative government was intentionally designed to keep things from being done. Among their greatest concerns, the nation's founders fretted that immediate passions could overrun long-term common sense. All along the path to change they erected high hurdles. It was not difficult for obstructers to derail the America's Future Act. Even though it was presented as a single piece of legislation, House leadership sent sections of it to nearly every standing committee, insuring extended review and in many cases, no review at all. Those on the losing end of proposed changes organized an advertising campaign designed to terrify the public. Lost jobs, lost revenue for communities, increased crime, bad people moving into good neighborhoods, higher taxes, failing banks. The plan's broad sweep allowed for an infinite number of narrow targets.

That November, the Republicans picked up a dozen seats to retain the House. They gained four U.S. Senate seats, one short of a majority. Republicans and Democrats now had fifty senators each. Democrats kept Senate control only with tie-breaking votes by the vice president, Roderick Rusher.

President Tennyson accepted much of the blame for the midterm defeats. Her job approval ratings dropped into negative territory, 43-49. Three weeks after the disastrous off-year election, Reed Guess announced that he had fallen out of remission. The brain tumor was growing. He would need more radiation. The governor of Connecticut, a fellow Democrat, would appoint a replacement. Tenny's best Senate strategist and deal-maker would be gone.

28

President Tennyson's third-year State of the Union address was substantively rich and packed with admonitions to Congress to move America's Future forward. The argument was sound. But given the change in the political climate from a year earlier, it was received more as a voice of desperation, a plea to save the ship, a stark difference from the buoyancy of its launch.

With Reed Guess no longer there to direct legislative traffic, Tenny lost a reliable conduit for moving White House programs through the Senate. Guess's replacement as majority leader, Sidney Alcorn from Oregon, had no majority to lead with the Senate now divided. Alcorn was not the tenacious leader who could overcome gridlock, and he and the president had not been close working partners when she served in the Senate. Senate action drifted inconclusively. Misunderstandings between the Senate and the White House increased. Washington's lobbying machine had adjusted itself to the wrenching proposals of the America's Future plan. Opposition obstructions erected during the past year were proving formidable.

In early February, shortly after Tenny delivered her third State of the Union address, a memo landed on the desk of Drew Vine, managing editor of the San Diego Beacon.

Drew:

See attached. I understand there is more to this story worth checking out. Please send someone.

I.P.

Attached was a clipping from a Mexicali newspaper. The article was in Spanish and it wrapped around a three-column wide photo of a strikingly handsome man who appeared in the photo to be about forty to fifty years old.

The first sight of him is captivating. Broad shoulders, open collar, gold chain, mildly hairy chest, thick and dark head of hair that says, "run your fingers here." His eyes, under dark and prominent eyelashes, are deep brown and penetrating. He's wearing a gold blazer, the jacket's gold perfectly accentuating his darkened features.

Drew Vine and most reporters at the Beacon were multilingual, a requirement for a newspaper so close to the Mexican border. The man in the photo is identified as Gabriel Montes, a Peruvian banker who handles wealth management accountants for Premier Group of the Americas, one of the largest financial firms in South America. Montes, a former soccer star, was arrested in Mexicali on charges of laundering money for one of the area's most violent drug cartels.

Why the boss wanted to send a reporter to Mexicali to follow up this story was unclear to Vine, but Irving Pounds owned the newspaper. Mostly Pounds stayed clear of the newsroom. But now and then he had what the staff came to know as "a project." Gabriel Montes, for some reason, was a project.

Dianne Worsley, Vine's reporter who drew the assignment, returned from Mexicali barely able to contain her excitement. In Montes' address and log book, police found the name and phone number of President Tennyson. Mexicali police were unusually cooperative with Worsley. They provided her with photos and full background information about Montes and the cartel. The White House wouldn't comment, but it didn't matter. There was enough for a long, above-the-fold front page story for the *San Diego Beacon*. The AP wire carried that story to publications throughout the United States. Montes became the focus of a media herd. His only response:

"Some things a gentleman simply does not discuss."

The relationship soon became clear. Tenny and Montes had been, and some speculated they still were, lovers. The president involved with someone deep into money laundering and drug gangs? The story took on a life of its own.

A hotel keeper in Cusco, Peru, near Machu Picchu, remembered them together there for a few days. An industrialist spoke of having dinner with them, together, in Buenos Aires. All of that was long ago. Fifteen years. Why would Montes still have her name and phone number in his pocket fifteen years later?

As a U.S. Senator, Tenny had been on a special committee investigating drugs and money laundering. Committee records were analyzed, revealing that Senator Tennyson had disappeared from her hotel in Mexico City during one committee trip and refused to say where she had been. A most unusual occurrence. Was she secretly seeing Montes? Were they still in contact? If not him, who?

All of this triggered old suspicions raised in her U.S. Senate and presidential campaigns, discarded then, but not so easily now.

As the cherry blossoms created their annual floral halo around Washington's tidal basin, Chris Santos, editor of the El Paso Daily, another newspaper in the Pounds chain, found a "project" on her desk. A former agent for the Drug Enforcement Agency claimed he was pressured to look the other way and abandon an investigation that involved Montes' bank, Premier Group of the Americas. The agent had refused to give up on the lead and soon after lost his job.

"Where did you get this, boss?" Santos asked Pounds.

"Overheard in conversation at a party I attended," replied Pounds.

The former agent, who asked that the newspaper not reveal his name, confirmed Pounds' news tip. And more. He claimed the White House was taking an unusually high level of interest in what was happening in the border drug trade.

Next came a widely-publicized arrest of midlevel drug cartel member Santiago Flores, captured by border guards as he tried to smuggle a van of high-powered weapons out of the United States.

Among his possessions was said to be a note from a higher up in his organization telling him that $20,000 had been paid for his safe passage. According to the note, arrangements had been made at the highest levels of the U.S. government. Apparently, someone on the border didn't get the same message.

By summer, journalists from publications that could afford it, freelance writers, and Republican Party operatives were swarming the border looking for evidence of White House interference in illegal drug and gun trafficking. Others were searching for, and finding, men who said they had had affairs with the president. Two congressional committees were checking the Banking Committee files for irregularities that might be linked to the president's time on that committee. The Treasury Department was trying to keep up with congressional requests for information that could link the president to money laundering.

***

"Hey, lady We had a deal. We were going to tell each other about our men, just as we did our boys."

"Who can remember?" said Tenny. "It's not that there were so many, it's just that so many weren't memorable or worth talking about."

The friends were sharing a late super in the White House, along with Fish, who had brought with her the disturbing news that the Judiciary Committee staff was looking into the drugs, guns, and money-laundering accusations.

"Not their jurisdiction, is it?" asked Carmie.

"Only if they want to build a case for impeachment," said Fish.

"Impeachment?" Carmie was appalled. "Because of a bunch of off-the-wall stories the media's been chasing?"

"Larry Anderson tells me he thinks they're trying to build a case for a full-scale impeachment investigation. Subpoenas, depositions, the works."

"They wouldn't!"

"Larry says he thinks they will and to get prepared."

Larry Anderson was the ranking Democrat on the Judiciary Committee. A veteran legislator, sometimes irascible, but a vote and voice the White House had learned to rely on.

"Hard for me to believe," said Tenny. "I'm still pretty popular and they'd be taking a big risk. They couldn't get enough committee votes to do it, could they?"

"Not sure," said Fish. "Zach Bowman, the chairman, is hurry-up ambitious. Wouldn't even be surprised if he was planning to run against you if you go for re-election. Larry's kind of a wild man, but he's with our staff all the time. He's our early warning system. Take it seriously and get ready."

"I don't know how to get ready," said Tenny. "It's all so far from real I don't even know what I'm fighting."

***

Ben Sage didn't know whom or what they were fighting, either. What he did know was a brilliant campaign when he saw one. For originality and effectiveness, the anti-Tennyson campaign he had been watching develop was hugely impressive. So impressive he found it hard to believe that any of his professional counterparts were masterminding it.

Ben speared an olive from the bottom of his martini glass. He and Lee were at the Big Fish in Rehoboth, making a quick escape from a day of high tension. Earlier, Henry Deacon, Tenny's chief of staff, had called to alert him that the House Judiciary Committee had scheduled a vote on whether to launch an impeachment investigation. Could Ben and Lee get ready for action, just in case it passed? The rest of the day was spent reorganizing their other campaign commitments. Then a quick flight to Delaware's Eastern Shore getaway. They needed some time to talk, to think, to get perspective.

"I just learned about the history of the martini glass," Ben said.

"Tell me," said Lee, "Another jokey accident?"

"No. The gin needs to stay cold to stay good, so that's why the long stem. The wide brim at the top helps the gin's flavor to open up. Then the cone shape keeps the gin and vermouth from separating."

"And why such a narrow vee-shaped bottom?"

"For the olives, of course. They can't just float around aimlessly. And the slanted side of the glass supports the toothpick. Brilliant engineering, don't you think?"

"I don't think about it at all. I just enjoy it."

"Lee, what do you think we're up against here? I don't know anyone who we compete with who could dream up and run a campaign as effective as the one they're running against Tenny."

"You don't think it's just the Republicans getting smarter?"

"Possible, but unlikely. What has me stumped is where they're getting all of this shit out of South America, Mexico, and all the places outside the U.S. Your guess?"

"The oil companies are my prime suspects. They work all over the world. They have their own FBI and local armies. They pay off everyone. And they've got a lot to lose if she wins the Future's fight."

"Maybe so. How about the banks? What goes for oil goes for them, too."

"Maybe both?"

"But these guys have never run campaigns like this before. They have enough clout in Washington to get their way without being part of an international conspiracy."

Ben drained his martini glass and motioned to the waiter for another.

"Is it that important to know where it's coming from?" asked Lee. "Isn't it enough to know what the Republicans are doing with all this stuff and try to beat it back?"

"No, it's not. We need to know who and why. Unless we know who we're up against, we won't know what to expect next. We'll just be running around trying to fix holes they punch in her. How do we get ahead of it and punch back?"

"Let's add the health insurance people to the list of suspects. They demolished the Clintons, even when health reform was at eighty percent in the polls. They're really good. Now Tenny's moving everybody to Medicare, pretty much wiping out private health insurance. That's plenty of motive and a track record of great campaigning, besides."

"Good point. But I think I'm leaning toward the oil guys because of the international angle. To collect evidence or invent it, they need to be deeply embedded in Mexico and Central America and South America. Contacts everywhere. Strong enough contacts to find nuggets of information others can't find, and to buy or intimidate people who usually can't be bought or intimidated."

"Yeah. You may be right," Lee said. "You know, I read Steve Coll's book about Exxon, *Private Empire*. He tells the story of a time when Lee Raymond was running the company and there was a lot of concern in America about gasoline shortages. One of Raymond's key guys suggests that the company should build more refineries here to make America more energy secure. Raymond says, why would I do that? We're not an American company. That's the way these guys think. The term banana republic started with all the military horsepower we threw into the poor Central American countries to make them safe for the United Fruit Company. These guys have been pushing smaller countries around forever. They're incredibly good at it. They may lose a battle now and then but they hardly ever lose a war they really want to win."

"Well I'm pretty sure this isn't about bananas. So are we settling on oil? Are those the guys we're fighting?"

"Not settling. But they're prime. They have the contacts and the power to do it. And they're smart enough to get others to pick up the tab so that their fingerprints aren't all over it. If it fails, you can be sure some of the guys in Congress will take the rap, not them. That's the way they play."

Plates of fried oyster appetizers interrupted the conversation. The two partners munched through them hungrily. Food for more thought.

Ben had spent all of his years in politics working in the United States. He had little experience elsewhere, the way some political consulting firms did. He had been thinking domestic politics, not international conspiracies. Until impeachment showed up on the radar. Now he was struggling with a whole new range of unfamiliar possibilities.

"One more thing," said Lee. "Who stands to gain immediately if Tenny is thrown out of office?"

"Immediately? The Vice President. Rusher," said Ben.

"Exactly," said Lee.

29

"NO!!" Congressman Anderson shouted.

In his frustration he repeated his vote three more times: "No! No! No!"

If he could, Congressman Lawrence Anderson would have yelled loud enough to sway the crystal chandeliers in the U.S. House Judiciary Committee hearing room. He considered all of this talk about impeaching U.S. President Isabel Aragon Tennyson pure nonsense.

After thirty years in the U.S. House of Representatives, Representative Anderson looked, sounded, and indeed was authoritative in many things. But for the last few sessions of Congress, he and his fellow Democrats had been in the minority. Even as ranking Democrat on the House Judiciary Committee, he had little power or authority. Years ago, when he was just a freshman member of Congress, Anderson also had a front row seat for an impeachment effort, Bill Clinton's. That was, as he saw it at the time, a shameful hunt for nothing more than dirty underwear.

Now, once again, members of the House Judiciary Committee were being asked to vote on whether to launch a full-scale impeachment investigation of a Democratic Party president.

It was July, months into the committee's inquiry. Committee staff had been sifting documents, traveling to U.S.-Mexican border locations, interviewing supposedly talkative drug dealers and cartel members, listening to current and former U.S. border guards and Drug Enforcement Agency agents. They were piecing together a story, a case, and none too quietly. Periodically there were leaks, exclusives. Always followed by official "no comments." Committee members were being briefed in executive sessions. The official public silence was more damning than the evidence. If this was too serious to discuss in public, it must be really bad. A petri dish for rumor and conspiracy theories.

The media chased anonymous tips, whispers, hunches. Media investments need pay days. And so scraps appeared often, most of them lightly sourced, or non-sourced, or spun from loose threads in unmatched socks. The total affect for President Tennyson was the creation of a lead weight, slowly dragging her into a sea of yet unproven guilt.

Finally, a press conference. Committee Chairman Zachary Bowman announced the committee had enough cause to ask the full House to approve an official pre-impeachment inquiry.

Representative Anderson's "no" vote was the seventeenth "no" on the roll call. There were three more votes to go, and only one more vote was needed to derail the Republicans from moving any further down the impeachment track. Before the roll call began most who thought about it expected the resolution to lose. The Republicans were used to bringing up votes just to embarrass the president, losing, and then bringing them up again. They had never tried for impeachment, until now.

"Mrs. Diaz."

Lenore Diaz, Latina American member from New Mexico, Democrat, first-termer, winner of her seat in an election so close it required a recount.

"Yes," said Ms. Diaz.

Yes? For a resolution that could wind up unseating her own Democratic president? A sister Latina?

A stunning vote. Republican members of Congress, watching on television from the cloakroom off the House floor certainly didn't expect it. Neither did White House staffers, watching from their offices near the Oval Room, or reporters covering this story.

A day earlier Lenore Diaz had received a brief, meaningful message. Either vote for this or your son Ralph pays. Ralph Diaz was serving three months in the Albuquerque Corrections Center for his role in a gang fight. The message was stark. No explanation. No qualifiers. But from the way that message was delivered Lenore Diaz knew it was not a bluff. Ralph was eighteen, a bit on the wild side like so many eighteen-year-olds, but a good son. It had broken her heart when the judge sentenced Ralph to jail. She blamed herself and her own political ambitions. Time bought at the expense of being with Ralph. Ralph already was paying a price for her career. She could not take a chance that the price would get even steeper. There were some very bad people in New Mexico. She knew who they were. And how bad they were.

The clerk moved on.

"Mr. Foster."

Darrell Foster was scared stiff. Foster didn't tolerate pressure very well. Foster the flake, his colleagues called him. You could never count on him. Easily swayed. Never consistent. Not particularly trustworthy even when he claimed he was with you. Diaz' vote put him in a place he did not expect to be. Foster's vote would be decisive. A congressman whose entire career *modus operandi* had been one of ducking, running and crouching as low as possible was about to be the judge, the last word on whether a popular president of his own party might be railroaded out of office.

"Mr. Foster."

Earlier in the day Foster had come to a decision. He planned to vote "yes," for the investigation. In his Maryland suburban congressional district, Foster had been fighting a growing reputation for being a mindless puppet for the president or whatever his party leaders wanted him to do. He had voted in favor of each bill the president had sent to the House—immigration, single payer healthcare, and others nearly as whopping big and controversial. Each vote had added to a growing legion of political enemies. By his count, the impeachment resolution was going down anyway.

A "yes" vote from him would show his independence with no consequences. How he voted wouldn't matter.

But he hadn't considered Diaz.

The pros and cons spun in Foster's head like tumblers in a slot machine. Create a months' long investigation that could remove President Tennyson from office? Incur the wrath of fellow Democrats? There would be a lot to answer for at home and right here in Congress.

But…congressional wrath could be short-lived because there's always another vote they want from you tomorrow. An impeachment hearing would be televised live, not bad for his reputation back in the district. He could always vote against impeachment itself later. And if Tennyson wasn't guilty of all of the messy stories about her, the investigation would clear her.

The clerk was looking his way. So was Judiciary Chairman Zachary Bowman. So were all of those television cameras. The eyes of the world. The voters in his district. Nowhere to hide and no more time to think about it.

"Yes," said Congressman Foster.

Foster's vote was like the starter's gun at a track event. House members gazed at the cloakroom television in disbelief. Suddenly, and for most of them unexpectedly, impeachment would rise to the top of the House agenda, and each member would have to deal with it.

The final "yes," from Arizona Republican Congresswoman Paige Lerner, came as anticlimax and only after heavy gaveling by Chairman Bowman.

The House Judiciary Committee had decided that all of the sordid stuff circulating in the tabloids and swirling in sludgy media backwaters would be transformed from rumor and innuendo into prime time coverage with live witnesses, under oath.

***

Ben Sage and Lee Searer watched the vote in their Georgetown office, surrounded by their staff. The air hung heavy, coated by the shock and uncertainty that usually follows the announcement of a death. No one said a word. No one could think of anything to say.

Ben felt something he had not experienced for a long time, and seldom in life. Nausea, evoked by dread. From countless past experiences he knew that when he was uncertain of an outcome, it usually meant he lost.

Ben's cell phone dinged within moments of the vote.

Deacon.

"How soon can you get here?"

"On my way."

"I'll pull together a core group."

"Deac, don't do or say anything until I get there."

"Not that easy. The media guys are all over Carlton in the press room. They want her. They'll take him. Christ, they'll take anybody."

"Resist it. Tell Carlton to close and lock the gates. No leaks. And for God's sake don't let her talk to anyone."

"Wait," a ridiculous notion just struck Ben. "Does she even know?"

"She knows. Fish called her right away. It's the only call I let in there. She's still with the OMB people about the budget. My guess is she treated the news from Fish like it was a social call."

Brief pause while they both considered the fact that the President of the United States had not watched her own impeachment proceedings on television, had not reacted when the vote went against her, and had kept working with the budget nerds even after hearing the news.

"Ben Do you think any of this is true?"

"I don't think so."

"I hoped you'd be more definite than that."

"Sorry. That's all I've got right now. Getting to either no or yes is going to take a lot of work. Lock the doors and get her cell phone away from her."

***

The next morning's meeting in the Oval Room was no different than others—six days each week whether in Washington, D.C., or traveling. It was a management tool Tenny picked up from the guys in the Pentagon. Meet at 7:00 a.m. No chairs. Everyone stands. Tight, specific agenda assembled by the overnight staff. Today's opportunities and crises. Things that happened while we were asleep that need tending or watching. Loose ends from yesterday. Here are the jobs. Who's doing this? What resources do we need to get it done? Objective? Deadline? Who's got responsibility? Anyone have anything else we haven't covered? Meeting adjourned. Seldom more than thirty minutes. Staff always. Plus, key players from inside and outside the administration who happened to occupy that day's hot seat. That meant Ben was there this morning, the day after the Judiciary Committee vote.

"Ben?" she said, when it was his turn to speak. "You'll work closely with Deacon and others on the House impeachment problem?"

"Yes, Madam President. We've already started. White House counsel needs to prepare a paper defining what can be done by government staff and what we'll need to outsource. I'll work with him on retaining private counsel that understands the politics of this. I'm arranging a defense fund from private contributors. Talking points have been prepared and distributed. We will keep your personal time and involvement at a minimum."

For Ben, Lee, their staff, and Deacon's, it had been a long night.

"Thank you," said President Tennyson. "Deacon, see that Ben is properly credentialed as a counselor to the president for the duration of this problem."

And then it was on to the federal response to the drought problems in Arizona.

Meeting over, Deacon pulled Ben aside.

"She wants to see you. Wait here."

Others filed out until there were just the three of them left. Tenny gave Ben a quick hug and motioned for him and Deacon to sit opposite her on the sofa.

"I'm going to say this upfront," she said. She had an earnestness that always accompanied tough situations. "I had that affair with Gabe. It went on for maybe a month and I loved every minute of it. He swept me away, that gorgeous, smooth-talking cad. It took a while before I found out he was a scoundrel and a dangerous one at that.

"So if the charge is did I have sex with that man, I plead guilty. Not that it's anyone's business any more than all the goings on among the guys. I was a private banker, held no public office and did what consenting adults do every day of the week. That's the beginning and end of it. Anything else you may hear will be a lie or a forgery.

"You know my relationship with Hal. Hal's going to be dragged into this—one more time. God, I'm sure he wishes he'd never heard of me. But at least he's in his last year as governor and won't have to deal with it in a re-election campaign. Ben, you know better than anyone that he did not appoint me to the U.S. Senate because we slept together. He appointed me against his better judgement because you talked him into it. Admit it!"

"You give me too much credit for that," said Ben.

"Bull shit. He knew we could wind up where we are right now, him being accused of appointing me as a consolation prize for not marrying me. Me being accused of being a slut. Ben, face it, you may have to testify to clear the air on that."

Ben started to speak but she left no commas or periods, took no breaths to give him an opening.

"There's absolutely nothing to the other stuff. The banks? Christ, I've got billions I don't know what to do with. Why would I risk everything to steal more? Drugs? Guns? Come on. I know I've brushed it off for months, thinking that if I ignore such crap it would eventually go away. I can't believe they actually got eighteen votes in that committee to set up an impeachment hearing. So, here we are. I'm not sure any of us could have stopped this earlier. They seem so determined to get me."

"Oh, they're determined all right," said Ben. "The House Judiciary hearings will be ugly. And the full House voting for impeachment is almost a slam dunk, since they've got control. We just have to stop it in the Senate, like Clinton did. They need sixty-seven votes you know."

In tough political situations, Ben, like Tenny, became all business.

"Madam President, we will hire our own investigators and our own research team to walk in their tracks. We need to know what they know to disprove anything they throw at you. Whatever happened, happened and we can't afford to be surprised when it comes up in the hearings or media headlines. We're going to dig as deeply into all this as they do. All of your personal finances and business dealings. All your travel in the years you were on the road. All the paper that's moved through the White House that has anything to do with any of this. Even, I'm sorry to say, all the men you slept with who might turn up to do you harm. Much deeper than we did for any of your campaigns. If they find anything that would hang you, we need to have found it first. Can you stand that kind of scrutiny?"

"Dig away. Ben, you know my flaws and weaknesses better than most people. Scratch them 'til they bleed. Make the worst case you can against me. But do it on facts. That's the only way I know how to fight back. About the sleeping around part. The fact is that over the years I've been with many men. Let's face it, I enjoy good sex. I'll try to remember them all for you to check out. I may forget a few who were forgettable. You need to find my former husband, Andres Navarro. I got a very nice letter from him after being elected. His contact information is in our data base. I don't think he'll be a problem. I made some deals when I worked with Groupo Aragon that I'm not proud of. That was years ago, and should have nothing to do with this. But I'll give you enough to get started just in case. My finances? Hell, I've got nothing to hide. Maybe just some embarrassing losing investments.

"Dig into all of it. We can win this on truth. But I don't know how we fight what they make up. I'm trusting you to figure that out. Win this campaign, Ben, but don't bother me with the details or take any more of my time than you absolutely need to. I ran for president to be president, not a criminal defendant. There are precious few days for that and I don't want to waste them."

She stood up abruptly. As Ben and Deacon walked to the door she stopped them.

"By the way, if I survive this I'm going to run for re-election."

They both spun in surprise. She had never said a word about re-election even though Ben had prodded her for months to do or say something to head off competition. Already two other serious Democratic candidates had announced and were building campaign teams and bank accounts. A wounded incumbent draws plenty of interest from those ready to bury the final sword.

"Just thought you should know. Oh, and while I have your attention, those pictures of me they've been running in the tabloids, the ones that make me look like a cheap hooker...I actually look pretty good in them, don't you think?"

She struck a seductive post, winked and lifted her skirt just above her knee.

President Tennyson had not been so oblivious to the media campaign against her after all.

30

The Nixon impeachment hearings had broken ground untouched since Andrew Johnson's trial in 1866. Twenty-five years after Nixon there was Clinton. Now, Tennyson. Much of what was mystery in 1973 had become almost routine.

House Judiciary Committee Chairman Zachary Bowman had not even been born when Nixon was president. New to the committee chairmanship, George Clooney looks, quick wit, unlimited ambition, Bowman was a good bet to run for president himself.

For the moment, he was at the center of the biggest political story in Washington. He would chair the hearings that would decide whether President Tennyson would be the third recent President to be impeached. Convening in Bowman's office this morning was Lawrence Anderson, the ranking committee Democrat, a polar opposite of the telegenic Zach Bowman. Receding line of gray hair, slightly stooped from age, and corpulent from too many nighttime fund-raisers. Anderson was from New Jersey, a safe place to be if you're a Democrat. He had been entrenched in Congress since his first election and had been through all this impeachment stuff before, voting in the House minority against impeaching Bill Clinton.

Also sitting in on this meeting was Bo Willard, Speaker of the House, and the one who would inherit the spotlight should the House Judiciary Committee find Tennyson impeachable. Willard had become Speaker when the House flipped back to the Republicans during the George W. Bush years. It took savvy to navigate a Republican House caucus since the emergence of a sizable right wing party-within-the-party. Willard was hell-bent for impeachment so that his friend, Rod Rusher, the vice president, could become president. What a great pair they would make. Even though they were in different political parties, on most issues they were of the same mind. As Speaker, Willard would be next in line for the White House, if they could get rid of Tennyson.

"I want to do this very quickly," said Bowman. "It's July. I'd like to see hearings in September and be ready for a House vote in October. I think we can finish this whole business by the end of the year. We don't want to drag this into the election year."

"No reason we can't," said Speaker Willard. "The committee votes out impeachment resolutions, the House votes on them. It goes to the Senate. The reasons for doing this are clear enough. I think everyone's ready to make the case."

"Then why even bother with the hearings?" asked Democrat Anderson. "You already have a guilty verdict. No need for a trial. But if you want to do this fairly, she has to have time to send up her own witnesses, hell, come and defend herself right here if she wants. We give axe murderers months to mount their defense. The president just gets weeks?"

"Hey, Larry, get off your soap box. How much more evidence do we need that she helped that old bank of hers launder the drug and guns money?"

"So you're going to parade a bunch of losers through here who claim that one of the richest people in the world risked her job as United States president to make a few extra bucks laundering money? Who believes that crap? And all the sex stuff. I guess we'll have a replay of Lewinski and publish a report called fifty shades of Tennyson. And what do you expect her to say, 'I am not a crook. I am not a whore?' This is all political bull shit and you know it."

"Let her defend herself with everything she has, Larry. She can afford the best lawyers, the best private investigators. And, hell, she's got the whole federal government to use against us. This won't be rigged. It's a fair fight."

Anderson slumped in his seat.

"Huh. Do what you want. I can't stop you."

Bowman turned to Willard.

"I'll need $10 million to get staff assembled and the investigation in gear. And I'll need temporary assignment from your chief counsel. Also, we'll need to build out a platform for the TV guys. Cody over here, my media guy, has been studying how they handled Clinton, and that's a good roadmap for us. We'll also need a separate room for the internet people, podcasters, and all."

"Can't they just cover it by watching it on TV?"

"No," thundered Anderson. "Everyone needs to be part of the circus."

"Larry, will you object to any of this?"

"Handle all the arrangements the way you want as long as our side gets its share of the money for staff and research. But don't mind me if you read that I've told the press we're going into this with a hang-her-first and then have the trial mentality. I've had my problems with the president, too, She's not the friendliest lady ever to be here. We go back plenty of years, since she was in the House. She used to drive me nuts there. Push. Push. Push. She's even worse now. But having differences in style and policy hardly makes her a criminal. There's a high bar for impeachment. This committee dropped it as low as Lewinski's drawers when I first got here. Now you're making it even lower so eventually every president can expect to be impeached if they wind up with the wrong Congress."

"Don't worry, Larry, we'll do this by the book. But from what I've seen, it looks pretty grim and we won't sugarcoat it. By the way, have you been in touch with the vice president?"

"No. Why?"

"Well I think you should. Over the next few months, anything could happen. Remember, after this committee asked the House to impeach Nixon, Goldwater and a bunch of other Republicans went to him, told him it was time to go, and he did. It never even got to the House floor. Not everybody stays 'til the bitter end, like Clinton. The vice president needs to plan his schedule to be around for whatever happens. You're the best one to tell him that."

"You're probably right. Coming from me he'll understand the committee is likely to take this all the way and that he's a good bet to be delivering the next State of the Union speech."

"Although his defense of her I saw on TV last night was pretty strong and looked authentic."

"What else would you expect from him? It's what vice presidents have to do. Until they don't."

***

The weeks between the House decision to hold impeachment hearings and the hearings themselves resembled the peak days of election campaigns—each side jockeying to command the heights of Mount Validity. Tenny's opposition was prepared for this combat. Within days of the Judiciary Committee vote, Republican support groups were on television with frightening ads of guns and drugs being trucked across the border into the United States with drivers showing White House passes to border guards.

Tenny's defense, caught off guard through wishful thinking and Tenny's refusal to take the impeachment threat seriously, moved quickly to play catch up.

A support organization was quickly formed to raise money and to manage her counter-attack. At the group's center was a small strategy team: Ben and Lee; Alistair Seltzer, one of the lead defense attorneys; Chip Fanning, CEO of Fanning and Frazier, a political research firm relied on for years by Sage and Searer; Henry Deacon; and Bruce Han, chief White House legislative assistant.

Platoons of respected leaders and organizations were enlisted for her defense. Campaign-style paid media was produced to compete with the opposition's. Mail and email blanketed digital and snail mail boxes. Supporters swarmed talk shows and wrote op-eds and letters. Tenny herself was on the move, obediently heading to cities and states the strategy team labeled pivotal.

Compared with the House and Senate Watergate hearings that led to Nixon's demise as president, the Tennyson hearings drew a meager television audience. Back then, before cable, before the internet, before smart phones, you either watched what any of three broadcast networks gave you or you didn't watch anything at all. When all three networks broadcast the same program, you had no choice. Besides, the Nixon hearings were historic, the first serious proceeding in a century that could lead to the removal of an elected president. While the Nixon hearings were rare, the Tennyson hearings were not. In fact, for many Americans, it was the third time they were asked to sit through an impeachment trial. The last one, Bill Clinton's, was considered a farce by most Americans, devaluing what was once seen as a solemn process. Now, the impeachment show was back for a rerun. Many found the game show "Jeopardy" more interesting than the jeopardy confronting the White House.

So it was a meager viewing audience that watched live while Judiciary Committee Chairman Zachary Bowman opened the impeachment inquiry with a brief statement of its purpose.

"For the past two months, committee staff has been reviewing certain allegations made against the president of the United States, which, if true, would rise to the level of high crimes and misdemeanors, the bar set by our nation's Constitution for impeachment and removal from office. Committee staff has interviewed dozens of witnesses, including the president herself, under oath. Staff members have traveled to various locations where the inquiry has taken us to obtain first-hand information and to review circumstances related to the allegations. Tens of thousands of documents related to this inquiry have been obtained, verified, and analyzed. All of this information has been reviewed by members of this committee. To summarize, our hearings will focus on the following topics:

"One. Was the president of the United States complicit in a scheme to launder money obtained illegally in a manner that violates U.S. banking, currency, and national defense laws?

"Two. Was the president of the United States complicit in a scheme to violate laws for the transport of illegal substances and weapons across the United States–Mexico border?

"Three. Did the president of the United States willingly misuse her high office to conspire with foreign nationals to enrich herself and her family and for other illegal purposes?

"These hearings will take testimony from those making such allegations, possessing documents alleging such crimes, and from those who will speak on behalf of the president to counter those allegations. The president will be welcome at any time to address these charges personally. The committee begins these hearings without prejudice or bias. We will form no judgements until all of the witnesses have been heard and the evidence presented. Now, counsel, please call your first witness."

***

At the other end of Pennsylvania Avenue, in a small White House office, the president's core strategy group was completing its first head count of U.S. Senate votes. Thirty-four senators would be enough to block the president's removal. Now the legislative staff was evaluating each Senator's current thinking. Others were suggesting ways to influence Senators' votes, through wives, children, close friends, contributors and pet projects. True, the current action was in the House. But Republicans were in the majority there. The president's defenders had little expectation that they could win either in the committee or on the House floor. But marshalling thirty-four votes in the Senate seemed possible. Even likely. That's where they focused their resources. In the midst of a lively exchange, suddenly, the chatter stopped. Deacon had turned up the volume on one of the room's three television sets. All eyes swiveled to it.

Filling the screen was a full-frame image of a startlingly handsome middle-aged man. His photos had been so widely published that anyone paying attention to the impeachment story would instantly have recognized him. For those who had not, the words on the screen spelled it out. Gabriel Montes. The camera pulled back to reveal him at the witness table being questioned by Katherine Polaski, chief Judiciary Committee counsel.

"I want to review this again, Señor Montes, because it obviously is important to our deliberations. You say you have been involved in a long-time affair with president Tennyson."

"Sí."

"When did the affair begin?"

"Twenty years ago."

"And you say it began when you both were young international bankers. Can you please elaborate on that?"

"Yes. We met at a conference in Peru. She and I were competitors for wealth management accounts in Latin America. She worked for Groupo Aragon. I was with Premier Group de las Americas. We were on the same conference panel. She was very smart, very quick. And quite beautiful to my eyes. After the panel, I suggested that we have a drink in the hotel lobby. That led to dinner. We talked of many things, including the ancient arts of Latin America. Her mother had been an art student and filled their home with many rare and beautiful artifacts. It became a passion, also, of Señora Tennyson. I could feel that passion she had for art. That raised my passion for her. I asked if we could have dinner the following night, too. But she was occupied.

"Before the conference ended, though, I had a chance to speak with her again. She was much in demand, representing a major

Mexican bank group and a member of the famous Aragon family of Mexico. A very rare combination of assets. Señora Tennyson, I asked, have you ever been to Machu Picchu? That got her attention. She had never been to this important site.

"I have many connections there, I told her. And it was true. The owner of the Cima del Mundo hotel in Cusco was a long-time friend. In fact, I had helped him finance his purchase. The chief of the major guide service was from my home city of Chiclayo, in Peru. I told the señora we could have excellent accommodations, with service and a tour such as others seldom enjoy.

"Señora was quite interested. She was scheduled to visit Buenos Aires, but said she would try to change the schedule. Señora Tennyson met me in Cusco three days later. We spent four days, seeing Cusco together, traveling to Machu Picchu, and enjoying one another's company."

"And it was then and there that your affair began?"

"Sí. It was quite romantic. Golden sunsets. Candlelight. Incredible vistas of a world that doesn't exist outside that valley. Everyone should experience it sometime with someone they love."

The audience and many of the members on the dais could not suppress laughter. Gabe was telling a love story and the listeners were enthralled.

"Christ," blurted Ben, out loud, to no one. He was not feeling the love, but rather a creeping sense of dread. These people were on stage with a very good show.

"Mr. Chairman!" Congressman Anderson thundered, "Are we conducting a daytime talk show here? Is this a soap opera? Oprah? Sex, sex, sex. So an unattached woman and this witness had an affair long ago. So what? What does this line of questioning have to do with anything related to this committee's inquiry?"

"Mr. Chairman," responded counsel Polaski, "the relevance of the questions will be apparent if you allow me to proceed."

"Proceed," nodded chairman Bowman.

A cutaway of Congressman Anderson showed him shaking his head in apparent disgust.

"Now, Mr. Montes, you say this was not the only occasion you met with President Tennyson romantically."

"No, no, no," said Gabe emphatically.

"She had to resume her business travels with that trip to Buenos Aires. I met her there, where we spent three very exciting days together. Two weeks later we met again in Mexico City where she introduced me to certain members of her family, including Don Miguel, her famous grandfather. A month later I was required to be in Los Angeles."

"Señor Montes, I want to remind you that you are under oath and that to not tell the truth is perjury punishable by a severe prison sentence and personal fine. What you have just described aligns with what President Tennyson has told our committee in her deposition. And in fairness to the president, I will point out we are talking about a period in which she was a private citizen, held no public office, and was a single, divorced woman. Your testimony to our staff diverges from hers after the Los Angeles meeting. I want you to fully understand you are questioning the veracity of the president of the United States, who also was under oath."

"Sí, I understand señora counselor. I can only say what I know to be true. I wish the lady no harm. I feel only fondness for her. In fact, I'm not embarrassed to say I love her."

The audience tittered with nervous laughter. Chairman Bowman rapped his gavel twice. Gently.

"Please go on and tell the committee of your contacts with President Tennyson since that time in Los Angeles."

"Well, as I told your staff. There have been so many. In the years since, we have spoken often, and corresponded. "

"What did you speak and correspond about?"

"After we stopped seeing each other romantically there were a few times where our travels took us to the same cities. There were a few evenings together. Not like before, but very pleasant. The tone changed from the excitement and freshness of a new romance to more of a businesslike relationship."

"Businesslike?"

"Yes. At first when we were romantically connected, she asked many questions about the bank that employed me, the Premier Group de las Americas. She wanted to talk about clients, prospects, much of it confidential. I am a guarded person but in situations where you give your heart, it's not easy to resist giving more. Like what's in your head. I regret that in the heat of passion I disclosed some trade information—clients, prospects, fees. Those kinds of things.

"And so you had a sense she was using you to gain a business advantage"

"I would not say such a thing. But I believe that was the result. Yes."

"And then when the relationship changed, the conversation changed?"

"Yes. I didn't know why. But she was more guarded than when we first met, and so was I. But once she went into your Congress, it was like before."

"Romantically?"

"No. I would not say romantically. Sexually sometimes, but not romantically."

"And what did you discuss, when you were talking?"

"She was on the committee that had an interest in the Americas and money. You know, how money passed around. Those kinds of things. Sometimes she would appear in Peru and would call, and we would get together. She asked many questions. She asked about accounts we had of what you might say were not quite usual."

"Illegal?"

"I don't know from illegal, madam counselor. Let's say different. Accounts that called some extra review to themselves. Especially she wanted what I knew about her own family company, Groupo Aragon. That surprised me. I didn't realize until much later that she had no contact with them for many years."

"No contact? With her own family company?"

"Sí. She told me during our time together that she had been forced out of the company and that it was her intention to get even with them."

"Let me understand this, Señor Montes. The allegation has been made that the president has done illegal things in office to benefit Groupo Aragon, a company her grandfather began and which employed the president and her father and other family members for many years. And is it your testimony that rather than trying to help Groupo Aragon she actually was trying to hurt the company, to get revenge?"

"Sí."

"Why?"

"Because she had wanted to run the company. The board didn't believe she was qualified and they dismissed her."

Only a few people knew the inside story of the dismissal of Isabel Aragon Tennyson. Few had thought to ask. The assumption was that she willingly had taken her large inheritance and moved on to other things.

"She told you this?"

"Sí. Pillow talk works from both sides of the pillow."

"And do you have other reasons to believe what she told you?"

"Sí, señora. It was confirmed to me by others in Aragon management when I asked. I gave your staff names to contact."

"So how did she intend to get revenge?"

"She was very successful. She told me and others of accounts held at Aragon, the amounts and the names. And she advised us how to take those accounts away and make them ours at Premier."

"And did you?"

"Quite successfully."

"So, to clarify, President Tennyson, then a United States senator, knew about specific Groupo Aragon accounts— for laundered money, for gangs in the illegal drug trade, for the illegal gun trade—run by people who murder and terrorize whole communities, and instead of reporting them to the authorities, she reported them to you so you could grab those accounts. And she did that as revenge for being fired by her own company. Is that your testimony?

"The story is perhaps more complicated, señora counselor. But it would appear so."

"And are those accounts still with the Premier Group?"

No, drug enforcement people in Mexico, working with yours, found those accounts, many of them belonging to Escuadrón de la Paz."

"The drug cartel?"

"Sí. They were disclosed after the arrest of Rafael Pecheco, who ran the organization. Premier paid suitable fines of course."

"And you, as the account manager?"

"After my arrest in Mexicali I paid fines as well."

"Do you still live in Peru?"

"Señora, I finally got the message. I was in a dangerous place and had to get out. I left the bank and moved to New York where I began my own private investment firm."

Committee counsel Katherine Polaski paused to sip from a water glass, moved a few papers on the table and let the damning weight of Gabe's testimony settle in. Live television took that time to get in quick station breaks and comments from their news staffs. Comments like "Blockbuster!" "Revealing!" "Sensational!" As Gabe's testimony wore on, the live television audience increased. Images of this gorgeous man and their president together flashed on the screen. What they did together strolled through the minds and fantasies of not an insignificant number of those on the viewing side of the tubes.

"Once again, Señor Montes," Polaski resumed, "I want to remind you that President Tennyson denies much of what you just told us. Under oath. At risk of being removed from office if it is proven she did not tell the truth. Why should this committee believe you?"

"Señora Counselor, I'm just a humble man, caught in the middle, trying to do the correct thing. You might say I romanced the wrong lady and it is more difficult than if I had to confront a jealous husband. As a gentleman, I destroyed the letters she sent me over the years, destroyed the emails after reading them, and when we signed into hotels I used names other than our own. I have given your staff the names and contacts of some people who I believe will agree with my story."

"We have spoken with them and some will appear in following days of hearings."

"One more thing that I didn't tell your staff because I wasn't certain I could find it."

"What's that?"

"My diary. It's not complete, but señora was an important part of my life for many years, and after our meetings I was inspired to write about them."

"You've found that diary?"

"Sí, señora Counselor. Here it is."

The commotion in the House committee room was audible. Her word against his would pit two even hands against one another. Credible written evidence, if confirmed, would add a heavy thumb to the balance—against her.

Committee Chairman Bowman rapped for order, and when he gained a semblance of it, he adjourned the hearing for lunch.

Ben's strategy group sat transfixed in the White House conference room. Gabe's testimony was stark, direct, with enough naive honesty to seem believable, enough sex to hold and build the audience, and enough questions about the president to raise anyone's doubt level.

Deacon, obviously flustered by what he just heard about his boss, the president, grabbed Ben by the arm.

"What do you think?"

"I'm just in awe at how good these guys are."

You don't think the diary is authentic?"

"Of course not. It's great theater and perfect timing. And it's going to be a bitch to disprove."

"And this guy Gabriel?"

"Tenny sure knew how to pick them. I hope there aren't a bunch more like him."

31

He was about ten years old, alone at home. Home was a three-story townhouse. Sitting in the first-floor living room. Doing something. Listening to the radio? Reading? Playing a game? Didn't matter.

He heard a noise from the floor above. Steps it sounded like. But he was alone. There couldn't be steps. Unless. But there were. Now he heard them on the stairs. Coming down the stairs.

Terrified, he forced himself to the stairwell and looked up. To this day, decades later, the image remains vivid. A woman. A strange woman. In a military uniform. Descending ever so slowly. One step at a time. Staring straight ahead. Zombie-like. Eyes wide. And what he could not forget, what he never forgot, were her eyeglasses. They were floating in front of her eyes, unattached to her head.

What did she want? Where did she come from? What should he do?

Until the universal antidote to unwanted dreams, escape to wakefulness, saved him from having to answer any of those questions. Why the floating eyeglasses? Why had that night of terror stayed with him through life?

For a while, in those pre-adolescent years, Ben had many nightmares. They all began with the same nocturnal brand. Like watching MGM's lion in the first frames of a movie, his nightmares introduced themselves with a whirling vortex. He was inside the eye of a multicolored tornado, spiraling down the funnel until he reached its tip. Then a nightmare would begin.

Tonight the vortex again appeared to him in dream, decades removed from his youth, introducing another threatening storyline that he quickly forgot once the light of wakening vaporized it in his mind. Ben jumped from his pillow, sweaty, heart pumping. Moments of undefined terror and the wonder that childhood fears had returned, packaged as before.

Ben sat on the edge of his bed. Alone, straining to untangle his thoughts and body from the last few moments. His room was dark as his dream. He reached for a light switch and struggled to unwrap himself from the tug of the sheets twisted around his legs.

Even though his bedside clock informed him it was barely 5:00 a.m., returning to the uneasy peace of sleep did not feel like an option. Better to face the nightmare of this day's waking hours.

32

Ben was no stranger to campaign attacks, and tough ones, and last minute ones, and well-financed ones. The longer Ben stayed in the business, the more attack ads there were, until it seemed that's all there were. Longer campaigns. More negative campaigns. More money and more avenues to spread bad news.

The campaign against Tenny was different from any of those. Here, it had become clear to him he was up against more than a single campaign or political party. This was taking on the smell of a legalized coup, managed and bankrolled by opponents who preferred not to be identified, working through their friends in the media and Congress, with some assistance by their allies within the government itself. Who designed this strategy? Who was running it? It's not easy to run a conspiracy. The more people involved, the more potential there is for leaks. People with secrets usually burst at the lips to treat their knowledge of a secret like valued currency. So far, in this conspiracy, they could find no one with loose lips. To Ben that said fright. Those involved were too frightened to drop clues about their involvement. What did Gabe say? He left Peru because he was in danger? From whom?

Until Gabriel Montes' testimony at the committee's first day of hearings, Ben felt his campaign was holding its own, keeping the president's poll numbers strong enough to prevent a collapse of support among fellow Democrats. President Tennyson's defense team had its own deep research effort in place and so far they had found nothing to contradict her own version of events. That version aligned with much of what Gabriel Montes had just testified to, including their time together in Peru and other meetings over nearly the next two months and the abrupt breakup, which, she testified, came after she had more background on Montes and was warned off by friends and others who knew him as a shady operator in the darkest corners of money laundering.

President Tennyson's research team found no contradictions, but on all the occasions Montes claimed they met, and which she denied, records showed both Montes and Tenny were in the same cities. Was he stalking her? Did they meet, or didn't they? Or had someone gone to a lot of work to rig hotel registers and other documents that aligned his supposed travels with hers? The witnesses Montes named to verify his story were a motley bunch. It didn't take much detective work to come to that conclusion. Ben and the legal team all felt they could raise enough questions about their veracity to at least win a draw with that round.

So far, so good. But what about this new element, the diary? If it proved to be authentic, and included names and dates and places that conform to Montes' testimony, and if the diary seems to have been kept at those times, not quickly prepared now for show time, it would be hard evidence, and hard to counter. It could tip the balance. And what did Montes write about their amorous encounters? Whether fact or fiction, it would make hot reading— like the book the Starr commission published about the blue dress and Clinton. That was downright pornographic. And did it sell!

Just as worrisome was all the talk about narcos and possible corruption of the DEA, prodded by higher ups in the U.S. government, a trail Republicans were trying to have end at the White House door. A few fired agents and other discontents would testify to such allegations, but a hard scrub of data could find nothing in the records to suggest any impropriety. Democrats on the Judiciary Committee were pressing to have these authorities called as witnesses to counter the charges.

Mercifully, there was a two-day break in the hearings to allow members of the committee staff to review the diary and authenticate it, or not, for the committee. Ben and the staff took the break time to revise their public campaign messages to fit the dialog as it was unfolding and to develop options based on what might be coming. He was at work on this with staff members in midafternoon when Father Bob Reynolds called. Bob Reynolds was a Jesuit priest and professor of theology at Georgetown University, the Catholic Church's flagship academic center in the Washington, D.C., area.

"Ben," said Reynolds. "I'm so glad I caught you. I was afraid that with the mess you have on your hands you'd be as cloistered as a monk, with your head in a prayer book and hoping for divine intervention."

Ben enjoyed Reverend Reynolds, or Bob, as he insisted on being called. Years ago, Reynolds had persuaded the diocese to hire Sage and Searer to develop a public relations and advertising campaign. As Reynolds explained it at the time, they had no intention of glossing over pedophilia or any of the other sins so visible in the Church's immediate history. Their goal was to restore confidence among the faithful—and just as important, restore the flow of the donations being squeezed ever tighter with each new ugly revelation. This was the first contact Ben could remember having with Bob Reynolds since then.

"Bob, good to hear your voice. I hope you've saved many souls since last time we spoke."

"Well that couldn't have been too many souls, after all it was only last month."

Before Ben could respond Bob Reynolds rushed on.

"You remember, well apparently you don't, that we're getting together tonight to work on the next steps in our campaign. Can't blame you for forgetting with all else on your plate. Anyway, I just got authority to move ahead with it. It's sure overdue. And it occurred to me I should remind you about it rather than trust your appointment book. By the way, Hank is in from Philadelphia and will join us."

Appointment? Tonight? Hank? He hadn't talked to Bob a month ago. He was sure of that. And who the hell was Hank?

Bob obviously was talking in code. Why? Through months of preparation for the judiciary hearings Ben never considered that his phone might be tapped. Bob Reynolds obviously suspected that it was and was talking gibberish just in case. Well if someone else was listening he already had let his silence go on too long.

"Bob sorry, these days I've got six phones ringing at once and somebody was talking into my other two ears. Who did you say was joining us?"

"You remember Hank. The graphics guy. He's staying with us for a few days."

Now Ben was sure that Bob was giving him signals and that the real topic was so sensitive they couldn't discuss it on the phone.

"It sure would be fun to see Hank again. Look, you were dead on. Tonight's meeting would have blown right past me. I see it now on my calendar. Let me cancel a couple of things. If I run into trouble I'll call you back, otherwise I'll be there. What time's best?"

"Any time after 7:00. And we're in a new place here now. Come to Healy Hall, Room 202."

In all the tough campaigns he'd been through, including presidential campaigns, Ben was fairly certain no one had ever tapped his phones. This obviously was a different kind of combat. How come the Reverend Bob Reynolds had figured it out? Maybe he hadn't. Probably he hadn't. It must have been "Hank," whoever that was.

That evening, Ben drove from his office in Georgetown to the University campus, usually no more than a five-minute trip. But now, suddenly conscious of the possibility he was being watched as well as tapped, he wound his way around Georgetown's narrow streets, an eye constantly in the rear view mirror. It didn't look like he was being followed. Then he realized they wouldn't need to follow him. If they'd listened to the conversation they knew where he was going. Ben, he said to himself after slapping his forehead, you've got a lot to learn about how to play in this league.

He parked on 37th street, bordering the campus, and walked the path across the grassy Copley Lawn to Healy Hall. Was he being followed now? He didn't think so. Fall classes were just getting under way and the campus was buzzing with new arrivals. The night was temperate, making the outside world appealing, drawing to it hordes of young company.

Healy Hall, an imposing, neo-medieval structure, was the backdrop for the movie *The Exorcist*. Its interior even provided scenes for the follow on, *Exorcist II: The Heretic*. While its exterior profile can be either picturesque or ominous depending on one's point of view, for Georgetown University, Healy Hall is a campus nerve center. Many of the world's most important leaders in politics, the arts, literature, and science have spoken in Healy's Gaston Hall auditorium. Healy houses monumental libraries that would hold their own for their architecture and collections with most university libraries. Healy is where Georgetown's president has his office. And it's where Father Reynolds wanted to meet him.

Ben entered the building through the main entrance and walked the stairs to the second floor. "Development office" was etched on the brass plate next to the number 202. The door itself was locked. He could see nothing through the door's glass. The lights were off.

Puzzled, Ben stood looking at the door. He was sure Bob said 202. Maybe there was another entrance. Focused on this problem he didn't hear the figure approach him from a dark corridor.

"Ben." It was a low, vaguely conspiratorial voice, out of the darkness in the stairwell behind him. Ben thought he was alone in the semi-darkened hallway of office suites, long-shuttered for the evening. The voice was so sudden and unexpected Ben physically jumped at the sound.

"Bob, you scared the shit out of me. Oh, Christ. Sorry for the profanity."

"Nothing I haven't heard before."

Father Bob Reynolds was a bear of a man, shaped like the football tackle he was when he played for the College of William and Mary. The years and too many covered-dish suppers had added girth, and with his shaved head and generally light facial features Bob had the appearance of a clerical snowman.

Ben started to say more, but Bob raised his fingers to his own lips and motioned for Ben to follow him—down the same darkened corridor from where he appeared. The corridor led to a stairwell. They walked silently down two flights of stairs. Then another door, unmarked, which led to another flight of stairs. Now they were in the bowels of the building. Near the boilers and water systems and radiant pipes that kept Healy Hall going. The corridors were wide. An opening led to a large, bare, gym-like space marked with a sign that read "Civil Defense Shelter."

Finally, Bob spoke.

"You know in the age of GPS and microphones that can record through walls you can never be too sure who's tracking or listening."

They walked a few more steps, to the end of the corridor. Bob opened a door to a small room, a meeting room capable of comfortably holding no more than a dozen people. As they entered the door, Ben was met by an unusually slim, almost pixie-like man with weathered features and, like Bob Reynolds, wearing the habit of a Jesuit priest. The visitor held out his hand like an old friend.

"Ben. So good to meet you at last. I've heard so much about you from my sister."

Ben had never met this man.

"Ben," said Father Reynolds, "Meet Father Federico Aragon."

Ben looked at him, puzzled, still not immediately grasping the significance.

"The president's brother."

33

Federico Aragon's olive features could not hide the cracks, the wrinkles, the used flesh that becomes nature's own when devoid of human comforts. He appeared to be a man in his sixties, fully gray, including eyebrows that seemed half again too large for his otherwise oval, slim face. His shoulders formed too small a hanger, causing his clothes to float around him. A small man in a big tent. While slight physically, when Federico spoke, what emerged as voice was a surprising contrast. Deep but soft, mellow, comforting. His trade was giving comfort to the discomforted. His voice and demeanor were in harmony with his work.

Federico interrupted Ben's awkward silence. He spoke near flawless English.

"Of course you're surprised to see me and in these circumstances. I am what you would call something of a marked man these days in Mexico. Hopefully, no one from there knows that I am here. Bob Reynolds and I were seminary classmates and during our years there and in later work we have become good and trusting brothers. My presence here must remain a secret, and so we could not let you know beforehand."

"The phone call…"

"My clumsy attempt to be an undercover priest," laughed Reynolds.

"Well it worked. I'm here and I managed to get here without telling anyone."

He turned to Federico. "So why, why are you here, and why in such secrecy?"

"Señor Ben, for many years now I have been what my people call the wandering priest. I move from village to village to serve those where there is no full-time parish. All around me there are the conflicts that come with politics and drugs, and cartels and even murders. But it's as if I'm in a bubble. I see only the wreckage left behind. I pray for victims, I help with births and sickness. I minister the old and the penniless and all those who remain faithful even though they live in conditions where no one could blame them for cursing God for abandoning Him. All of the players in the drama around me know that my singular mission is the Church's mission, no others. It doesn't hurt that they know I am the grandson of Don Miguel Aragon, with whatever that might mean. Even years after his death, many violent people fear retribution if they were to harm an Aragon. It gives me a measure of safety others might not have. In fact, at times, the criminals even help support my mission."

Bob motioned them all to sit. The room was fitted with a simple pine table and six hard backed pine chairs. On the table Bob had placed a bottle of wine and three glasses. Two of the glasses had been in use before Ben's arrival. Now, Federico poured himself another.

"Excuse me, this wine is quite good. I enjoy comforts, you see. I haven't forgotten how."

Ben was taken with this priest. He spoke with ease and feeling, and despite his physical size, he had a commanding presence. The peasant priest was himself no peasant. He was an Aragon.

"So, let me explain why I'm here now. Isabel, my sister, is in a great deal of trouble, and I can help. You see, while my eyes may not reflect recognition at the evils around me, I still see them. My ears hear them. Those whom I comfort tell me many things. They know me, my background and the fact that Isabel is my sister. They know the people who are now saying that she was involved in guns and drugs and they know these are all lies. Some have been paid to lie. Others have been threatened. These facts are known where I travel."

"Have you evidence? You simply saying it would be dismissed as a brother trying to help a sister."

"The court you are in, Ben, is not a legal court. It's political. And I believe I have collected and can continue to collect enough evidence to win in the political court. The question I have for you is at what point should I present it? I will do it now, or I will return when timing may be better. I will do it publicly and in any forum where it will help Isabel."

Ben refilled his wine glass and looked hard at this unlikely man who was promising to save the Tennyson presidency.

"Why are you contacting me, and not your sister directly, or people on her staff or our legal team?"

"Isabel would send me back to Mexico with an armed guard if she knew I was here, and especially if she knew I was walking on dangerous ground. We are very close. She cares deeply about my welfare and worries constantly about my travels through dangerous areas. Whatever I do publicly must be done in a way that she suspects nothing in advance.

"As for why I wanted to speak to you, it is because of the danger. If I were to contact anyone in your government or your legal team, they would know immediately. They are everywhere. Of all those helping her, you are the least likely to be watched by them. And if you are watched, Bob Reynolds is your client. You being with him is a business call. I believe this is the safest way to get my message to all of you. Now I have. Discuss this with those defending her and let me know when and where to appear. But it should be a time when it makes the most difference, when it can move the most of your public and the votes she needs to survive and clear her name. If it's too soon they will have time to defame me and others and find other ways to question my evidence."

"Who are 'they'?"

Federico looked quite surprised at the question. Ben didn't know?

"The rich. The powerful. The strongest and most dangerous interest group in the world."

"Rich and powerful? Do you mean banks, oil companies? Who are they?"

Again, Federico was struck by the question.

"Señor Ben. The wealth of the world is held in very few hands. Some are in my country. Some are in yours. They are everywhere. On every continent. And they are into everything. Oil and banks, yes. But they have fortunes they inherited. They are dictators and others from corrupt regimes. They own and control great parcels of land and great industries. Look at the people who run the drug cartels and who thrive in the world weapon trade."

"Are you saying these people are connected?"

"They have more in common with each other than they have with any nation they live in. They are their own interest group, powerfully influencing what others do in finance and trade and transportation and everything else that matters to them, even military actions, even selective enforcement of laws where that suits their interests. Everyone talks about the one percent, or maybe the tenth of one percent. These are the hundredth of one percent. So few but so powerful. Did you know that just sixty people—sixty—have as much wealth as three billion on the lowest rungs of income? Of course, not everyone in this class is so motivated by greed or use their power selfishly or criminally. But many do. I know this from my own experience with the Aragon Company. I was once apprenticed to be one of them.

He paused for a minute to take another sip from his wine glass, enjoying his brief encounter with the spirits inside.

"Isabel knows these things, too. That's why they are trying to destroy her. As long as she is president of the United States she is a threat to them."

Ben turned to Bob Reynolds.

"Do you agree with Federico, there's a conspiracy among an element of the super-rich to bring down the president?"

"Ben, the Church is everywhere, too. We see things we don't or can't talk about if we want to stay on our primary targets—saving souls and helping the poor. We do what we can, but we're not big enough to take on the people Federico's talking about. If we openly tried it would go hard on the Church and even harder on our people. We're totally aware of this problem and danger."

For the next two hours, Federico described to Ben the nature of his evidence, the names of others who would testify on Tenny's behalf, the pressure, the bribes, the threats, all connected with those testifying against her.

They knew of Gabe's affair with Tenny. He didn't know how they found Gabe, but once they did, they set up the arrest in

Mexicali to own him. Gabe was a fraud. Hotel registers had been forged to show Tenny and Gabe as guests where they never were, at times they never were there. Drug enforcement people who testified were doing so either because of cartel threats or for pay or because they or their families were being blackmailed.

How did Federico come by all this information? His connection with President Tennyson was well known. His friends throughout the region began warning him as soon as she was elected president. Questions were being asked. People were being made offers. Villagers don't need fiber optics to communicate with one another.

They parted as they met, with handshakes in the evacuation center, sealed from GPS and unwanted listening devices.

"Where will you go now?" asked Ben.

"Back to my mission. It would be suspicious to everyone if I did not keep my schedule."

"Where do they think you are?"

"Houston. At a week-long retreat Jesuit priests attend each year. We wear hoods a lot, you know. It's hard to tell one of us from another when we are together. It's quite a good disguise."

Federico could be as impish as his sister. It must run in the family, Ben thought.

"And how do we find you again?

"Through me," said Reynolds. "Tomorrow I will sign a contract with your firm to update our PR program. You'll have business reasons to be in contact with me on a regular basis. It won't appear suspicious. I'll know how to find Federico on short notice."

They left Federico alone in the small room while Reynolds escorted Ben up the stairs. Before they reached the top landing, Ben stopped and turned to Reynolds.

"How is this peasant priest able to come to Washington in secret and have enough cover so that anyone else might think he was at a Catholic retreat in Houston?"

"The Church is a big organization, Ben. We've got a lot of resources."

"So you're not the only man of the cloth who's in on this?"

"Me? No, he laughed. I'm the messenger boy."

"Who else knows?"

"He's got a lot of fellow priests in Mexico. The confession booths are quite a grapevine of information—sort of like an ancient internet."

"And these priests can act politically on their own?"

"In a tightly structured organization like the Catholic Church? Hardly."

"You mean," here Ben hesitated before saying what just popped into his head.

"The Vatican knows and is trying to help us?"

Father Reynolds gave him a wink along with a final handshake.

"The Church greatly admires President Tennyson."

34

The small strategy group gathered in the conference room of Delacott and Seltzer, the lead law firm handling Tenny's impeachment defense, listened transfixed as Ben related the details of his meeting with Federico Aragon. A number of those present being lawyers, Ben became the object of rapid cross examination. Federico's manner of telling. Did it seem authentic? Did he perspire? Fidget? Stumble at inappropriate times? How strong were his sources? Would they be accepted as confirmation? Some at the table remained skeptical that Federico's testimony would be credible, given his family relationship.

Alistair Seltzer, the lead litigator and the face of the defense, saw nothing but opportunity in Federico's testimony and fended off the concerns of others on his team. Their case was thin enough. They could use all the help available, and if Federico was as convincing as Ben described, a collared priest who could handle hostile cross examination would at least increase the level of doubt about the charges. Doubt was their first line of defense. The more uncertainty, the less likelihood of the opposition getting to sixty-seven votes.

The Senate vote was genuinely in doubt. Revealing Federico in that forum, at the right moment, could break the impeachment fever. There were two beneficial effects of waiting until near the end of the process to reveal Federico. It would give the opposition little time to discredit him before a final vote. And it would keep Tenny from protecting him by quashing his appearance. Although it was exceedingly irregular, the accused could not know about her most important defense witness until he was called to the witness stand. They all would have to deal with her wrath afterward.

***

Chairman Bowman ran a tight ship. The House Judiciary Committee compressed its hearings into three weeks, a fraction of the eight-week marathon the public endured during the Clinton impeachment. With Clinton, the public ultimately overdosed on relentless carping and turned aggressively negative against the Republican accusers. This Republican leadership was determined not to repeat that mistake. Also driving the accelerated committee timetable was the presidential election year calendar. President Tennyson had now made it clear to all that, unless she was removed from office, she would run for re-election. The Republicans felt they had to dispose of President Tennyson before year's end, before the primaries gave her more forums to raise her positive profile.

During those tightly scheduled three weeks, a conga line of remarkable witnesses snaked in and out of the witness chair. Juan Manuel Ibarra, a clerk at Hotel Bolivar in San Salvador, verifying a signature for Gabriel Montes, one room, king-size bed, two people, on a night Montes' diary said he and Señora Tennyson shared a room.

Carl Tessen, a Chilean bank examiner, testifying that señora Tennyson committed fraud in withholding vital information as the Temuco bank merged with Groupo Aragon.

Jesus Guzman, identified as a regional cartel boss, shown on video, face in shadow and voice garbled to hide identification, testifying he had connections inside the management of the U.S. Drug Enforcement Agency helping move heroin across the border from Ciudad Juarez to El Paso, Texas.

The governor of California, Harold Thompson, denying that he appointed Isabel Aragon to the Senate because of their "personal" relations.

No, said the governor, Ms. Tennyson did not blackmail him into the appointment with threats to expose their history. And no, he knew of no situation where the president used her body to gain any advantage during her terms in Congress or their work together in the L.A. Lights movement.

Richard Legar, an American who worked at the Fiesta Hotel restaurant in Tampico, testified to seeing President Tennyson, then a U.S. senator, meeting a man there. Legar was from San Diego, California, and was certain the woman he saw was his senator, but because he feared the criminal climate of Tampico, he was afraid to approach her. She obviously did not want to be recognized. He didn't know the man, but it could have been Montes. Senate records showed her in Mexico City on that date. Why the subterfuge in a place as dangerous as Tampico if she had nothing to hide?

Committee counsel Polanski also presented a thick file of executive branch documents that committee staff authenticated as having passed through the Department of Treasury and the Department of Homeland Security, messages that could be interpreted as coded instructions to clear a path for Mexican contraband. Was the White House tampering with border enforcement and banking practices in ways that helped cartels and Latino banks? The paper trail was suggestive, but not clear cut.

How do you respond to such charges? Deny. Deny. Deny. But it was like taking a scissors to smoke. The charges were sensational. Those making them seemed so certain. A few pieces of hard evidence were like anchors, holding the looser accusations in place and making it difficult for the defense to sweep circumstantial testimony aside.

Worse, it was good theater. Novel entertainment. As the hearings continued, the committee's viewer rating increased. Networks were finding they could charge more for advertising during the live daytime hours and the nightly reruns of the day's testimony. That was all they needed to give the hearings more air time and to promote them more heavily.

The president had given her deposition early, heeding advice from her strategy team not to appear live before the committee. That would only draw a larger audience and subject her to the hostile questions of the committee's Republicans. The growing wall of testimony refuting her sworn statements prompted a decision to have her return for a second round of closed-door depositions. Many of the lies had to be challenged. Her research team provided strong rebuttals, backing up her own memory and testimony.

Would Tenny's denials and the weak case against her allow her to survive? No one on her team felt particularly confident. As Federico correctly pointed out, this was a political fight, not a legal one. The media sowed considerable doubt about Tenny's integrity. The accusations were grafted onto embedded nativist prejudice against Tenny's Latino background. A strong minority of Americans still hadn't overcome that hurdle.

On straight party-line votes, the House Judiciary Committee approved three articles of impeachment.

Article One accused the president of illegally interfering with the proper enforcement of border security by using her office to directly abet the movement of weapons and narcotics across the United States-Mexico border.

Article Two accused the president of participation in an illegal scheme to hide drug cartel money from authorities.

Article Three accused the president of lying to a committee of Congress about her involvement in these alleged crimes.

The action would move to the House floor, where Speaker Bo Willard and his Republican majority were waiting with barely concealed glee. The Democrats had sent President Nixon off to inglorious early retirement. Republicans had failed to return the favor with Bill Clinton. They would not miss this time. Willard lost no time in scheduling the debate.

During the Clinton impeachment, more than 200 members spoke. Willard expected no fewer than that for and against President Tennyson. Even with tight speaking time limits, the whole process would likely take three weeks. No one on either side of the debate believed the outcome was in doubt. This was a battle the President was not likely to win in the House. And she didn't.

The day the House voted to impeach President Tennyson was also the day Senator Reed Guess died.

Guess died at home, his family at his side. Tenny had been a frequent visitor there, and for weeks earlier at Bethesda Naval Hospital. The call informing her of his death was no surprise. For the past two days he had been in a coma. But the finality touched her as deeply as the deaths of her own mother and father had. She rested her head on her desk in the Oval Office and did something she rarely did—let tears flow freely.

The Senate went into temporary recess so that members could travel to Connecticut for the final services. Tenny was there as well, delivering a eulogy for her friend, the man whose untimely cancer diagnosis made it possible for her to be president.

35

Removing a president from office is not civil war or a military coup, but it is wrenching to democracy. The majority of voters have elected a president. Now a majority of Congress is asked to override that decision. Because impeachment awls to the very core of a democratic process, the Constitution sets up a number of safeguards and hurdles before a president can be removed. The chief justice of the U.S. Supreme Court, not an active political figure, presides over the Senate trial. Senate rules require each senator to walk to the front of the chamber and sign an oath book pledging to do "impartial justice." The vote needs to be overwhelming: two-thirds of the body, 67 of the 100 senators must agree. There is no cross-examination. Senators submit questions in writing. The Chief Justice reads them and the prosecution and defense answer them.

The House sent ten "managers" to the Senate to argue for the removal of President Tennyson. Eight defense lawyers represented the president. For two days the prosecution argued its case. On the third day the body was stunned to see President Tennyson in the Speaker's well. An enormous risk, but a calculated one. The defense team looked ahead and saw only uncertainty. Every argument in its arsenal would need to be deployed, including the president herself.

She stood alone in the Speaker's well of the United States Senate, stripped of the trappings that go with the State of the Union address and other symbols of presidential power. A lonely figure, armed only with a lapel microphone in the fight to salvage her honor and her legacy. No written speech. No teleprompter. No aides handing her notes.

But President Tennyson didn't need any of it to keep 100 Senators, a packed visitor's gallery, and a television audience counted in the tens of millions riveted on her performance.

For thirty-eight minutes she held the floor, extemporaneously answering each of the impeachment articles voted on by the House. Point-by-point, she defended herself, with names, dates, and context. While her presentation was heavy with facts, it also was light with personal vignettes, even humor when she discussed her relationships with men. And no surprise, considering the pummeling she had endured through the U.S. House impeachment proceedings, she often surfaced barely concealed anger.

The usually staid senators could not suppress smiles and even some laughter as she dismissed the charge that she helped former Peruvian banker Gabriel Montes launder Mexican cartel money.

"Did we have an affair?" she said, "We certainly did, and it was a great one while it lasted. As most woman and even many men will agree he's a handsome and charming devil. But he's also a lying, thieving scoundrel. It took me a few months to catch on to the real Gabriel Montes. When I did I promptly ended the relationship. Mr. Montes stalked me for years afterward with notes and phone calls. His testimony that we resumed a relationship or that we have had any contact since I stopped seeing him is total fabrication.

"Numerous handwriting experts have testified that the hotel registers he presented as so-called evidence were doctored to make it seem we were there on later dates. Analysis shows that his so-called diary was created not over a period of years, but over the course of a few days to fool gullible people who preferred not to accept the scientific proof of its forgery. I'm stunned that the majority of the Judiciary Committee would fall for this charade. If this were a court of law none of what he presented as evidence of my involvement with him or money laundering on his behalf would be accepted. There is no evidence of it. There is no case. There are no grounds for this article of impeachment.

"For those of you who are happily married, I envy you. But let me ask, did you have relationships with others before marriage? Were there some relationships you would prefer to forget? And for those of you who no longer are married or have never been married, have you had relationships that are no longer enduring? That's life, isn't it? We move on, don't we? These are not criminal acts. And neither was mine with Mr. Montes."

In comparing her love life with theirs, the president connected with many of the senators sitting in judgement. Her comments evoked considerable nods, smiles and more than one senator to exhibit momentary embarrassment.

Countering charges that the White House had interfered with border enforcement of drug and weapon control laws, the president reaffirmed what her counsel had argued during House impeachment hearings, that incriminating agency documents were forgeries.

"Ask yourselves," she demanded of the senators, "why on earth would I do such a thing? Where is the motive? Money? Really? I've revealed my wealth. Check it out. My interest in getting more

Americans hooked on drugs? I spent six years of my life working the streets of Los Angeles, helping drugs' victims. Helping the gun trade? The NRA has spent millions trying to defeat me in elections. It makes no sense at all. I have no answer for how those documents got there or who put them there. But I do have an answer for whether I or anyone I instructed tampered with border security. The answer is an emphatic *no*."

In interviews that followed her speech, the president's supporters were ecstatic.

Senate President Pro tem Stuart Alcantra said, "I believe she secured her position today. From beginning to end, it was one of the most powerful presentations I've heard in my thirty-six years in the Senate."

Senator Lisle Garabali of New Jersey said, "She came through the fire stronger than ever. She's like steel."

When the president completed her testimony there was no applause. Neither was there anyone to immediately challenge anything just said. She spoke long enough to consume the morning session and require a break. It was the ultimate in media management. All of the day's stories were about Tenny and her defense.

The media generated by Tenny's performance flowed like fine champagne. She had delivered many perfect edit points for broadcast news to clip and air. Her frankness was jarring and rang of truth and authenticity. Her energy was compelling and contagious. The print media, which for months had feasted on ominous stories about her, radiated with writers and editors won over by her. It was a great day for the home team.

Ben had known her for twenty years, through multiple political campaigns, countless speeches on her own behalf and for other candidates and causes. With her Senate defense she had reached the top of the mountain.

It was too early to declare victory, but the scent of it was in the air. Federico was scheduled to deliver his evidence the following Tuesday. After Federico's testimony, Ben planned to double down on the media campaign to win public support.

That was on Friday. On Saturday, the defense team met to discuss Federico's appearance and final arguments. With momentum clearly on their side and poll numbers confirming it, Ben allowed himself a second martini Saturday night during dinner with Lee. Later, back in his apartment, still in an upbeat frame of mind, he watched the movie *Moneyball* for the third time. He loved that movie. The path to success in sports was presented as he had walked it in politics. Decades ago, in his first political campaigns, Ben had to overcome generations of campaign dogma. Until then, campaign decisions were about feeling things in the gut, getting Charley in ward six to deliver, distributing enough campaign pins and bumper stickers and yard signs. Ben was a pioneer in changing all of that.

He demonstrated that gut decision making worked much better if based on polls and other research data. He was one of the first consultants to go all-in on television ads, even if it meant no money for bumper stickers. In *Moneyball*, past performance was dissected and analyzed, and where it competed with the gut of the long-time team scouts, the numbers won. And so it was in politics. For his first six years in the business Ben didn't lose a campaign. Not one. No matter the odds or how steep the hill to climb.

Tonight, Ben emptied much of the bottle of his favorite gin while he watched baseball parallels of his own career flick by.

So when the phone rang at 7:30 Sunday morning, he was groggier than usual. At his age, getting up was more of a process under any circumstance. Feeling the first aches and pains of the day. Compounded this morning by something he seldom felt any more. An alcohol-driven hangover.

"Ben, Deacon."

That woke him up. Deacon? At this hour on Sunday morning?

"Federico's dead."

"How?"

"Bullet in his brain."

"Oh my God, they murdered him."

Ben was standing now, fully awake. Ice replacing blood in his veins.

"They found a suicide note."

"Suicide? Federico didn't commit suicide."

"The note said he realized his sister was guilty and he couldn't live with the shame."

Ben sat back on the bed. Legs weak. He suddenly felt a powerful urge to defecate.

"Does she know?"

"She's in with the White House counsel team now. I think she's working on a letter of resignation."

36

In little more than half an hour, Ben managed to compose himself, pick up Bob Reynolds in a taxi and arrive at the White House. The front lawn was shoulder to shoulder with television cameras and media people waiting for anything, a blowing leaf, a passing sentry, or expectantly, a chastened president prepared to make a statement.

Ben and Bob Reynolds didn't pass through that gauntlet. They entered on the National Mall side where the White House cooks and cleaners and other functionaries enter and leave. If they were seen by media eyes, they were not recognized. Ben was counselor to the president, a familiar figure to White House security. Reynolds was used to faking his way past surprised guardians. Few want to quibble with a priest, especially when accompanied by a known insider like Ben Sage.

The West Wing was in a state of paralysis, an army without marching orders, not knowing whether to gird for a fight or turn over their swords to a conquering enemy. Phones were ringing but few knew what to say other than, I'll call you back. Ben stopped at Deacon's desk.

"Where are we?"

"They've been in there for about an hour. The only others except her counsel are Lawson and McKitrick from the national security team. I'd guess they brought her more details about what happened. "

"How did she take the news?"

"With a stony stare. No screams, no tears, no words at all. I'd say if that bullet had hit her brain, not Federico's, that's how she would look in the first seconds after. Like she was either instantly dead or only temporarily upright before the body recognizes that it's all over."

"We're going in."

"You can't. She said absolutely no one. Including me."

Without a word, Ben grabbed Reynolds by the arm and sprinted into the Oval Office, past a very surprised Secret Service agent at the door, who quickly collected himself and barged in after them.

The president was at her desk. The White House counsel and national security executives were seated in chairs facing her.

"It's all right," said Tenny when she saw Ben and Reynolds, "Leave them be."

The guard retreated.

"Sorry, Ben. I can't talk with you now. You'll have to leave."

"Not until you hear what Father Reynolds has to say. This is Father Bob Reynolds, a friend of Federico's, a great friend. Federico trusted him to deliver a message to you if anything happened to him."

She stood up, startled.

Without waiting for an invitation to speak, Reynolds told of Federico's secret visit to Washington weeks earlier. The letters, the copies of emails, photos from hidden cameras, the audio recordings. The network of priests and other Federico loyalists who had been collecting this evidence for nearly a year, ever since the first rumors began. That's what he hoped to deliver in person at the critical time, to break the back of the conspiracy. He was supposed to be here today. He was planning to go public with all of this right here in Washington Tuesday. That's why he was murdered.

Tenny stood staring at Reynolds, both arms on her desk for support, leaning forward, straining forward, as if with effort she could hear Federico himself.

"Madam President, please understand, Federico was incredibly brave to do all of this while ministering inside the climate of death and torture that raged all around him. It's to Federico's lasting credit and the bravery of many others that all of this testimony was collected and recorded for you. You must continue this fight or else Federico's death and the probable death and torture of others will be for nothing."

She stared at Reynolds for a moment, sat back down and closed her eyes.

"He didn't commit suicide. I know that," she said quietly.

"It is a sin against God to take a life, even one's own," said Reynolds. "He didn't commit suicide and he didn't write that note. How could he, when his life for the past year has been dedicated to saving yours."

"Our counterparts in Mexican intelligence also don't believe it was suicide."

She rose from behind her desk and walked to the curved bay window looking out on the National Ellipse. Her back was to everyone else in the room.

"I've prepared my letter of resignation. Even if everything you say is true, after today my reputation is ruined. People will always doubt. Even if I survive the Senate vote, how effective can I be?"

The gravity of the moment pressed down on everyone in the Oval Office. It became harder to breath, to think, to talk. Ben broke the silence.

"You can't resign. You simply can't."

He moved around the desk to face her.

"Federico spoke of a conspiracy, and when I asked him who was behind it, who were the "they," he said the rich and powerful. You're their target because you were once one of them. You know what they do and you know who they are. That makes you dangerous, really dangerous to them. And indispensable to everyone else. If you go now the rest of us are their victims. It's not just your fight."

"He loved you," said Ben. "But he also saw you as a vehicle to bring justice to the very people and causes he'd devoted his life to. He enlisted a small, dedicated, heroic army to protect you. It's their fight, too. Theirs, mine, everyone's. Everyone who trusted you. Who still trust you."

Reynolds had been present to comfort the afflicted in countless moments of grief. Now he did what his life's instincts trained him to do. He stepped toward Tenny and grasped her hand. Her head bowed from the weight of her sorrow. Her hand tightened in his. The room remained quiet while they appeared to silently pray together.

Deacon burst through the door.

"Sorry to interrupt, Madam President, but you've just had an urgent message. I felt you should see it immediately."

He handed it to her.

She read the note and closed her eyes as if to shut out everything she had heard and seen this ghastly Sunday morning.

The note read "May God be with you and guide you in your hour of sorrow. Father Aragon was our brother, too, and we, as all who knew him, grieve. We pray for him and for your continued stewardship of your great nation."

It was signed, Monsignor Alfredo Moretti

Without disclosing the contents of the note, Tenny turned to Father Reynolds.

"Who is Alfredo Moretti?"

"The Holy Father's personal secretary," said Reynolds.

Apparently Reynolds had been in contact with a higher power before getting into Ben's taxi.

37

The camera crews began gathering on the White House lawn shortly after sunrise. Overnight desks picked up the story of Federico's death from Mexican news sources. The initial stories featured the damning suicide note with little questioning of authenticity. The note was universally seen by the media as the death knell for the Tennyson administration.

Network anchors and their A reporting teams were roused from their Sunday morning beds to handle what clearly would be one of the biggest news events in years. Throughout the morning hours, news editors scrambled to fill time until hard news came from the White House. Members of Congress who had been on the front lines of the impeachment effort were like hounds unleashed, recapping the worst of the accusations with glowing self-actuated auras of righteousness as early diviners of corruption. Tenny's most devoted supporters were cautious in their defense, this morning's high watermark being to urge everyone to forgo judgment until the facts were known—responses dredged from a well of sadness rather than spirited conviction.

In the absence of news, there was rumor. A White House staffer seen carrying a box to her car. That set off a pack chasing the idea that staffers were told to empty their desks. Someone said they thought they recognized a doctor entering the White House through the adjacent executive office building. That could only mean that the president was physically or emotionally in distress. A standard 8:00 a.m. changing of the security team at the vice president's residence sent cameras racing there on the presumption that the Secret Service had been alerted about a change in command.

The media anticipated a resignation and wasn't shy about passing on that expectation to the public. Sunday morning talk shows cancelled their planned guests so that their crews and anchors and all their resources could stay focused on what was happening at the White House. That presumption was justified by two events. White House press secretary Carlton Bliss had confirmed that the president was with top members of the White House counsel staff and also with leaders of her national security team. These meetings certainly would be needed prior to any formal resignation. Then, at 11:00 a.m., the leadership of Congress appeared on the front lawn, in full view of the cameras. Their unity made its own statement. They walked silently, faces grim. None would answer questions.

When they filed into the Oval Room, Tenny rose, greeted each of them with hugs, and with tears in her eyes.

"Madam President," began Senator Pro Tem Stuart Alcantra, "please accept our deepest sympathy for the loss of your brother."

Still standing, she hushed Alcantra with a wave of her hand.

"Thank you, Stuart. Thank you all. I know why you're here, and I'm willing to abide by your judgment. But before you make that call, I'm going to leave you to talk privately with George McKitrick and his intelligence team about what they've learned from Mexico. They are in the cabinet room waiting for you. Let me introduce Father Bob Reynolds, who I imagine you don't know. He has information you should be aware of. Please use my office. I'll be in my residence. Call me when you're ready to talk." With that, she, Carmie, and Fish, who had arrived to comfort her, were gone. The others remained.

It was a cloudless November day in Washington. The lack of cloud cover sent temperatures into the mid-20s. Despite the cold, thousands of people had gathered in Lafayette Park, around the Ellipse, along Pennsylvania Avenue, waiting, sharing what appeared to be a memorable moment in history. No waving signs in support or to protest. In fact, there was the silence of mourning. Mourning for what? Promises either not kept or unfulfilled? Hopes dashed, again, with the pain of disappointment? A mourning for a country, a process, a friend gone bad? At 1:18 p.m., the congressional delegation reappeared on the White House lawn, this time ready to speak to the cameras, and through them to the by now tens of millions of Americans drawn to the drama unfolding at the White House.

Senator Pro Tem Stuart Alcantra, Democrat from Wisconsin, the longest serving member of the Senate, was the lead spokesperson for the group. He had no prepared speech, but from long experience before cameras and crowds he needed none.

"This is a time for honesty, for total candor, for the absence of partisan politics and pettiness. That's the spirit that motivated all of us to come here today. We came to suggest that in light of the tragic death of the president's brother, and the circumstances of it, the president should consider resigning her office in the best interest of the people of the United States. That was our assessment of what we knew then. But during the past two hours we have been made aware of new circumstances, new evidence, all of which raises serious questions as to whether the death of Father Federico Aragon was in fact a suicide and whether the note left at his side was authentic. We have seen written documents and spoken with Mexican authorities that place the matter in much doubt. The president was as frank with us as we were with her. In fact, she offered to abide by our judgment on whether she should resign the presidency.

"After discussing this among ourselves we advised President Tennyson to remain on the job she was elected to do. The evidence and whatever information may yet be revealed should be presented through the Senate's consideration of the articles of impeachment now before it. The full Senate should be given an opportunity to resolve this question in the constitutionally proscribed way.

"We all extend to the president and her family our deepest sympathy for her loss. Given the fact that the future of her presidency is being litigated in the Senate, and that the Senate is the forum for the presentation of facts and evidence, we will take no questions. Thank you."

The members quickly retreated to the White House door where two black SUVs waited to spirit them away.

The media crews, the anchors, the thousands on the streets and the tens of millions connected electronically had been waiting all day for a final chapter of the Tennyson presidency. Instead, as the day ended, they were left with nothing but the expectation of more to come.

38

There was no precedent for all of this. No rule book. The House had made its case for impeachment, published its report, cast its vote. That record now had to be considered against the evidence supplied by the late Reverend Federico Aragon. Much of it was authenticated in the days following its release to the Senate leadership. The Mexican government was cooperating fully. President Isabel Aragon Tennyson was hugely popular in Mexico. She was, after all, a native daughter, the strongest and most successful advocate for immigrant rights, a woman who had been generous supporting Mexican art and scholarship and those in need. If she were to run for president of Mexico she would be a landslide winner. Mexico's leaders understood all of this. Their popular support now was tied to hers. Federico's death and a suicide note that at first seemed to be a smoking gun in the case against President Tennyson now increasingly appeared to be the strongest evidence on behalf of her innocence. Indeed, her victimization.

In the two weeks since that dramatic Sunday, public opinion polls had shifted wildly. From narrow approval of her on the eve of the Federico's death, to free fall in the days following the original reporting. With the new evidence the polls showed a recovery for her of sorts. That recovery would have been more robust but for a massive right-wing campaign to stunt it.

Opponents were everywhere with suspicions of CIA complicity, cover-up, corrupt Mexicans coming to her defense, forged documents. Conspiracy theories were rich Internet currency. All of this fed into the now riveting debate on the floor of the Senate, where managers for and against her continued to argue the impeachment indictment, all being telecast for an audience of hundreds of millions, in the United States and around the world. Tensions and audiences were building. A final vote deadline was scheduled within a week.

When Ben rushed Father Reynolds to the White House, he hadn't seen the evidence Federico had left behind. His only information had come from the conversation with Federico. In the days since the drama at the White House he had time to review that evidence thoroughly. Aside from the details, a number of questions continued to puzzle him.

How, for instance, did Federico, a single, penniless priest, traveling alone in the poorest byways of Mexico, manage to recruit and organize so many others to his cause? What he presented was a significant portfolio, collected over many months, obviously requiring more travel and money than Federico had time for and possessed. Ben kept thinking of that wink Father Reynolds had given him at the end of his meeting with Federico, when he asked whether the Vatican knew about this. The timing of the message that arrived at the White House after Federico's murder was exquisitely perfect to influence Tenny's decision. Was there a war room in the Vatican mirroring their own? Was the Pope himself aware, or even directing it?

And that led to the second question. The campaign to remove the president was too clever and on too grand a scale for it to be a creature of domestic politics. Certainly the Republicans knew opportunity when they saw it and jumped aboard with glee and relish. At this very moment, they were fighting hard in the media and on the floor of the Senate to finish the job. But those were not the guys who recruited Gabe and the others to testify against Tenny, or who created bogus written evidence that backed up lying testimony. Republicans certainly did not kill Federico. This was the stuff of intelligence professionals. Working at whose bidding? Was it so crazy an idea that there existed a sort of super-wealthy Spectre as in the James Bond books and movies?

Tenny quickly recovered from her bout with doubt and her flirtation with resignation. Once she had decided to remain in office and fight efforts to remove her, she went into full campaign mode. She regrouped, composed herself and asked the networks for five minutes the following night to deliver a message. It was a message that expressed her love for Federico, her pain at his loss, assurance to other nations of U.S. leadership continuity, and a willingness to abide by the Senate's decision, whatever it might be. That was a lot to pack into five minutes, but she did it reverentially, and forcefully.

Then she hit the road and the phones to shore up public support and to put pressure on senators who her team believed still could be persuaded to vote against the impeachment resolutions. Ben and Lee had mapped out a full schedule, and she agreed. She was theirs, just as she was during the campaign that elected her. But she insisted on one detour. The leaders of the immigration reform movement had scheduled a long-delayed victory party, shelved until the Supreme Court made its final judgement on the act's legality. That judgement was in, the act was preserved, and now it was time to party. Tenny was not going to miss it.

Henry Deacon, her chief of staff, was scheduled to accompany her that night, but a crisis in the South China Sea kept him chained to his desk. Rita Gonzales, Tenny's long-time top aide on immigration policy went to the hotel early to help the advance team with arrangements. It was unusual for Tenny to travel alone, but everything about the last few weeks had been unusual. She headed to the Washingtonia Grand hotel with just her security escort and the knowledge that tonight would be tonic after all she had endured in recent weeks.

39

She arrived at the hotel later than scheduled. The president had hoped to be there for the earlier cocktail party, to shake hands, stand for photos, share the evening personally with those who meant so much to her and her campaign to win immigration reform. No matter, she would stay later. This was a festive evening. Pleasure does not keep time as rigorously as pain.

A two-story elevator ride lifted the president and her security team to the ballroom floor. Hotel manager Glen Freiberg greeted her as the elevator doors opened into the hotel's enormous kitchen, alive with staff in the final stages of preparing the largest sit down dinner the new hotel had ever served. As was her custom before making any public appearance, the president asked to take one last look at herself before becoming the center of attraction. Freiberg escorted her to a bathroom to the left of the elevator doors. Check your hair, your lipstick, assess your appearance and how you will look close up on television. Take a few deep breaths to calm yourself. It was a ritual she followed through her political career.

Four minutes later, a brisk walk through the kitchen with frequent handshakes—cooks, waiters and other staff, many of whom themselves secured by the new immigration law. Now she was behind a curtain veiling her from the banquet floor, greeted by long-time friend and ally Leon Rivas, chairman of the Immigration Reform Coordinating Committee. They embraced warmly and exchanged whispered words.

"Ready?" he asked. She nodded.

"Great night," he added.

She breathed deeply and closed her eyes.

Rivas cued the evening's master of ceremonies, Florida Senator Carson Coulter. Coulter had been filling time on stage, introducing notables, raising the emotional temperature of the crowd for the president's arrival. With the signal from Rivas, Coulter lifted his arms dramatically as if to levitate everyone in the room.

"Ladies and gentlemen," his rich baritone boomed, "the president of the United States."

A brassy "Hail to The Chief" bounced off the ballroom's hard surfaces, amplifying both the sound and the excitement. President Tennyson strode quickly onto the stage, an energetic, hands-waving entrance, the image of victory.

The moment she stepped onto the stage was a rush back in time. Time when her presence ignited spontaneous crowd combustion. Her first campaign for Congress in Los Angeles, the victory march through California for the Senate, the amazing Alamo presidential campaign launch and the tens of thousands who would come to see her, touch her, hear her words as she went from city to city running for president. Tonight, for the first time since descent into the ugly world of impeachment, she could feel the love, and the trust, and the expectation. Worn thin lately, but not tonight. Tonight was hers. These were her people.

The ovation was deafening, sustained, overriding the orchestra. Many in the room had lived their adult lives with the uncertainty of place and belonging. For so many, the war now was over. Victory achieved. This was V-J Day and for tonight, this ballroom was Times Square.

Television cameras were live, as they were at most of the president's events these days, recording what could be the last moments of her historic presidency. The images shown now were caviar to cable television directors, a rich visual feast of expressive faces, tears, embraces. The president, triumphant, love enveloping her, love she requited with each air blown kiss.

Then the cameras went dark. Black. Suddenly and ominously. All of them at once. Those watching on television could no longer see anything.

Those in the ballroom saw hell.

The explosion shattered the south wall of the ballroom. Through that opening rocketed a fireball so intense it incinerated those directly in its path. Lethal black smoke roared through the wall's splintered openings. The ballroom's thunderous cheers dissolved abruptly into total silence. It happened so quickly. Too quickly for screams. Now, only occasional shattering of falling glass. A throat, gagging. Little else. Table salads dressed a sea of bodies. Exit signs blinked red, too late for warning.

Lincoln Howard, the Washingtonia Grand's chief of security, quickly regained his feet and raced up two flights of stairs from the security office to the ballroom level. The dark cloud blowing through the ballroom doors flashed scenes etched in his memory from two tours in Iraq. Howard ducked into a bathroom, surprising three women standing immobile at the sinks. "Get out!" he shouted to them. "Get out of the hotel!" They ran. He grabbed fistfuls of cloth hand towels, soaked them in water and raced into the ballroom through a door closest to the stage, wet towels covering his face.

Howard was no stranger to dead and wounded bodies. But his years in the Marine Corps never produced a scene like the one at the other end of his flashlight beam. It was as if a deranged choreographer had positioned a vast expanse of bodies on the floor, bodies partially hidden by white table cloths. Shrouds. Shrouds adorned with memorial wreaths of flowers, scattered from dinner tables by the force of the explosion.

Despite the arc of horror framed by the blackness beyond flashlight range, the stench of something, what, chemicals of some kind, he took a few tentative steps on a floor now slippery, sticky with salad oil and vinegar, water from overturned vases, wine, the color of blood, mixing with the still bleeding bodies all around him. Howard edged into the ballroom swinging his light's beam, searching for movement, any sign that someone was alive, anyone who might claim priority for removal from this grotesque tableau.

Back and forth he swung his light, one delicate step after another, feeling the terrible softness of draining life under his shoes. Then he saw her. With disbelieving eyes, he saw her. On her back, as still as the parquet floor beneath her, a woman in a green suit, right sleeve hanging from her shoulder, skirt pock-marked with what appeared to be charred holes from tongues of flame, blood painting her forehead and cheeks. The president of the United States was in the tight beam of his flashlight, for the moment, a star, spot-lit, the center of his attention, his alone, her eyelids tightly shut. Nothing about her suggested life.

Howard lifted her gently, arms tightly wrapped around her as precious cargo. Once in the light of the hotel lobby he carefully laid her on a sofa and used a wet towel to wipe blood from her cheeks and forehead.

Only one television remote truck survived the blast, the one from local Channel 6. Gloria Graham, a tech intern pressed into on-air commentary, was the only voice of live coverage. Harley Littlefield, a Channel 6 videographer, manned the only live camera at the scene.

Littlefield's daily grind was covering traffic accidents long over and fires long extinguished. He had learned long ago to be inventive about how to make stale stories seem interesting. Here he needed no camera tricks. Everywhere he turned there was anguish, panic, smoke and suffering. He was in the front row while the show was still in act one. No shortage of powerful images. He headed for the large glass main entrance doors of the hotel. Gloria had no choice but to go with him, terrified that she might have to interview survivors, responders, anyone at all. Gloria had never interviewed anyone and never planned to. Her ambition was to one day be in the truck, turning dials, not on the street in the midst of chaos.

The main lobby was a sea of bodies and walking injured. No ambulances yet, no emergency workers, no fire trucks. Not even a wailing siren. Hotel employees and guests were braving the remnants of smoke to carry survivors from the ball room. Sounds of pain wove around excited voices. The lobby's rich golden carpet was washed with pools of fresh blood. Hotel workers were arms deep in blankets, sheets, and pillows. Everywhere, a chorus of ring tones from cell phones never silenced.

Harley Littlefield was recording all of this on the camera he shouldered, transmitting it through the long trailing cable that tethered him to the Channel 6 truck directly across the street.

Gloria followed his lead, trying to add voice to the images on the screen.

"So many victims. Oh, so many look so bad. So hurt. And more coming out of the ballroom all the time. It looks like whatever happened, happened there, in the ballroom. I'm looking for Peg Merchant, our news director. She was in the ballroom. And Bill Crawley, our cameraman, was there, too. I hope they're okay. I don't see them here. I hope the ambulances get here soon. Injured people are even giving first aid to each other."

Harley continued to scan the room with his camera, recording quiet bedlam. Faces in pain, improvised tourniquets, rescuers with towels for masks braving entry to the still smoking ballroom. The ballroom was his destination, too, the apparent center of the carnage. As he edged closer to the ballroom entrance, Gloria moving as best she could ahead of him, trying to stay in camera view, his viewfinder came across a tall man, dressed in suit and tie, guarding a figure on a sofa. He focused tightly on that cameo.

"Gloria!" he shouted abruptly. "It's the president."

Gloria turned where Harley motioned. She had seen so much in the last few moments. She heard herself speaking as if a disembodied presence, barely thinking words before she spoke them. Was this really happening, or was it just an intern's dream? If this was happening, was it really the president? Yes, it was. It was her. Before she realized what she was doing, out of pure instinct, she tried to conduct her first interview.

"Madam President?"

No answer. The image of the president seen by tens of millions watching on television was startling, particularly for those who only moments before had seen her clothed impeccably, chin high, awash in love and triumph. Her hair now a mat of gray ash and dust. One cheek charred, the other bloodied. Her wool suit jacket, the color of healthy green summer grass, ripped to the lining at the right shoulder, her matching skirt riddled with what appeared to be burn holes from the erupting blaze.

"Madam President?" Gloria repeated.

Lincoln Howard held his arms out to wave off Gloria and Harley.

"Please," he pleaded, leave her be."

The sound of sirens suddenly filled adjacent streets, uniforms appeared, men and women with medical bags and equipment. Gurneys, oxygen tanks, people in full fire gear, hoses. Help had arrived.

A team of Secret Service agents swept into the lobby. Lincoln Howard waved them toward the president. Harley's camera showed two agents lifting the president, one carried her toward the lobby door. They didn't speak nor did they ask anyone's permission. Harley's camera followed them as far as he could until another Secret Service agent blocked his way at the door.

***

In 1981, President Ronald Reagan was rushed by ambulance to the George Washington University Hospital suffering from gunshot wounds. Now it was another president, Isabel Tennyson, lying in the same hospital's emergency room, the entire building in downtown Washington ringed by police cars, Secret Service agents, remote television trucks with extended antennae, and adjacent streets filled with people waiting for word of her condition. She was thought to be alive, possibly even conscious, but no one could be sure. Speculation filled news casts. Some who had been at the hotel recalled seeing Secret Service agents carry her from the lobby, not waiting for EMT workers, equipment or even a stretcher. The fear of further explosions or building collapse motivated a quick exit. She had arrived prone, in the back seat of a black Suburban, sirens screaming, at the hospital's emergency entrance. Medical crews were waiting.

Now there were more sirens, more Secret Service agents parting the waiting crowds. A recognizable face, Vice President Roderick Rusher, emerged from one of the caravan's limousines and walked quickly through the ER entrance surrounded by guards. Rusher had insisted on this visit. Oscar Samoza, his chief of security this terrible night, could do little but comply, even though no one was certain that the threat of more bombs, more violence, was over.

"Control of the U.S. government is at stake here," said Rusher. "I have to know her condition and not rely on reports." Rusher had spent decades in Congress. He knew how suspect second-hand reports could be in times of unexpected crisis. He had to see for himself.

Chief surgeon Maurice Winegard was leading a surgical team behind doors where even the vice president was not permitted. It was hospital director Sarah Isaacs who met Rusher and gave the preliminary evaluation.

"Concussion, broken ribs, broken collar bone, broken left leg, multiple cuts, some deep. The medical team is evaluating her for possible blood on the brain, internal bleeding. She was barely conscious and in shock when she arrived. Now she's under sedation while the team works on her various injuries. Fortunately, Dr. Winegard was delivering a dinner seminar for new medical residents when the hospital was alerted to prepare for an unknown number of blast and burn victims. Many of our top people were already here."

Rusher thanked Isaacs. His chief of staff, Beverly Rawley, would be here soon and remain as long as needed with an open line to him. For now, said Rusher, he would give the public this news: the president is alive, her injuries are being treated and her condition is being evaluated. More information will be given as soon as it's available. Isaacs agreed that this was all that could be said for now. It was too soon to know whether her injuries were life-threatening.

Ten minutes later, after hospital staff alerted the media that there would be an announcement, Vice President Rusher delivered the president's condition report. With these additions: Rusher, his family, and all Americans were praying for the president's recovery; no effort would be spared to determine the cause of the explosion; and he, Roderick Rusher, would be at the helm until President Tennyson was able to resume her duties. There would be no gap in continuity for the United States government.

There was general agreement that the vice president handled this night of crisis with composure, respect, and the assurance required for an anxious public.

40

Crime scene investigators arrived in the second wave of emergency vehicles. If there was one bomb, there could be two or more, with fuses delayed to cause maximum fatalities. Experience in Iraq and Afghanistan changed investigation protocol. Tread with care, expect the worst. While fire fighters worked to extinguish the blaze, bomb squad specialists from the FBI, the U.S. Army, and other agencies combed three square blocks around the hotel, searching for anything suspicious, anything that could be that second, or even third bomb.

The direction of the explosion was obvious, the hotel's south side, where the rail tracks were located and damage most severe. Television trucks, police vehicles, motorcycles, the entire presidential vehicle entourage and the bodies of many who arrived with them, formed a scene of carnage from which no one appeared to have survived.

By dawn, fire still smoldering but no longer an obstacle, bomb crews were able to climb to the uprooted tracks and twisted steel that faced the hotel. Four rail cars were lying at various places along the track bed, two were blown completely off the tracks onto the pavement 20 feet below. Rail crews were working at fever pitch to remove some type of milky substance still draining from damaged tank cars to adjoining streets.

One tank car had been cut in two by the explosion. It now lay on its side, two gigantic wads of steel. Little science was required to determine that this car was the source of the explosion. By noon, investigators concluded that the explosive device was an IED, an improvised explosive device, the most deadly weapon used against U.S. troops in Iraq. The bomb had been attached to the underside of the rail car, a car transporting ammonia nitrate.

In a cruel duplicity of popular applications, ammonium nitrate is both a valuable and widely used soil additive that enhances crop growth, and an extremely dangerous compound that mining companies use to blow off the tops of mountains. One of the worst disasters in U.S. history, one that all but destroyed the port of Texas City, Texas, in 1947, was triggered when 2,600 tons of ammonium nitrate aboard the cargo ship *Grandcamp* exploded so powerfully that it broke windows forty miles away and brought down two small planes flying at 1,500 feet. Ammonium nitrate was used by Terry Nichols to destroy Oklahoma City's Alfred P. Murrah Federal Building, an explosion felt fifty-five miles away and recorded at 3.0 on the Richter scale.

Who attached the explosive to the rail car and why remained a mystery to be solved. This much was clear to those walking the ruined tracks even as fire fighters worked to extinguish the last glowing embers around the hotel: It was an act of terrorism.

41

Members from both chambers were gathered on floor of the U.S. House in an extraordinary special sesssion, not for the purpose of hearing a presidential speech or an appearance by a visiting head of state, but to pay tribute to fallen colleagues and to respond to an attack aimed at the heart of the U.S. government in the center of the nation's capital.

Florida Senator Carson Coulter had died in the explosion, moments after introducing the president at what was to have been the celebration gala. Four members of the U.S. House, honored guests seated near the dais, where the explosion's force was most deadly, also were killed. So was Rita Gonzales, the president's long-time staff member who had labored through the Senate years and early months of the presidency to achieve immigration reform. Most members of the Washington, D.C., police patrol that escorted the president to the hotel had been killed instantly. They were parked and waiting directly across the street from the obliterated tracks and took the full force of the blast. The death toll included Secret Service agents, media people, hotel workers, members of the band, dozens of guests standing and cheering their president as their final acts on earth. Hundreds more had been treated for injuries, many remained in local hospitals, some in critical condition.

Before a watching nation, religious leaders of all faiths paid homage to the victims from the well of the U.S. House. Vice President Rusher spoke with emotion about his visit earlier that morning with President Tennyson, who had been moved to the Bethesda Naval Hospital for longer-term recovery from her head injuries, now diagnosed as serious, but not life-threatening. Her body had been battered. Healing would take time. Rusher praised the president's strength and courage and promised that the terrorists, whoever they might be, would feel the full force of retribution from the United States government, a promise that drew an extended standing ovation from the assembled members of Congress. It was a day of sorrow, a day of resolve for a nation always quick to unite when under attack.

Following the joint session there was another meeting. House and Senate leaders of both parties met in the ornate Capitol office of Democratic Senate leader Sidney Alcorn.

The subject of this meeting was impeachment. At the time of the blast, the U.S. Senate was within days of a decision on whether to remove President Tennyson from office. Now the nation was in mourning, the president was hospitalized, there were funerals to plan and attend. National shock to be calmed. Assassination attempt or not, the charges against the president remained to be resolved. The House had voted. The U.S. Constitution required the U.S. Senate to act. But it could not act now. The assembled leadership decided to delay a Senate vote until the president's medical condition became more certain. Best case, after she returned to the White House. The day of judgement would be delayed. It could not, though, be avoided.

42

A busy rail freight line crosses the Potomac River from Virginia to reach Washington, D.C. at 14th street, in the district's Southwest quadrant, about a half-mile from the White House. Once in the district, the tracks turn to the east, roughly paralleling many government agencies and the National Mall with its many museums. At 7th street, the tracks turn diagonally southeast, along the riverfront. This rail line, running through the heart of the nation's capital, is an important link in rail's north-south traffic corridor. It also has long been a controversial link, one that the city's leaders and federal safety experts have tried to relocate for its obvious dangers to local and national safety.

After years of effort an agreement was struck. The line would be moved to less congested surroundings. Hazardous material transport through the city would be avoided. The agreement had been signed last year. Construction of the new route was under way. A year too late.

Despite the agreement, it was commonly known that the rail line would occasionally ship hazmats on this corridor, generally with advance notice so that in the unlikely event of a spill or derailment, emergency crews would be available. In fact, the day before the explosion, officials were notified that a small amount of ammonium nitrate was on the transport schedule. The Secret Service asked that the shipment be delayed until the president left the Washingtonia Grand hotel.

Clay Bergman puzzled over this. Bergman was chief of the FBI's national security branch and the designated lead officer assigned to investigate the explosion. Pressure was intense to find the bombers. The U.S. military was on alert to respond, and in fact, eager to respond at any definitive sign that this was an al Qaeda or

Isis operation. Many congressional voices were demanding action, even without firm evidence. Who else could it be?

Bergman was not so sure. No one had claimed responsibility. That was unusual for terrorist groups after a successful operation. And this was no hit and run event like the Oklahoma City bombing. Someone had access to avoid detection while attaching the bomb to the rail car. The car exploded precisely when it was opposite the hotel and exactly at the time the president was speaking. The device was not timed to explode; it was remotely detonated. For Bergman, this operation had all the earmarks of an inside job.

While the labs continued to analyze the twisted remains of the tank car for finger prints and other clues, Bergman and his team scanned railroad employee lists and interviewed the train's crew and rail officials. Yes, rail officials were aware of the request to delay shipment of ammonium nitrate. Yes, the request had been relayed to operational people both verbally and in writing. Each member of the operational staff was quizzed. None had an explanation for why the request was ignored, why the car was sent, why, in fact, the train had come to full stop opposite the hotel at that critical moment.

The train's operating engineer ordinarily would have been a prime suspect. But he had no role in sending ammonium nitrate on this particular run. Perhaps it was opportunistic. He knew the cargo from the train's manifest. He could have planted the bomb without raising suspicion. Maybe. But he needed an accomplice to press the trigger. Backgrounds were checked, phone logs requested and received. Nothing suspicious.

While there were other possible avenues to pursue, the deeper Bergman's team delved into rail operations, the more convinced he was that the answer lay in the control room, with four people on duty that night, anyone of whom could have ordered the train crew to stop where it did, when they did.

The break in the case came from an alert D.C. traffic cop. Officer Jerry Riles was driving west on Independence Avenue when the explosion rocked his car. Disoriented by the source he pulled to the curb just as a speeding car careened onto Independence from 2nd Street and raced west at high speed. Instinctively, Riles clocked the speed and snapped an image of the car. Then, seeing the explosion's fireball, he followed its source to the hotel. All night Riles remained on duty at the hotel. It was two days later, after learning about the IED device and its remote trigger, that Riles recalled the speeder. He checked his instruments, saw that he had captured the license plate number and forwarded it to the FBI investigators.

"Turk Winslow?"

"Yes, that's me."

Winslow was at home when two members of Clay Bergman's FBI investigation team arrived at his door.

"FBI," said agent Bryce Dent.

Winslow's eyes widened and immediately lit up the words "guilty of something" for the trained agents on his doorstep.

"We're here to talk with you about the explosion," said Dent.

"God," said Winslow, "How on earth did you find me?"

Winslow had been caught totally off guard, expecting from all media reports that the bomb trail would lead to Middle Eastern Islamic terrorists, not to his suburban Virginia home. He had pushed the button that triggered the tanker car to hurl death and destruction through the Washingtonia Grand, a confession impulsively made, impossible to withdraw.

Hours later, Clay Bergman and six other agents arrived at another suburban Virginia home, this one belonging to Paul Rendowsky. Rendowsky was the railroad's night traffic supervisor. At work, a day earlier, he had denied any involvement. Now Winslow had involved him.

Turk Winslow and Paul Rendowsky were members of a Virginia militia group whose members considered the new Immigration Act treasonous. They were convinced that unless Congress repealed the law, the United States would soon be transformed into just another Latin American country. An act of terror by home-grown patriots, they believed, would convince Congress that the opposition would never tolerate the inevitable invasion. President Tennyson, whom they considered a secret agent for

Mexican interests, had steered this threat through Congress. With her out of the way, her successor could end it.

When they learned about the event at the Washingtonia Grand they realized that with a single bomb they could not only strike down the hated president, but also destroy the leadership of the immigration reform movement. It was too rich a prize to pass up. Timothy McVeigh and Terry Nichols blew up the Murrah building hoping to trigger a right wing revolution. Winslow and Rendowsky's goal was more modest. They just wanted to repeal a law.

Rendowsky had gone to work the afternoon of the explosion, like all afternoons, after picking up his young children from school and depositing them at home, just across the Potomac River, in Arlington, Virginia. Coworkers at the railroad reported he performed that night, as any other, with no outward sign of nervousness or tension. Winslow had sat in his car, alone, six city blocks from the hotel, watching a video stream of the banquet on his cell phone, waiting for President Tennyson to take center stage before activating the explosives.

It took only four days from explosion to the filing of criminal charges, not just against Winslow and Rendowsky, but also against five other militia members who took part in the conspiracy.

43

In ancient China, when there was flood, plague, pestilence, hunger and other hard times, it was commonly believed that the ruler had lost the mandate of heaven. That's when empires were overthrown. In a twenty-first century context, even though economic times were improving, the bombing seemed like a final dreadful act in a particularly fretful reign. Members of Congress were anxious for a breather, some time to inhale and get relief from an unending push for controversial change, much of it unpopular and threatening to their own careers.

Counterintuitively, the hotel attack on Tenny weakened her support among many of the Democratic Party senators she needed to fend off conviction and removal. Think of it as sensory overload. For nearly three years, they were shoved into the center of a legislative caldron, forced to make definitive decisions on long-stalled issues—extended healthcare, immigration, reining in of the big banks, serious climate initiatives, the most massive infrastructure program in U.S. history, election law reforms, and for the past two years the massive America's Future Plan, which forced them to choose among every powerful interest group in Washington. In tandem with the hard choices and possibly career-ending votes, the senators had to defend the president against a roaring bonfire of rumors and testimony that linked her with drug cartels and gun runners, sordid tales of sex for profit, the strange circumstances of her brother's death, and now, all that capped by the worst terrorist attack since 9/11, aimed not at the United States as a nation, but at the president herself.

Three weeks had elapsed since the assassination attempt, six days since President Tennyson was released from the hospital, far from healed but determined to return to the White House. She arrived in a wheel chair, a boot protecting her broken left leg.. Her bandages required freshening twice a day. Her left arm was elevated by a sling to keep her repaired clavicle in place. The days immediately following the explosion remained a blur to her. There was a period of short term memory loss. Episodes of odd behavior. Now that was behind her. Her mind was clear. She was back in charge. For how long was a matter for the U.S. Senate to decide. The final vote would be held in two days. The Senate had resumed its debate about her future.

The last day of summation on the impeachment resolutions dawned without a clear picture of how the saga would end. The mood was not positive in the West Wing. Internal head counts had every senator's commitment, except for four. Tenny needed two of those four to survive. With one last shove, Senator Jane Lyman of North Carolina could be persuaded to oppose the resolutions. She feared a primary against her in next year's election and she knew that a coalition of women's groups that had always supported her could head that off. Fish was delegated to broker such a deal.

Ken Geary, from Montana, said he wanted to be with Tenny. But his wife, who remained in Bozeman while Geary served in Washington, was surrounded by fiercely anti-Tenny friends and neighbors. She told her husband she would be mortally embarrassed if he sided with the president. Family harmony would be at risk. That deal was much harder for an outsider to broker.

And those were the most likely two votes.

The other undecided senators were long-time opponents, Democrats who had not supported Tenny in the presidential primary and gave only lip service after she defeated their favorite, Rusher. Now if Rusher ascended to the Oval Office, they would have a friend in the White House and an altogether more productive working environment for themselves.

That should have been enough to put them in the conviction column. But in each of their states, Iowa and New Hampshire, Tenny was more popular than the national norm. Voting against her carried electoral risks and both were up for re-election next year. Ben's advertising and PR efforts had squeezed them hard locally. That succeeded in freezing each of them from making a declaration of intention. There was still hope.

On this day of summation, Ben wasn't sure they could get two, or even one of the uncommitted votes. When you're a winner, you know it. You feel it. When you're not, you hang your hat on hope…a very thin reed if you are out of options to do anything more about it.

Tenny didn't have such doubts. She was a winner. She always had been a winner. How could a Latina woman who wound up president of the United States consider herself anything but invincible? After Federico's murder she plunged into deep despair. For a time, she considered the possibility that her streak of fortune may have outlived its expiration date. But the fact that she had survived that massive explosion, which killed and maimed just about everyone on the stage with her, an explosion aimed explicitly at killing her, removed her doubts for all time. A slight hearing loss, a few facial scars that one day could be surgically erased, a mild concussion that required her to take care not to have any further head trauma. Minor stuff compared to all that went on around her. No, this was her destiny. She would not, could not lose.

***

In his office in the Executive Office Building, Vice President Rusher was decidedly on edge. Everyone around him knew it. His staff, his family, his Secret Service detail. For the thirty years he had served in the Senate, he learned how to be an accurate judge of voting strength. Because many of his former colleagues still served there, he had a pipeline to information few others could tap into. He knew exactly where the vote count stood and who remained in doubt. Publicly, he fully supported President Tennyson. He had been properly deferential during the weeks of her incapacity. Twice he had visited with her at bedside. Privately, he had tasted the power of the West Wing. It was delicious.

During the months' long slog from Judiciary Committee hearings to now, the eve of the final vote, Rusher had played the good soldier. Privately, carefully, ever so carefully, he did what he could to undermine her. It was a risky game in an arena where there was little trust, even among supposed friends.

For Rusher, everything about the past two and a half years had been risky. Agreeing to join a ticket with a woman he personally disliked and whose political agenda was far from his own, the humiliation of taking second place to someone who didn't have a tenth of his knowledge and experience about how things worked, who knew nothing of foreign policy, and then having to bite his lip until it bled watching her get that damn fool agenda passed through Congress.

Tennyson didn't seem to care what he thought. She was so convinced of her own righteousness. It was like she knew the ten steps to heaven and she was climbing them, unconcerned with any advice not to be so almighty certain. Except for occasions where the two of them had to share a stage, they didn't. They didn't have breakfast, lunch or dinner together. Their families didn't socialize. He went on obligatory trips around the country and around the world. They were cordial, like urban neighbors with nodding acquaintance but too busy to stop and talk.

One of those obligatory trips before impeachment fever infected the House Judiciary Committee was to Nigeria, eight months ago, for the inauguration of its new president. He led the U.S. delegation that included four members of Congress, the secretary of energy and a half-dozen corporate types closely tied to Nigeria's oil and mining industries. At the reception following the formal ceremony, Pete Garner, Texas Global Oil Company's CEO gripped Rusher's elbow in a friendly gesture. They had known each other and worked together for more than a dozen years. Rusher was one of the shrinking number of senators who oil men felt really understood their industry and could be counted on for support.

Garner steered Rusher to a corner of the cocktail reception where they could be alone among the crowd.

"That president of yours is a real handful, Rod."

Rusher smiled, nodded knowingly and shook his head in easy agreement.

"That she is. I hope she doesn't do so much damage it can't be corrected later."

"You mean the next election?"

"Of course. I don't see how she can be re-elected with all the wreckage she's causing."

"We can't take that chance. Our assessment is she could be re-elected."

"Good heavens. What a dismal prospect. Well, it won't be with me on the ticket. I never should have agreed to be on it in the first place."

And then, Garner's words sunk in.

"What do you mean you can't take that chance? What's your alternative?"

"I wondered whether you knew. You should. We're going to make you president. Impeachment. You should know it's coming and it's all set up. You're going to be president before the term is over."

"Impeachment! What's she done?"

"That's all being taken care of. Some of us are handling the details. I can't tell you anymore, and probably shouldn't anyway. But you need to know so that when some things come to your attention that you may not understand, you'll know why. It may be that we'll need some help from you and your people."

"To do what?"

"Be a conduit for some information. Confirm a few things. This is all in good hands. You're going to be president, Rod. Count on it."

Rusher remembered that conversation nearly word for word. As it turned out, he wasn't asked to do much. He verified a few erroneous dates and names of people who supposedly were in places they actually weren't. Some notarized papers to generate. Simple stuff, but the kind of things "truth" depends on.

Three months before the Washingtonia Grand explosion, with impeachment very much on track and being artfully managed toward its conclusion, Rusher was in Mexico City, the president's representative at a conference on world hunger. Rusher had little to do there. Hordes of others in the U.S. delegation were talking soil nitrogen levels, genetic modification, and other language of the new agriculture. Rusher's role, similar to most events he attended, was merely to wave the U.S. flag and to excuse the president from having to make the trip.

The opening conference reception was hosted by Para-Gon, the energy and chemical division of Groupo Aragon. It was an evening featuring Mexican food delicacies, carefully calibrated not to seem too opulent for a conference about hunger, but impressive enough to appeal to the delegations from the eighty-four attending countries.

Javier Carmona, long-time CEO of Groupo Aragon was there to welcome the delegates, sharing the stage with the president of

Mexico and Vice President Rusher. As they sat together, waiting to be introduced, Carmona leaned in toward Rusher and quietly invited him to his private hotel suite for brandy and a cigar as soon as social etiquette permitted them both to leave the reception.

Rusher was well aware of the entwined history of his president and Groupo Aragon. It was hard to miss, given all the sordid testimony passing through Congress on the way to an impeachment vote. That testimony also peaked curiosity. There were things to be learned from this man, Carmona, one of the most influential business people in the world, and no doubt the repository of many secrets about President Tennyson.

Later, in Carmona's suite, they sat on the balcony smoking fine Cubans and drinking Armagnac. Carmona was in an ebullient mood, talkative about his company, world affairs and his history with President Tennyson. Carmona knew much about conspiracies from decades of masterminding them and attempting to foil them. All his instincts born of that knowledge warned him to not say what came next. But he could not resist. The future president of the United States was sitting here, on his balcony. The two of them, alone. How many times in life do such opportunities occur?

"Señor Vice President, we appreciate your participation in our project to make you the next president. We look forward to your ascension."

Rusher was startled. The only personal contact he had had about it was from Pete Garner, months ago, in Nigeria. Since then, papers and contacts related to the president had floated through his office. He dutifully signed off on and forwarded documents he otherwise would have questioned had it not been for Garner's heads-up. Garner had said "some of us are handling the details." But he didn't know who else. He could assume, though, that oil people were certainly involved. That was encouraging. Oil people were very reliable and dependable. Carmona was also an oil guy, through his Ener-Gon division. Not just oil, but huge worldwide chemical operations. That and Aragon's many other interests put him in a much higher league than Garner.

"May I ask the nature of your participation," asked Rusher, cautiously.

Carmona laughed, unable to restrain his claim to bragging rights. Rusher would have to know the incredible debt he was about to owe to Carmona.

"In America, you might call me the ringleader. Señora Tennyson I knew as a little girl. She was bright, lively, and pleasant. But as a woman, she is most dangerous. We knew that before anyone else. From the beginning I warned my close friends that something had to be done. Fortunately, others agreed.

"I want you to know you are in the best of hands, Señor Vice President. The small group of us who are managing this project have all the wealth needed to support it, and all the contacts required to make it successful.

"My card, with my private phone number, Señor Rusher. Please, contact me whenever you believe I can be of assistance."

Rusher hardly knew how to respond. But sitting in the richly paneled suite, drinking expensive brandy, smoking a Fuente Don Arturo AnniverXario, the finest cigar he had ever smoked, listening to one of the richest men in the world tell him that he and his friends were organized to make him president, Rusher could only say, "Thank you." No further questions or answers were necessary.

For Carmona, it was mission accomplished. The next president of the United States, just as the current president of Mexico, would be beholden to him.

That was three months ago. Before Federico's murder, a development that terrified Rusher, who, for the first time, sensed the danger in the game that was being played on his behalf.

That terror was compounded when he was told of the hotel explosion. Waves of guilt washed over him then, and remained until the FBI found the militia clowns who had detonated the bomb. That was all behind him now. Tomorrow, as planned, as predicted, Rusher felt confident that Carmona and those Carmona had enlisted in this cause, whoever they were, had spent their money wisely and that they would, in fact, succeed.

44

Attorney General Robin Birch was frantic this morning. If tomorrow's Senate vote removed the president from office, as seemed possible, the attorney general's role would be central to the transition. Already understaffed and deeply enmeshed in countless major investigations and ongoing proceedings, Birch had no time for distractions. If the president was removed, she most likely would be sent packing, too. Rusher would want his own AG, and right away. She had diverted six key staff people to plan and manage the transition, if it came to that. Now here was the national security director asking her to make the forty-five-minute drive to NSA headquarters in Fort Meade, Maryland, for a talk.

"Can we do this tomorrow?" she pleaded.

"I need to see you right away," was the curt message. "No. It can't wait. I'll send a chopper for you."

Birch climbed aboard the chopper, accompanied by two staff aides, a number of work binders and considerable apprehension. A request like this meant serious trouble.

Robin Birch was surprised that President Tennyson had appointed her out of a very talented group of other possible candidates. Her background was corporate law, financial corporate at that—the very target that had been in Tennyson's sights all the while she had been in Congress. Birch had represented some of the very people Tennyson considered the biggest obstacles to reform. When Tennyson called Birch for an interview they had pulled no punches with one another. The new president was out to shrink the banks, toughen Dodd-Frank, get a twenty-first century version of Glass Stegall passed, and she needed an AG who was so familiar with all of the ins and outs of global corporate banking that she would not be tricked, fooled or bought off. The key question was whether Robin Birch shared those goals.

In fact, she did. She had become increasingly soured on the whole megabank enterprise. She voted for Tennyson and was excited that someone who might actually take up reforms was elected. Not many of her colleagues knew of Birch's passion for reform. She wasn't overtly political. But one of her clients, Carmen Sandoval, knew. Carmie was outspoken, a known friend of Tennyson's. It was easy to share private hopes and doubts with her. After the election, Carmie steered Tenny to Birch with confidence that she would be a good fit for their agenda.

None of this, of course, had much to do with the activities of the NSA. Birch guessed that the summons to the meeting had something to do with domestic terror. Maybe a potential attack NSA had in its sights. One of those accompanying her on the chopper ride was a key FBI terrorism expert.

Birch was ushered into the NSA director's office. Her aides were told to wait outside. It would be just the two of them.

"Can I get you anything?" asked NSA Director Kenneth Kloss, "coffee?"

"No."

"I'm having a double espresso and suggest you have one too. You may want to fortify yourself for what I'm about to tell you."

Kloss used his office coffee machine to make his drink, then gestured to her to sit next to him on a sofa. He pulled a digital device from his coat pocket.

"I know being here's an effort for you, with a possible transition tomorrow. But after you hear this you'll know why this couldn't wait. You had to know this now."

Kloss punched the play button.

45

The U.S. Constitution mandates that a Senate impeachment trial be presided over by the chief justice of the U.S. Supreme Court. That role fell to Brian Kamrath, who had led the Court for the past ten years. It was said of Kamrath that the best thing about him as chief justice was the fact that he looked like a chief justice. A trim, tanned outdoorsman, Kamrath had been plucked from the Tenth Federal

Circuit bench and appointed to the Supreme Court by then President Marcus Lowell. Kamrath and Marc Lowell had been Yale classmates, partying together for years. Brian Kamraths's family had been rooted in Boston for six generations. But Kamrath felt constricted by life in New England. After his obligatory two years in a Wall Street law firm he moved to Colorado where the skiing was better, where the hiking trails were longer and more challenging, and where there was more opportunity to floor the hot Porsches he loved to drive.

Brian Kamrath proved an effective corporate lawyer at a time when Denver was transitioning from an overgrown western town to the financial capital of the Rocky Mountain west. Kamrath was not a particularly driven personality. He did not burn the midnight oil or give up weekends and vacations to make a few extra dollars. Despite that, his legal practice thrived. For decades, he had settled into a very appealing routine. Tennis or hiking or skiing on weekends. A month during summer steering his sloop, the *Betty Bee*, along the Maine coast. He and his wife and two daughters would migrate to Camden, Maine and their rustic, comfortable cabin, just two blocks from the dock where lobstermen brought their daily catch.

For Kamrath, corporate legal work was both lucrative and incredibly boring. So when his good friend, Colorado Senator Robert Rager, asked whether he would like to be considered for an opening on the Tenth Circuit, Kamrath was interested. The new job gave him considerable time freedom and flexibility, and he found it for the most part only mildly challenging.

Then came the retirement of Supreme Court Justice Joseph Jacobs, the call from his old friend, Marc Lowell who explained that he was being pressed to appoint any of three ideologues, none of whom he agreed with. Kamrath, on the other hand, came from the same New England Republican DNA as Lowell. Proper Republican. While legal scholars rolled their eyes at a Kamrath appointment, no one could find anything particularly wrong with the way he'd lived his life nor with decisions he had written, speeches he had made, or clients he had represented.

And besides, Kamrath looked like a Supreme Court justice. He charmed the Senate Judiciary Committee at his hearings and displayed just enough irreverence to charm the media as well. Two years later, Chief Justice Alfred Wagner died suddenly, and President Lowell moved Kamrath into the presiding chair.

Now here he was, Brian Kamrath of Denver, Colorado, in December, in Washington, presiding over an impeachment trial and not a bit happy about it. For one thing, he considered the charges against President Tennyson thin and suspect. If this were his case to decide on the Tenth Circuit, he would have dismissed it long ago and spent the summer where he should be, in Maine, on the *Betty Bee*, eating lobster fresh out of the traps and corn three hours off the stalks. But it wasn't his trial or his say. He was merely a figurehead, plunked down to establish and maintain decorum in a chamber that had lately lacked much of it. Tomorrow it would be over, one way or another, and he could begin thinking seriously of the two weeks the family would spend at Aspen over the Christmas holidays.

Finally, after weeks of testimony interrupted by the delays necessitated by Federico Aragon's death and the Washingtonia Grand explosion, the Senate was ready to render a final judgement on the fate of President Isabel Aragon Tennyson. The public already had made its judgement.

Judgement 1: the public was weary of the story, seemingly the same story each day after the early revelations. She was being pummeled like a boxer on the ropes and the public just wanted the beatings to stop.

Judgement 2: Whatever prompted the impeachment process, while originally shocking and at times pornographic, the public was unconvinced that President Tennyson was either a crook or a sexual pervert. Since Washingtonia, her favorability numbers had been rising. Now they were as high as they had ever been, except for the weeks after her election.

Chief Justice Kamrath sat through it all, saying little, answering parliamentary questions, and trying as best he could to adhere to precedent. After the summations, Kamrath announced that the roll call vote would take place tomorrow, the appointed hour of noon, when the Senate would reconvene for this, their only piece of business. Kamrath then adjourned himself to his comfortable apartment in Washington's upscale Kalorama neighborhood, its balcony overlooking busy Connecticut Avenue and the National Cathedral.

As the chief justice, Kamrath had a small security guard to protect his person, and also, among other things, to periodically sweep his apartment for listening devices. There wasn't much contact with neighbors, although they were friendly enough. He drew little attention to himself. The locals were used to political celebrities. Rarely did anyone create a fuss when they saw him.

Kamrath was packing up for a quick exit from Washington after tomorrow's vote when his private cell phone buzzed. It was the attorney general.

"Mr. Justice, General Birch. Sorry to disturb you at home but Ken Kloss and I have to see you on a matter of the gravest importance. May we come to your apartment in about half an hour?"

Strange. The attorney general and the head of NSA, coming here? On short notice?

"Can you give me a preview? What topic?"

"Can't say by phone. But I assure you it's important and very time sensitive."

"Well, of course," he agreed.

He didn't know Attorney General Birch very well. His legal world had been in the West. Birch was what Kamrath was groomed to be, a New York corporate lawyer. Their paths seldom crossed, though his impression was that Birch was an excellent lawyer and certainly a great choice for what President Tennyson was doing to rein in the banks.

Ken Kloss, on the other hand, was an old buddy. Kloss, a retired Air Force general, had been head of the North American Air Command at Colorado Springs. They belonged to the same local golf club. Their wives became good friends and the couples socialized together. In fact, the Klosses and the Kamraths had dinner right here in this apartment not six months earlier. That's probably why Kloss felt comfortable asking to meet here. He knew it was secure, and away from prying eyes.

Birch and Kloss came with company. Two technicians swept the apartment for any bugs that might have been installed since the last sweep. All clear. Then they were gone, leaving three of the most important figures in the U.S. government alone at the dining room table.

"Let me get right at it," said Kloss.

"As soon as we heard about the explosion at the Washingtonia we enhanced all of our monitoring. We needed to know if this was a solitary act or a major effort to take down the government. We monitored everyone of importance in the DC area."

"Even me?"

"Even you. At a time like that we have no idea what's happening. The prelude to a major attack on a disrupted leadership? A coordinated effort to bring down the top leaders in government? We just don't know. So, yes, we monitored your phones and computers, too. But we were particularly alert to calls made to or received from foreign countries. One of our devices blanketed the vice president's home. And here's what we heard:"

Kloss punched play on his digital recorder and played this conversation:

"What have you done? I didn't sign up for this."

"What do you mean?"

"Murder, not impeachment, that's what I mean."

"The bomb. The bomb. You didn't have to kill her."

"Kill her? Why should we kill her? Nothing's changed since we spoke. The plan's working. It's all working just as I told you it would. I know nothing of a bomb."

"Then who?"

"Wait. Where are you calling from?"

"My residence. My cell phone. It's secure."

"Secure!? There are no secure lines, you damn fool."

The party on the other end abruptly hung up. One of the voices was immediately recognizable to Justice Kamrath.

"The vice president knew there was a conspiracy to get rid of the president and he was in on it?"

"Pretty evident, isn't it? But that's not all. We tracked the person on the other end of the call. It's Javier Carmona, CEO of the Aragon Group, the president's old family company."

"Really? Her own company trying to depose her?"

"It gets worse. After the vice president's call, Carmona heard about the explosion. Not knowing whether the president was alive or dead, Carmona sort of panicked. It could have been one of his operatives who went rogue on him. He had to know. So he made a number of phone calls himself, even after warning Rusher about phone security. Listen to these:

"Peter, you heard?"

"Heard what?"

"I think your president is dead."

"Dead! No! What happened?"

"You don't know, then?"

"Javier, what are you talking about?"

"I just had a call from Rusher. He says she was killed. Sounds like a bomb."

"My God! Why should I have known?"

"We need to know whether any of our people are involved."

"Do you think that's possible?"

"Anything's possible with, well, with those we're working with."

"You mean the cartel guys? I thought you had them under control. After what happened to her brother…

"Stop! It's best we say no more. We'll talk later."

"Who's Carmona talking with?" asked Justice Kamrath.

"Pete Garner, Texas Global Oil."

"Texas Global!"

"There's more."

Kloss punched play again.

"Jack. Pete. You heard?"

"Shit, I heard all right. What have those Mexican idiots done? First that priest, now this. We were going to win the vote."

"*Carmona called me. He heard it from Rusher. I don't think he had anything to do with this one.*"

"*Who, then?*"

"*Carmona thinks maybe some of the cartel guys got nervous and needed to make sure. You know, if she survives and beats the vote there's a trail of stuff that could lead right back into their laps.*"

"*We weren't going to lose the fucking vote. It was all arranged.*"

"*Time to start burning paper and wiping out hard discs, just in case.*"

Kloss hit the stop button.

"That's Peter Garner talking to Jack Hurley"

"Jack Hurley! Blue Bank's Jack Hurley! My God!"

"One more," said Kloss.

"*Javier, Pounds. I hope this isn't what it looks like. That you people took a shortcut.*"

"*Not me. Not anyone here. I'm checking up and down our group now. So far no one is involved. They say it and I believe it.*"

"*I hope to high heaven that's true. I promise you, if you or any of the people you've enlisted in all this are responsible I won't defend you. I was aghast when I learned about the president's brother. Just sick about it. You assured me you had nothing to do with that. Now this. You know what this means, don't you? Every intelligence agency in the government will be crawling all over to find out who did it. Well, when they come asking questions about how I got all those news stories that set her up I'll tell the truth. We hated that woman. I wanted to run her off, not run her over.*"

"*Please. Stay calm. We'll talk when I know more….Wait. Wait. I hear now she might not be dead.*"

The conversation ended.

"Is that who I think it is?"

"Yes, Irving Pounds."

Kamrath was as focused now as he had ever been in life.

"There are other calls," said Kloss. "We've counted eleven people who very clearly are part of the conspiracy, half of them like Carmona, not even Americans, none of them foreign government people but all them well known and personally powerful. They didn't set the bomb. They were far too clever for that. But they were involved in a scheme to take down the president and replace her with Rusher. And with a deeper dive into all this we're likely to find that Federico Aragon's murder was totally connected."

"Good lord! And you're here because you think I need to stop the impeachment vote tomorrow?"

"Someone has to. Or else this crowd will wind up running the country through the vice president, who obviously is one of them, and would be in debt to them. This is nothing less than a coup to take over the United States government."

Kamrath walked to the open balcony window. Long seconds passed.

"The Constitution is written, for the most part, in very general language, leaving much room for interpretation. That's what gives so many of us judges lifetime employment. But when it comes to impeachment, the words are detailed and specific. The chief justice presides and the Senate decides. That's it. Cut and dried. I'm powerless to intervene in the process other than to see that it happens."

"But you can meet with the Senate leaders before the session and give them this information," said Birch.

"Yes, I can. Then what happens? They call off the day's vote while they consider the evidence and the options. Do they tell the real story and place cuffs on the vice president? Or is there a cover story because it gets entangled in partisan politics? With this Congress, that's the most likely outcome. What a mess that would be. We have to think through all the consequences of anything we do."

"But what if we go to the media in the morning, before the vote and just reveal what we've learned," Birch pressed on.

"Well, you're the attorney general with a lot of skin in the game. Her guy. Excuse me. Her woman, making a last ditch effort to save her. Ken here loses credibility to protect the nation's security because the other side will accuse him of interfering with a political decision. And me? What am I doing here? I review cases that require interpretation of the Constitution. Where's the case? What interpretation is in question? There's a delicate line here between legality and politics, and if we make the wrong move, or possibly any move, the credibility of all our institutions are compromised."

"But we can't just let this happen," said Birch.

"We don't know that it will. The vote tomorrow could go either way. If she's retained, you can go to her with the evidence and decide how to move the case through the normal criminal process. If she's not.... well let's hope we don't have to face that."

"You will talk with the Senate leadership tomorrow, before the vote, won't you? Ken and I will stand by to be there with the evidence and help."

"I just don't know," said Kamrath. "I just don't know. There's nothing in the Supreme Court manual that tells me how to proceed. I guess I have to set my own precedent."

NSA Director Kenneth Kloss and Attorney General Robin Birch picked up the digital player and their papers. They had no idea what to do when they decided to consult the chief justice. After consulting him, they still didn't. Obviously, neither did he.

46

Crowds assembled early. Many carried signs supporting the President. Others demonstrated noisily for her removal. Some brought babies and small children to witness history. A Mexican-American contingent numbering in the hundreds marched up Constitution Avenue from the White House wearing tee shirts emblazoned with the words, "Impeachment? Never!" By noon, thousands of demonstrators encircled both the White House and the Capitol. The line for seats in the visitors' gallery formed the moment guards opened the Capitol doors. The few fortunate enough to be ushered into the gallery found many seats already occupied by members of the House, congressional and Senate spouses, staff and others who jumped the lines of priority.

There would be a delay, the chief justice announced. The climactic Senate session would not begin at noon. He was said to be meeting privately with the speaker of the House and the president of the Senate, presumably about transitional issues should the vote for removal pass.

Delay increased anxiety. In the White House Carmie and Fish joked and shared stories with the President, thin veneer to blanket the tension of the moment.

The vice president went through the motions of an ordinary business day, but it was not an ordinary day and he was not his usual genial self.

The one hundred senators waiting to cast historic votes were themselves on edge. For months, each had been pressured by mail, email, phone calls and visits. Aggressive media buys had flooded their local stations, raising the stakes no matter how they choose to vote. The senators wanted it done. Over. Behind them.

Those in the galleries, some who had been waiting for three hours, grew increasingly restless, constrained from demonstrating impatience by an enhanced crew of gallery guards.

Delay provided time and space for arguments and fist fights among opposing sides mobilized on the Capitol lawn.

Cable TV filled its space with pointless interviews and repetitious review of the events that brought matters to this decisive moment.

Shortly after 1 p.m. the chief justice and the congressional leaders emerged. Events then moved quickly. The clerk called the roll. All 100 senators answered. There was only one item of business on the agenda and Chief Justice Kamrath went right to it.

Head counts, for and against, had been reported in the media for weeks, as one senator after another declared where he or she stood on conviction. Now those votes were being cast. Ninety-six votes accurately followed the script. Only four senators who entered the chamber that day were officially undecided. The time for decision expired when their names were called.

The final tally was announced:

67 to remove President Tennyson. 33 against.

With announcement of the final tally, Carmie and Fish walked to the wheel chair where the president was seated and embraced her. Long, hard embraces. Her White House years, the last months of impeachment turmoil, Federico's death, her own miraculous survival, all seemed now to blend into exhaustion. She had just become the first president in the history of the United States to be removed from office by the United States Senate. At this moment of loss she felt little else but relief that the ordeal had ended.

"I suppose I should go on TV and announce my resignation," she said.

"I'm announcing mine, too," said Carmie. She sat next to her friend, arm around her shoulder. "We go together. We're still alive with plenty of life in us. This may be over," she said, sweeping her arm around the room, "but this," pulling both their heads together until their cheeks met, "is just beginning a whole new chapter."

Deacon entered, as respectful as if he were confronting death.

"Madame President, the chief justice just called. He asked that in the interest of orderly transition, you not submit your resignation until arrangements are made."

"Do they know when?"

"Apparently not. He just ask that you do nothing until he calls back."

"I imagine there's a thousand cameras downstairs waiting for me to say something."

"He asked that you do nothing, not even talk to the press."

"Well, there's something the chief justice can't object to. Have the staff pack my bags. I'll be ready to leave when it's time."

Contingency arrangements for Tenny already had been made. A helicopter was standing by to take her and Carmie to Andrews Air Force Base. From there, Air Force Two, the vice president's plane, would fly them to Los Angeles. A friend's seaside estate in Malibu would be a halfway house for her return to a new life. Whatever that might be.

***

By pre-arrangement, Vice President Rusher presented himself in the Chief Justice's chambers an hour after the vote. A small group would witness the swearing in. Mrs. Rusher, the attorney general, the president pro tem of the Senate and the Speaker of the House. It would be closed to the press and public, a decision that provoked an uproar from the media, which was hardly appeased by the fact that a reenactment would be scheduled afterward in the cavernous House rotunda. Only one person was present who was not on the previous list of transition witnesses, NSA Director Kenneth Kloss.

Rusher, in his finest navy blue Brooks Brothers wool suit and brick red tie, entered to mild applause from staffers lining the halls. The door closed behind him.

"Mr. Vice President," said Kamrath, looking every bit the chief justice he was, smartly robed and as an erect as a statue, "I realize you are here to be sworn in, but before we do, Director Kloss has something you should hear."

Kloss hit play on his recorder.

The vice president's words tumbled into the room.

"What have you done? I didn't sign up for this."

"What do you mean?"

"Murder, not impeachment, that's what I mean. The bomb. The bomb. You didn't have to kill her."

"Kill her? Why should we kill her? Nothing's changed since we spoke. The plan's working. It's all working just as I told you it would. I know nothing of a bomb."

"Then who?"

"Wait, where are you calling from?"

"My residence. My cell phone. It's secure."

"Secure!? There are no secure lines, you damn fool."

Each word hit Rusher's body like a dagger.

No one spoke to interrupt the moment. Justice Kamrath had met earlier in the day with Speaker Willard and Senator Alcantra and had played these tapes for them. They agreed then that if the removal vote failed, the president would handle the next moves personally. If it succeeded, they would be here, now, like this.

The vice president moved quickly through triumph at the expectation of becoming president to shock at hearing his own compromised voice, to anger that now he was the center of a what appeared to be a conspiracy to deny him this office. But Rusher was an old pro, not easily deterred.

"Thank you, Justice Kamrath, may we now move on to my taking the oath."

"Not yet said Kamrath. The attorney general has something to say."

"Mr. Vice President, you are under arrest for treason, for threatening the president of the United States, for lying under oath to the Congress of the United States, for violation of your oath to uphold the Constitution and for entrapment of the president to do criminal harm. Each charge is a felony. You have the right to remain silent…"

That was too much for Rusher. He interrupted the reading of his rights.

"What is this nonsense," he angrily exploded. "The Senate has voted, President Tennyson no longer is the president and I am in the next in line. I demand to be sworn in."

"I'm sorry, Mr. Vice President," said Justice Kamrath, "I cannot swear in as president someone who is charged with treason and other felonious acts. President Tennyson is president until she resigns and the resignation is accepted by the Congress. Neither action has occurred."

"This is outrageous." Rusher's eyes darted to the others in the room. Ominously, no one else appeared surprised by this drama except for Mrs. Rusher, who gripped Kamrath's desk, until someone helped her to a seat.

"Yes, it is," said Kamrath. "It's outrageous that you would plot to overthrow the elected president in concert with foreign nationals who have organized a monstrous set of lies against her."

Attorney General Birch spoke up.

"Mr. Vice President, we have two choices here. I can take you from this room in handcuffs and you can fight these charges through the courts, or you can resign as vice president and all charges will be dropped. You can say you were an innocent victim of a scheme for which you were unaware, but on learning of it you did the right thing by exposing it and resigning."

"You're blackmailing me. The attorney general of the United States is blackmailing me. The chief justice of the United States is blackmailing me. This is patently unconstitutional," roared Rusher. "There's absolutely nothing in the Constitution that supports any of this."

Kamrath reached into his inside jacket pocket and dramatically pulled out what appeared to be a tally sheet.

"Let's see here. I've got at least five votes that say it is constitutional," said the chief justice. I couldn't reach Justices Padillo and Arlen this morning. But I did speak with Justices Dillingham, Steele, Chang and Redwood a few hours ago. Their votes and mine add up to five. How many votes do you have?"

Rusher was stunned. He was being railroaded by the chief law enforcement officer of the United States and the chief justice of the Supreme Court.

"But the Senate has impeached the president. It's done. It's over," he pleaded.

"Not exactly said Senate pro tem Alcantra. Before this meeting I spoke with two senators who voted for impeachment who now have decided to change their vote. Since the Senate makes its own rules on this matter we can certainly vote for reconsideration. Once this story becomes public, I imagine just about everyone will want to change their vote."

"Mr. Vice President. Your choice?" asked Justice Kamrath. "Jail? Or pats on the back all around that you wound up on the right side after all?"

Epilogue

The forecast was grim, but typical for an Iowa January. Ten degrees and chin deep snow. Stowed on Air Force One was their heaviest winter clothing. The passenger list included the traveling staff, members of the campaign media, Ben Sage and President Tennyson. Weather or not, Iowa would be voting in four weeks. The events of recent months denied Tenny a proper start for her re-election campaign. If she survived impeachment, she had said, she would run. But it would have been presumptuous to actually begin campaigning for a new term while the Senate was considering whether to end her current one.

As a sitting president, her primary election victory most certainly would be assured. But not if she took voters for granted, not if she failed to show up at the town hall meetings and familiar road stops where she was expected. Louis Gorland, Arizona's governor, and Arnold Ledbetter, a digital age billionaire, both had been in the field since summer, counting on Tenny to be damaged goods, maybe an ex-president, possibly being so fed up with the whole business that she would say to hell with it and not run, even if she could. In politics, there are few free passes to power. If she wanted a second term, Tenny would have to work for it.

And she wanted a second term. She really wanted it. Her wave of weariness ended within moments of Chief Justice Kamrath's call informing her of the remarkable turn of events that would preserve her presidency. Her wounded leg felt so much better. Even her head wounds looked like they would heal a lot faster. Winning is its own tonic. Within twenty-four hours, Ben Sage and Lee Searer were in her office with instructions to pull the re-election team together, set up a travel schedule, get polls in the field, develop a strategy. Three weeks later, they were on the road.

"Before you shake the first hand," said Ben, "Tell me you're doing this for the right reasons. Not just to settle scores, or restore your own image or because you can't think of anything else to do with your life. Not being able to answer the simple question why you want to be president has brought down more than one candidate. It shows. It's deadly. This may sound like a silly question after all you've been through. But you have to answer it and answer it convincingly. Why do you want to be president?"

Ben and Tenny were sitting together in the president's private area of Air Force One, separated from the 120 reporters covering this, her first actual campaign swing, and from her own traveling staff. They were reviewing the schedule, the speeches, the names of key people who would meet them on the ground.

From her window seat, Tenny looked down 30,000 feet to the snow covered checkerboard of the Midwest landscape. Farms and farm homes clearly visible in the sun's bright reflection. Life down there. Real life. But made impersonal through distance.

"There was a time when I couldn't answer that question. I was at a crossroads in my my life and went to Carmie Sandoval for advice. She said I'd been seeing the world from 30,000 feet. I had to get on the ground, where real people live to find the answer. She sent me to Hal and to the barrios of L.A. Within days, hours maybe, I knew what I wanted to do.

"Now here we are, at 30,000 feet. Ironic that you're asking me this question. And you should. This time I know the answer. I'm going to finish what I started. Twice now I've underestimated the power I was trying to change. That won't happen again. Frankly, Ben, I had stars in my eyes when I was elected president. I felt I could do anything. Queen Isabella could write a check or whatever they did in those days and send Columbus on his way. If she had a problem, she could cut off heads or send the Spanish Armada out to fix it. I guess somewhere in my genetic makeup, those ideas haven't died with time. I thought if I said do this, it would happen. I thought if I had a challenge, I would overcome it. Anything. Everything.

"I gave them plenty of openings to bring me down. I wasn't on guard. I was careless. I didn't have enough allies. I went after them like the Light Brigade, charging at top speed into the valley of death.

"But, I came out alive. Thanks to you, and Kamrath and others and incredible good fortune to still be alive. They corrupted my family. They murdered by brother, my dear, sweet, brother. And with all their money and power they're still the most destructive force on earth. We've wounded them with all this exposure, with all they did to try to impeach me. They're weaker than they were yesterday. One more term, four more years, I'll have more protective armor, more weapons to fight them, more allies. We're going to get them, Ben. We're going to get them.

"We're going to rewrite my America's Future plan to include a much tougher fight against the corrupt and greedy bastards. By the end of my second term they will be on the ground, my foot on their back.

Hearing her own words, she suddenly paused, reminded of something. Her head tilted back on the cushioned seat rest. Her thoughts drifted to another place, another time.

"Ben, have I ever told you about the Mayan warrior princess Ix Wak Chan Ajaw?

The Latina President's Main Characters

U.S. President Isabel Aragon Tennyson
("Tenny"; "Senora Aragon Tennyson," "Senora Tennyson"; "Bell")

Sid Farnham
Secret Service control officer on night of bombing

Lincoln Howard
Washingtonia Grand chief of security

Roderick Theodore Rusher
Vice President of the United States

Carmen ("Carmie)
Isabel's best friend

Queen Isabella of Spain
Duke of Aragon (Ferdinand)

Miguel Aragon
Isabel's grandfather ("Papa" "Papa Miguel" "Don Miguel")

Maria Rosa
Isabel's mother

Malcolm Tennyson
Isabel's father

Federico
Isabel's brother

Andres Navarro
Isabel's husband

Rafael Celeste
Mexican soap opera actor

Javier Carmona
Top executive at Groupo Aragon

Hal Thompson
Isabel's mentor

Ben Sage
Political strategist

Lee Searer
Ben Sage's business partner

Bert Wilmont
Los Angeles city councilman

Sheila Fishburne
("Fish") Congressperson from Alaska

Reed Guess
Democratic Senate majority leader

Henry Deacon
President Tennyson's chief of staff

L. Irving Pounds
Media mogul, Hal Thompson's father in law

Sally Pounds
Hal Thompson's wife

Susan Cipriani
Reed Guess's campaign manager

Jack Hurley
CEO of Blue Bancorp, U.S. financial giant

Pete Garner
CEO of Texas Global Oil

Gabriel Montes
Peruvian banker

Congressman Larry Anderson
Ranking Democrat on the House Judiciary Committee

Congressman Zachary "Zach" Bowman
House Judiciary Committee chairman

Bo Willard
Speaker of the House

Bob Reynolds
Jesuit priest

U.S. Senator Stuart Alcantra
Senator Pro Tem

Robin Birch
U.S. Attorney General

Kenneth Kloss
Director, National Security Agency

Brian Kamrath
Chief Justice, U.S. Supreme Court

Ix Wak Chan Ajaw
Mayan warrior princess

Author's Notes

For anyone who might try to identify a real life political figure in these pages, don't. This work is as it is represented, total fiction.

Now let's add a few asterisks to that legal disclaimer.

President Barack Obama, President Bill Clinton, Pope Francis and a few others you encounter in this novel obviously are real people. I've appropriated them for purposes of the story, common practice in historical fiction. Otherwise, the characters either have been born whole through my imagination or are composites from my experience. I've met quite a few interesting people during my years in active political combat. Parts of them have been grafted onto other parts. But no one, living or dead is a replica of a single individual, or intended to be. Except for Alena and Laura, who tend bar at the Big Fish restaurant in Rehoboth, Delaware. They are real people in a real restaurant and are exceptional at their work.

Some of the events I've fictionalized here are my recalls from actual political events. One example: The incident where "U.S. Senator Hamel" pays for prostitution services with his credit card. That actually occurred during one of the campaigns in which I was involved. I've created Senator Hamel and placed him in California to fit the story. The incident happened elsewhere. The real life senator was defeated in the next election.

To ease every reader's mind, I should say there is no Washingtonia Grand hotel, or no hotel at all at the location I've described. But there are railroad tracks, and cargo moves over them on a regular basis, and some of that cargo is hazardous. The tracks are perilously close to the Capitol building, the White House, and other important private and government venues. All true. And there have been accidents.

I am well aware of the constitutional and other legal impediments for the impeachment process to end as I have concluded it in *The Latina President's* final chapters. But with fiction the author has license to imagine his or her own reality.

Finally, or I should say, firstly, my love and gratitude to my wife, Sylvia Bergstrom, who saw nothing unusual about an 80-year-old man announcing he intended to write his first novel, and then giving him non-stop encouragement to actually do it.

About the Author

For more than thirty years, through over two hundred campaigns, Joe Rothstein was at the center of U.S. politics. He was a strategist and media producer for former Senators Tom Daschle of South Dakota, Patrick Leahy of Vermont, Don Riegle of Michigan, Bob Kerrey of Nebraska, Tom Harkin of Iowa, and many others in the campaigns that brought each of them to the U.S. Senate. At its peak, Rothstein's political consulting firm could count 10 percent of the Democrats in the U.S. House as his clients.

Rothstein is a former editor of the Anchorage, Alaska *Daily News*, and he is currently chairman and editor of the international news aggregator and distribution service EINNEWS.com. His political opinion columns are published at www.uspoliticstoday.com.

Joe Rothstein lives in Washington, D.C., with his wife, Sylvia Bergstrom.

A Request

Now that you're here, I imagine you have an opinion about *The Latina President*. Love it? Hate it? Like the story, disagree with the political points of view? In this era of easy feedback options, more readers than ever are weighing in with comments about what they've read. I'd welcome your take on my novel. Amazon, Good Reads, and countless other public venues are exciting hubs for reader reviews. Please use one or more to share your opinion of *The Latina President*.

And while you're at it, consider contacting me directly. I'm easy to reach. Let me know if you would like me to send you advance copies of my next novel. You can also follow my ongoing political commentary at www.uspoliticstoday.com.

Joe Rothstein

202 857-9742

jrothstein@rothstein.net

CPSIA information can be obtained
at www.ICGtesting.com
Printed in the USA
LVOW05s1351290817
546817LV00005B/606/P